G000243181

Nick Thorpe is an award-winnin[g]
Adrift in Caledonia and *Eight Men an[d]*
range of media, including the (
Telegraph and BBC Radio 4. He liv[es]

For more information, visit www.nickthorpe.co.uk or
follow him on Twitter, @urbanworrier, and also on
www.facebook.com/urbanworrier

Praise for Nick Thorpe

'Thorpe is an accomplished storyteller . . . thoroughly
entertaining'
Daily Telegraph

'If you enjoy chuckling during your armchair travels, my
advice is: Rush and Reed'
Tim Severin, *Washington Post* for *Eight Men and a Duck*

'It beats all those tales of travel writers foot-slogging through
exotic lands in search of profundity and enlightenment'
Independent on Sunday

'His insight and humanity, together with an honest lack of
certainty, make him a companionable guide'
Sunday Express

'His is a spiritual journey as much as anything else . . . assisted
by some bouncy writing, a sharp eye for detail and a slight
earnestness you can't help but warm to'
Daily Mail

ALSO BY NICK THORPE

Adrift in Caledonia

Eight Men and a Duck

Urban Worrier

*Adventures in the Lost Art
of Letting Go*

NICK THORPE

ABACUS

First published in Great Britain as a paperback original in 2011 by Little, Brown
This edition published in 2013 by Abacus

Copyright © 2011 Nick Thorpe

The moral right of the author has been asserted.

All rights reserved.
No part of this publication may be reproduced, stored in a
retrieval system, or transmitted, in any form, or by any means, without
the prior permission in writing of the publisher, nor be otherwise circulated
in any form of binding or cover other than that in which it is published
and without a similar condition including this condition being
imposed on the subsequent purchaser.

A CIP catalogue record for this book
is available from the British Library.

ISBN 978-0-349-12085-0

Typeset in Centaur by M Rules
Printed and bound in Great Britain by
Clays Ltd, St Ives plc

Papers used by Abacus are from well-managed forests
and other responsible sources.

MIX
Paper from
responsible sources
FSC® C104740

Abacus
An imprint of
Little, Brown Book Group
100 Victoria Embankment
London EC4Y 0DY

An Hachette UK Company
www.hachette.co.uk

www.littlebrown.co.uk

For C

There's a river flowing very fast. It is so great and swift that some will be afraid, and try to hold onto the shore ... But the river has its destination. The elders say we must let go, push off into the middle of the river. Keep our eyes open and our heads above the water. See who is in there with us ... And celebrate.

THE HOPI ELDERS

Some drink deeply from the river of knowledge. Others only gargle.

WOODY ALLEN

Contents

Prologue

It's Friday afternoon and I'm sitting cross-legged beneath the apple tree with Charlie, who is a kind of guru. Today we are practising, once again, how to stay in the present moment. Of course, it ought to be impossible to be anywhere else – and yet I'm finding it fiendishly tricky simply to rest here in the dappled sunshine. I keep thinking about the last sentence of a newspaper article I've just submitted, wondering if it should have been a little punchier. My guru sits and gazes at me with compassion. It's a little unnerving, but he really does have the most incredible eyes – deep brown pools of intense connection and playfulness. Nevertheless, I find myself noticing the straggly hedge behind him, wondering when I'll find time to give it a trim. At this point, without breaking eye contact, he leans forward and licks my face.

Now I'm definitely in the present moment. Spluttering with laughter, I push Charlie away and throw him his ball. He leaps after it as joyfully as if it were the first created thing in the universe.

I can't be the only one with a four-legged muse. Which of us, watching a family pet tearing across open country or curled contentedly in front of the fire, has not felt that bittersweet stab of joy mixed with something close to envy? What is it about this slightly malodorous cocker spaniel that moves me so? Is it his passionate curiosity about the world, his total focus on following a scent, his endless capacity for play? Or perhaps it's just that straightforward way he has of getting exactly what he needs. Often, turning from the kitchen sink, I'll find him sprawled shamelessly on his back in the unwavering belief that I have nothing better to do than to tickle his belly. Strangely, he turns out to be right. I sink my fingers into his shaggy coat and give him the massage I would so richly enjoy – and in his abandonment to it, I somehow receive a little of it myself.

It's difficult to say when we humans first began to take on the anxious, preoccupied demeanour that characterises modern Western society. Some blame the Industrial Revolution, when we began to ignore our natural rhythms in favour of endless productivity. Others might scroll back much further and argue that it's part of the evolutionary leap that brought us language and consciousness, and the potential to engage with concepts and comparisons rather than simply things, people and places. Certainly, Charlie gives no indication that he is fretting about the morality of his brazen advances on a local poodle, or his ongoing addiction to discarded fast food. As far as I know, he does not lie awake at night wondering if there is a Dog Almighty. There is only the joy of chasing squirrels, the aroma of bacon, the warmth of his bed.

This also explains, of course, why we humans are mapping genomes and exploring space, while dogs are still sniffing each other's backsides. They don't win Nobel Prizes, or negotiate peace deals or, indeed, 'achieve' anything in the sense we have come to understand it. But it's also true that dogs don't tend to start wars or systematically destroy their own ecosystem. And after a quick glance at the expressions of commuters struggling home in the rush hour, you can't help but think we've paid a heavy price for the control we like to believe we exert on life. The statistics only confirm what the British economist Richard Layard calls the 'deep paradox' at the heart of Western society: that despite unprecedented prosperity, medical advances and freedom to chart our own lives, we are no happier now than we were fifty years ago – and noticeably more prone to depression, alcoholism and crime. Huge numbers of us are plagued with anxiety, addicted to tranquillisers or shopping or work, running to stand still.

It seems that our harried culture encourages fretting from an early age. I should know. I'm told I was always a slightly anxious child, sorting my Lego into colour-coded boxes, sticking rigidly to my exam revision wallcharts, and generally avoiding sport in order to lessen the possibility of failing at it. My young adult years were littered with people telling me I should relax a little, loosen up, stop thinking so hard about everything. I was once flattered but a little surprised when a girlfriend told me I was 'a real warrior'. Nobody had ever said that before. 'Not "warrior",' she clarified. '*Worrier!*' The relationship ended soon afterwards.

Later, I developed a private addiction to self-help books. While others secretly feasted on chocolate or swigged from a bottle hidden in the top drawer, I would get an almost physical high browsing furtively in the Mind, Body, Spirit section, bingeing on books promising to change my life in seven easy steps. They never did, of course. But the prospect was enough to keep me coming back, in the hope that the next title – *Feel the Fear and Do it Anyway* or *How to Talk to Anyone* – would give me that elusive key to eliminating the bits of my life that didn't work, and perfecting the rest.

I know I'm not alone in this desire to control my environment. It's human instinct, a feature of workplace politics and family feuds alike, and most of us question it only when the first fractures begin to show in our relationships, our bodies, our much-cherished certainties. Depending on your perspective, that modern milestone known as the midlife crisis can be a coming of age, a navel-gazing indulgence or an existential curse. But if it doesn't do irreversible damage, it can also be a blessing – a wake-up call. Because almost forgotten within each of us, waiting to be called forth, is something rather like a small dog. Let's call it the soul: our purest, truest, most uncomplicated self. We keep it on a pretty short leash most of the time, dress it up and train it to perform for audience applause, or starve it to within an inch of its life. But it remains essentially a loving creature, ready to emerge and lick an open face.

This is the story of how I began to play a little more with my soul, and eventually to befriend it. I hope it brings at least a morsel of encouragement to others with a Rottweiler-like tendency to be their own worst enemy. My actual dog was only one of many mentors in this journey, which began the day I realised that the struggle to control my life had become a war against myself. It opened up a series of questions that seemed to me to have wider relevance: What happens when we let ourselves off the leash? Will life grind to a halt if we stop pushing so hard and get playful instead? Can we trust our deepest desires or do we need a robust legal system or omnipotent deity to save us from ourselves? What will happen if we allow ourselves to be really honest with the people in our lives? Is vulnerability a curse or a gift? Ultimately, can we learn the capacity for contentment, or is it as arbitrary as hair colour, a trait we're born with? And while we're at it, will we ever be free of all these nagging existential questions?

Exhausted with my perpetual schemes for self-improvement, I decided to spend a year learning to loosen up. I would travel at home and abroad in search of alternative role models: balloonists, clowns, adrenalin junkies, naturists, travellers, schoolkids, hippies, monks, spiritual teachers. Some had abandoned the conventional treadmill altogether, but others had found a way to dance with everyday pressures, rather than flee them. All of them believed that fear was better harnessed than suppressed.

The philosopher Alexis de Tocqueville once memorably compared our task in life to that of 'a traveller journeying without ceasing towards a colder and colder region; the higher he goes, the faster he ought to walk'. I have come to believe that precisely the opposite may be true – and this book is my attempt to prove it.

What follows, then, is the story of my experiment in letting go, a crash course in kindness to oneself, an alternative to relentless trying. This book is for you if you have ever felt tired of the haranguing voices in your head, if that endless list of jobs means you never quite get round to relaxing, if you sometimes wonder where the last ten years went.

Or if you're simply envious of your dog.

I

Habits of Highly Ineffective People

Edinburgh

'We often discover what will do, by finding out what will not do; and probably he who never made a mistake never made a discovery.'

SAMUEL SMILES

The day I lost control was a sunny Monday in August. I remember the moment vividly. It was mid-morning, and I was hunched at my computer, eyeing the approaching juggernaut of another deadline. I had been obsessing over final adjustments to a book manuscript for about two weeks, and felt about as healthy as roadkill. This in itself was not particularly unusual. True, the shallow breathing and shooting pains under my arm were new, and the migraines had been getting worse, along with an unexplained dull pain below my ribcage. But the general territory was familiar: I now had two newspaper commissions stacked up, and was determined never to blow a deadline. I looked at the clock: 10.30 a.m. Another working lunch, then. I couldn't allow myself to stop.

Or so I thought.

It was around 11.15 a.m. when, with a jolt, I realised I had been in a sort of trance for some time. Wearily, I focused my gaze back to my computer screen, which was surrounded by sheaves of paper, half-drunk cups of coffee, unopened bank statements and *The Seven Habits of Highly Effective People*, the latest in a succession of self-help books I had entirely failed to put into practice. I looked down at my hands lying motionless on my lap like loafing employees and angrily willed them back to work.

But that morning nothing happened. The hands stayed where they were.

This was new. This was definitely new. I tried again, but to no avail. It was as though the order from my brain hadn't reached the ends of my arms. I stared at my hands again, suddenly fascinated and appalled. Was I having some sort of stroke?

Over the years I thought I had developed a rather effective fight-or-flight response to mounting pressure: either a) work much harder or b) climb on a plane or boat and escape to somewhere unusual with no inbox. Indeed, by alternating a) and b) for several years, I had improvised a half-decent career in travel writing, and sheer willpower had always won through in the end. But that morning I found myself facing the humiliating possibility that I was no longer at the helm of my own life.

I had been freelancing for a few years, enough to lose the idealistic gloss of starting out on my own, but not quite enough to have mastered it. Indeed, I was always darkly amused when people in office jobs talked wistfully about 'being your own boss'. It made the rather large assumption that the one inside your head was always going to be more likeable than the flesh-and-blood tyrant down the corridor. Whereas, in truth, my internal industrial rela-tions had recently been worse than any I'd known in newspaper offices. The more tired I got, the more savagely I found I snarled at myself to keep going. But that morning it was as though two parts of me were deadlocked. I found I could flex my fingers fine, but nothing would induce them to type another sentence. A sense of something like wonder overcame me. It was less like a stroke than a strike.

I dragged myself away from the picket line and staggered downstairs to see Ali, who is a professional counsellor and also my wife. This conflict of interest unfortunately makes it difficult for her to offer me her impartial services without also noticing the fact that, for example, I haven't yet got round to hanging out the washing. But she knew a case of exhaustion when she saw it.

'Nick, how bad does this have to get before you get some help?' she said, when I told her what had happened. My tendency to overwork was not new in our marriage, and it made my impulse towards self-sufficiency doubly hard for her. In truth, neither of us really understood it. While Ali instinctively reached out with snail-like antennae, constantly seeking connection, I was more crablike – emotionally armoured and approaching problems sideways, if at all. 'You've been wandering round like a zombie for days and you've barely spoken a word,' she said. 'Please, stop and look after yourself – for my sake if you won't do it for your own!'

I should probably have gone to see a doctor. But I had seen a lot of doctors recently for the persistent migraines and the mysterious ache in the gut, and for a battery of clinical tests with Ali, which revealed no biological reason why we had not yet been able to have children. I didn't want another weary shake of the head, another polite suggestion that I try to relax a little more. I guess I wanted to believe that my working habits needed, well, just a little more work. That someone could help me fix my malfunctioning will-power like a faulty accelerator pedal on a car.

So I called a life coach.

The sudden rise of life coaching is one of modernity's more puzzling trends. There are thousands of people offering their services in Britain, but it's not as if life is some new fad or phenomenon, like line dancing or sudoku. On the contrary, life has been on the fixed menu for quite some time now. So why the sudden need for people to tell you how to do it? Yet the humiliating truth was that I wasn't scoring at all highly in the rudimentary business of being alive – at least not according to the fourteen-page online questionnaire I was required to fill in before my first appointment. Devised by someone called Angela Court Jackson, it covered everything from belief in God (shaky) to the state of my fingernails (chewed).

'So how do you feel,' asked Angela, a couple of days later, 'about scoring *zero* for effectiveness?'

We were sitting either side of a scented candle in her sunlit home office, a place of tamed, symmetrical in-trays and fresh white walls, on one of which a framed print of the Chrysler Building was thrusting aspirationally skywards. I had picked Angela out of the hundreds of Google results because she sounded professional, lived just round the corner from me in Edinburgh, and gave her first session free – but looking into her concerned, sisterly face that morning I had a sudden premonition that I was in danger of becoming the sort of person who stuck motivational Post-it notes on the fridge.

'To be honest, I thought some of the tickable statements were a bit absolute,' I said defensively, flipping through my answers. 'I mean, can anyone *honestly* say they reply to *all* correspondence quickly and speedily? Or that they're able to ask for what they want from *anyone*? Or that they *never* put things off?' I had cravenly re-negotiated the two newspaper-feature deadlines only that morning and was feeling enough of a failure as it was.

Angela smiled soothingly. 'It's not about getting ten on each section. But I would say if you're scoring zero it's probably an area you need to look at.'

What exactly *was* effectiveness, anyway? It sounded like something you'd look for in toilet bleach, not a human being. Yet I had to admit I was intrigued. Never having allowed myself the indulgence of an inner MOT before, I was anxious to know what other qualities might have dropped off my life while I wasn't looking.

Joy, apparently.

I look forward to getting up virtually every morning? Er, nope.

I have enough pleasurable time to myself every day? I often have fun? I felt sad just talking about it. When did life suddenly get so serious?

We spent the next hour surveying a few initial thickets in the vast jungle of my potential self-improvement. As I talked, oddly emboldened by the fact I had never met Angela before, I noticed she was picking out certain phrases and writing them on a piece of paper:

sometimes wakes up with a sense of dread
fear of letting people down
slight directionlessness
on the edge of something ...

Every few minutes she tentatively suggested 'challenges' I could set myself. Most were mundane and obvious – get a health check-up; think about a system for filtering incoming emails; hire a book-keeper to log my tax receipts – so obvious, in fact, that I was fairly sure I would never get round to doing them. Others were plain bizarre – try Hopi ear candling and investigate Botox injections for possible migraine relief. Eventually, since we were already in strange territory, I cut to the chase and told Angela about my hands going on strike.

'If I were a company I'd be a pretty crap one to work for,' I summarised.

Angela chuckled sadly. 'So, here's a challenge: how can you as boss, change the culture of your company? Maybe throw in a few bonuses?'

I thought about the 'boss'. He started life as a kind of metaphor, but I had to admit that his voice was worryingly recognisable to me. He was a sarcastic perfectionist who had grown so relentless in his criticism that I honestly couldn't imagine life without him. If I were not at my desk by 9 a.m., he was already writing off the day as wasted. And I could barely type a sentence before he popped up like that infuriating animated paperclip in early Microsoft programs: 'Hello! That intro looks even more banal than the last one! Do you want to start again?' Most of the time I wanted to smother him. But Angela shook her head and said something that would come back to me many times in the months ahead.

'You've programmed this inner critic for a reason,' she said. 'I don't know if he motivates you to get to your desk on time, or what – but on some level he works for you. So stop trying to push the voices down, and let them come up – and try thanking the critic. Because maybe some of what he is saying is of value. I'm wondering if he might quieten down a bit once he knows he's being heard.'

I stared at her. I didn't know which was more alarming – the fact that we were both talking about an imaginary character in my head or her suggested remedy. And yet her advice was so counterintuitive and strange that I had a feeling it might turn out to be very wise.

I tried it out on the critic as I cycled home. 'Spare me the flaky New Age hokum,' he was muttering. 'People pay money for that?'

'Thanks very much for your thoughts,' I said, keeping my (imaginary) voice bright and level like a call-centre worker's. 'Your opinion is very important to us, and we'll take it into consideration.'

I waited for a comeback. But, for the moment at least, the critic seemed to have hung up.

'You look like shit,' said my brother Dan with his usual affable bluntness later that evening. 'How about a bit of clubbing later?'

We were sitting in a bistro in a backstreet off the Royal Mile, where Dan had been doing the Edinburgh Fringe on his way to meet his partner Carole at her relatives' in the Highlands. Having run the gauntlet of some singing chimney sweeps and a partially clad woman handing out flyers for 'The Groove', he was on his third pint and determined to coax Ali and me out to a nightclub. Across the table, Ali was looking pleasantly tipsy over her glass of wine. I was as sober as a nun and struggling to keep my eyes open.

'There's no way I'm going clubbing,' I said wearily. Nightclubs had always seemed like alien territory, mainly because I was unable to drown my inhibitions in alcohol without simultaneously triggering a migraine. As I reminded Dan, the last time I had managed to let go on the dance floor – after someone added a double vodka to my Coke at a family wedding – the surviving footage seemed to show me energetically miming a primary-school sack race. The memory made me wince almost as much as the colossal headache that followed.

'Yeah, but you enjoyed it at the time, didn't you?' said Dan. His disappointed look made me want to avoid eye contact. 'That was a Nick we hardly ever get to see! Bit of a shame, if you ask me.'

Five years my junior, Dan had always been the rebel in the family, and I envied him for it. In many ways, he had grown up as a kind of anti-me. I mastered the Rubik's cube; he bought an air gun. I took the cycling proficiency test; he built a skateboard ramp. I spent my summers on Bible camp; Dan hitched to Glastonbury. We both studied art at school, and our portfolios said it all: mine full of fussy, almost photographic still-life drawings; his alive with swirling psychedelia. I still pictured him as a teenager in his bedroom, long-haired and surrounded by candles, graphic novels and batiks of marijuana leaves. Yet despite, or possibly because of all his mind-expanding experimentation, he had grown up to become the sort of friendly, well-balanced guy that everybody loved. Nowadays he worked in social housing for an English city council while collecting vinyl and growing vegetables on his allotment in his spare time. And every so often he took off to explore far-flung places with his backpack. We had that in common, at least.

'Been anywhere exotic recently?' he asked now.

'I'm not sure. Does Donegal count?'

The previous month I had been a guest at possibly the oddest film festival in the world – three days of screenings about journeys in home-made boats, in the improbable and rain-lashed location of Tory Island, nine miles off the Irish coast. My ticket to this esoteric convention was a voyage I had taken in 2000 from Chile to Easter Island on a slowly sinking vessel made of reeds. Rash as it had seemed to trust myself to this experimental form of transport in the company of several equally unqualified shipmates, it had turned out to be a thoroughly life-enhancing experience, and one I always assumed was fairly unique. But sitting in a blacked-out village hall,

watching footage from literally dozens of journeys made in everything from animal-skin coracles to ancient galleys, I concluded I was
simply one of a well-established breed. There was now even a
pseudo-scientific name for our endeavours: archaeonavigation.

Standing soberly in the bar one evening listening to men (and
they were almost always men) from across the globe debating the
reliability of square versus lateen sails or boasting about the alleged
scientific merits of their *Boy's Own* adventures, I was overcome by
a creeping sense of the absurd. Why were we all so intent on such
improbable feats? What were we really trying to prove? It seemed
to me there was an elephant in the room with us, and across its
rump were branded the words *midlife crisis.*

Dan laughed uneasily at the tale. 'Don't knock a good honest
midlife crisis, bro. Better to build a reed boat than buy a Ferrari.'
He took a sip of beer. 'Don't tell me you're losing the wanderlust?'

It was a fair question. I had always loved travel for the way it
opened my mind to other people and how they lived, and distracted me from the existential questions of ordinary life. Then a
couple of years previously, I had spent a wonderful summer hitching around Scotland by boat – a glorious excuse to engage with my
adopted country, and which had changed my whole relationship
with it. And for the first time in the ten years since I had come up
from London to start work, I knew it was somewhere I wanted to
put down roots, start a family. Old habits die hard, of course, and
I had taken a few trips since then – a voyage down the Peruvian
Amazon, a commission in Montenegro and, more recently, the
Irish film festival – but increasingly I had the feeling that my travels were an avoidance of the real issue.

'According to the life coach, I need a bit more than a change of
scenery,' I admitted to Dan now. 'More like a personality transplant . . .'

'You went to a *life coach*?' cut in Dan, trying to hide a smile. 'Nick, you seriously need to loosen up! What about taking an ordinary holiday instead? You know, relax with a good novel, sample the local cuisine, recharge the batteries ... ?'

I felt Ali's hand rest supportively on my shoulder. 'Nick gets a bit panicky without a project,' she said. 'Put him on a sun lounger and he'll be twitching in minutes.'

It was true. Ever since I first tried my hand at freelance travel writing, I had found it impossible to take any trip without trying to cram in a writing assignment. It saved me from the angst of doing nothing in a world that registered only movement, achievement, speed. But it wasn't very conducive to romantic meals. I patted Ali's hand by way of apology. She put up with a lot. If only I could learn to be as laid-back as Dan.

'How do you relax, then, oh great guru?' I said.

'Oh, just the usual stuff,' shrugged Dan, draining his glass as he got up to go. 'Beer, friends, travel, the great outdoors ... some more beer ...'

He made it sound easy. I had all the ingredients apart from beer – so how had life become so arid and joyless recently? 'Actually, I wouldn't underestimate the beer,' said Dan, cheerfully. 'Why do you think most of the world heads for the pub at the end of the week?'

'That's the problem,' I concluded. 'I've got to learn to loosen up *without* alcohol. Maybe I should make that my next project.'

I was being flippant, but when I looked up at Ali, she was eyeing me thoughtfully. '*That* is the best idea I've heard all day.'

I am seven years old. It's a warm summer's day, and I am in the garden of my childhood home. I'm lying face down on an inflatable lilo which all but fills the paddling pool. Somewhere in the background I can hear my two younger brothers chattering to my mother, and nearby the low hum of bees. Gazing down into the water over the end of the airbed, I watch the patterns of sunlight dancing on the blue bottom of the pool, where blades of cut grass move gently backwards and forwards. The sun is warming my back, and the soles of my feet. There is nothing else but this simple moment.

It seems such an inconsequential scene – nothing happens, and nobody speaks – and yet I have returned to it often over the years. It remains so vivid that even now I can reach down and feel the cool water. Why does it still lure me so powerfully?

Perhaps, it occurs to me today, because I have found a time before judgement. A time before my critic learned to measure my life against itself. It fills me with a yearning so strong that my eyes turn wet and blurry. It is a kind of homesickness. I want to go back there.

Compared with that carefree, weightless time of childhood, I feel like a sherpa, laden with baggage, staggering up a mountain path. I am so very, very tired. Tired of carrying so much, controlling and marshalling it ever upwards.

I need to let go of something, and soon.

2

Learning to Fall

Cornwall and the Cotswolds

'The desire for safety stands against every great and noble enterprise.'

TACITUS

I was perched on a narrow cliff ledge. Thirty feet below me the Atlantic slapped and shouldered the mottled granite, spitting spume. I groped for a cleft to steady myself, my left leg wobbling uncontrollably.

'Don't worry if you can't find a fingerhold,' came a voice from above. 'Just push outwards and jump.'

It was springtime, and many months since my first humiliating lapse of willpower. It had taken me this long to realise that what had happened at my desk on that August morning was not a one-off blip, but an irrevocable change. As autumn darkened into winter I had grown more cautious in taking on newspaper commissions, giving myself space to crash whenever the now familiar symptoms of stalling and panic returned. Inevitably, my income waned. Ali kept a tactful watch on me – but I hid the problem as much as I could. On occasion, I wept angrily in the shower.

I did my best to apply Angela's advice, staving off 'the critic' with insincere thank yous as a caveman might wave a firebrand at a persistent wolf. A one-off £235 Botox injection yielded mixed results: the migraines continued, but my frown vanished – indeed, I barely recognised the man in the bathroom mirror, so blank and emotionless did he appear as he reached for the painkillers. Hopi ear candling was considerably cheaper, but produced only a disconcerting hissing sound and hysterical giggling from Ali, who walked in on me lying on the sofa with what looked like a lit cigar in my ear.

More usefully, however, I had also discovered I was far from alone in my mysterious incapacity. According to a government website, more than 13.5 million working days were lost each year to 'self-reported work-related stress, depression or anxiety' – a catch-all covering the amorphous conditions that employers seemed instinctively to suspect as bogus. As someone muttered on a radio phone-in: 'We didn't have stress in my day – we just got on with it.' I felt guiltily that this was probably true – and if you worked for yourself, who else was there to blame if you lost your drive? Yet many more were hanging on by their fingernails, according to my mother, who was dispensing record numbers of antidepressants at her pharmacy. It was like an epidemic that everyone was trying to hide.

Eventually, as winter turned to spring, I had determined to hide no longer. I would follow what my body was so transparently telling me and make a virtue of surrender. I would turn my affliction into a new project: a year of letting go. And I would begin it all by jumping off a cliff.

There were various reasons why this felt like a good idea at the time. On one level it seemed a bold and symbolic act that epitomised the devil-may-care spirit I was hoping to bring to the year ahead. It would be a cathartic statement of intent, an actual cliff to parallel the ones that had been turning up with alarming regularity in my dreams. In a typical nightmare the previous week, I had found myself hanging from a pinnacle on a mountain when cracks began to appear. A huge slab tilted outwards, and I fell with it, screaming.

At the same time, Ali and I had found ourselves at something of a demographic cliff edge. Heading towards our late thirties, we were at an age when our chances of conceiving naturally were plunging rapidly, and even IVF turned out to be a high-stakes gamble. As one of the 10 per cent of infertile couples whose condition is simply 'unexplained' – everything in apparently working order, but nothing happening – we assumed we'd have a better chance of conceiving by IVF than those with blocked tubes or low sperm counts. So it was a bit of a shock, on turning up for our initial consultation, to discover that the opposite was true. With no obvious cause to the problem, it was harder to intervene medically to fix it. Apparently we had a one-in-ten chance of conceiving through IVF. We had taken a long hard look at the highly medicalised road ahead – timetabled sperm production, hormone injections, egg-harvesting every month, and then the agonising wait to see if the minuscule odds had paid off. The consultant didn't try to put any gloss on it. 'Once you're on the list you can keep coming back until you can't stand it any more,' he said with a rueful smile.

After a lot of thought, we had decided to cut our losses. Neither of us had any desperate biological urge to pass on our genes or have children that were 'our own blood' – we simply thought we'd be good parents. And there were hundreds of children out there already waiting. Why not give one a home? And so, in a shared burst of idealism, we had taken a running jump off the fertility cliff-face. We removed our names from the IVF list – and signed up instead for adoption classes.

Yes, there was something pleasingly unequivocal about a cliff. It offered nothing in the way of gentle change, only abandonment to the forces of gravity. Once you had jumped, it was too late to change your mind. The increasing momentum would see you through, no matter what awaited you at the bottom.

None of this alleviated the physical charge of terror I now felt hanging off an actual cliff at the rugged southwest corner of Cornwall, while a man in a crash helmet tried to talk me into letting go. It had been a long journey to get here, almost as far as it was possible to go in Britain before falling off the end. After catching the train from Edinburgh to London, we had borrowed my mother's car and watched contentedly as suburbia receded and the world got slowly greener: the Home Counties morphing into Salisbury Plain and Devon moorland, then the pleasure of Cornwall's zigzag seascape, notched with fishing villages. Holing up in cosy B & Bs, we had spent a day or two walking the clifftop paths – Ali for pleasure, me to get the measure of what lay below. Finally, the options had narrowed towards the jagged westernmost point, and this particular ledge, not far from Land's End.

It was too late to back out now, and I took a kind of masochistic comfort in that. Besides, I wasn't the only one craving a questionable adrenalin hit. According to the newspapers, it was a youth craze: throwing yourself off cliffs or piers for fun. They called it tombstoning – an unnerving reminder of the sometimes fatal results. But Sam Starkie preferred the term 'coasteering' – a sort of mountaineering-for-the-coast, with the added assistance of neoprene wetsuit, buoyancy aid and safety gear. As watersports instructor to the unhinged, Sam was damned if he was going to let a few kamikaze renegades spoil a good honest adrenalin rush for the rest of us.

'Kids are always going to jump off things for kicks,' he argued, peering over the cliff edge above me, waiting for me to stop quivering and leap. 'We've just come up with a way to do it safely.' As if to persuade me, he tossed his waterproof rucksack over my head and down to the foaming waves, where it bobbed and turned over. Unable to climb up or down, I decided I had no option but to follow it. Gripping my spectacles, and uttering the obligatory scream of insane abandon, I launched myself into space.

They say the hardest part is letting go, but it isn't true. The hardest part was falling, out of control, towards deep water. I gasped involuntarily as my body plummeted downwards, accelerating horribly until the soles of my trainers smacked the surface and all was suddenly enveloped in a chilled explosion. I had a momentary blurred glimpse of bubbles rising from turquoise depths, before my buoyancy aid returned me cork-like to the surface. I cough-shouted and punched the air in delight, enjoying the adrenalin tingle and the sensation, for the first time in months, of stress expelled rather than accumulated. Turning, I found myself eyeballing a quizzical grey seal, riding the same swell.

'How many ways are there to get this close to nature?' grinned Sam, surfacing nearby after his own much higher leap. 'We've even seen basking sharks this year, eh, Dad?'

A pensioner with a silver goatee waved his agreement from just beyond the next swell, sculling happily away from the cliffs on his back, as if in a heated outdoor pool in Marbella. Privately, I felt a little ambivalent about Sam's decision to bring his dad. Somehow our risk-taking seemed less edgy with him around – like taking your mum to see Eminem. And yet he had been the first to leap. Ali, on the other hand, had politely declined to join us, content to camp out in a coffee shop with a good novel.

But now what? We kicked away from the cliffs, enjoying the tumult of waves at play, watching shags and gannets diving into the water around us. Coasteering was an exciting but slightly silly thing to do: a hybrid of rock-scrambling, swimming and bodysurfing, all in what the coastguard graphically called the 'tidal impact zone'. I looked over my shoulder, out towards the headland of the bay, where an unnervingly large wave was swelling in the distance.

'Keep your legs bent when the sea pushes you against rocks, and use the swells to climb out,' said Sam, seeing it too. He was enjoying himself, but I noticed he wasn't taking as many chances as it had first appeared. As well as a thick wetsuit, buoyancy aid and tough trainers, he also carried radio and rescue equipment in his floating rucksack. I braced my legs against a sloping rock and waited for the swell of the breaker to shoulder me up onto it. It arrived with an angry hiss, and I heaved forward, grabbing a cleft as the foam began sluicing back through my legs. But the force was too great and I leapt back into the swell with it to avoid the cheese-grater effect of being dragged over barnacles.

'Quite a buzz, huh?' said Sam, grinning at me between the bobbing toes of his rubber trainers.

We climbed another cliff and leapt off again, one after the other. You had to focus on a rock offshore, watch the lift of its seaweed skirt to gauge the slight undulation of the inbound wave, then time your outward leap so that the swell beneath would carry you away from the cliff, not into it. With a bit of practice we all exited safely and scuttled crab-like along the rocks near the water-line, making for a beach where we could climb a steep cliff path in our wetsuits.

'We're basically just continuing the tradition of Cornwall's smugglers,' said Sam as we picked our way over the rocks and began our ascent. 'They used to anchor offshore, and come into these coves in small boats. Then they had to haul their contraband up the cliffs in total darkness without getting spotted by the excise men waiting at the top.' He paused. 'Though admittedly they didn't have to do it in neoprene.'

Indeed. And there was another key difference. Smugglers risked the danger of the cliffs because of the financial rewards of their illegal booty. Whereas, centuries later, we were doing it simply for kicks. Much as I was enjoying the bodily sensation of release, I couldn't help thinking it was a sign of imbalance to subject oneself to danger for such frivolous reasons.

'Why do you think people are so keen on this stuff?' I asked as we made it up to the top and wandered back along the cliff path towards Sam's black Transit van, emblazoned with the name Vertical Descents.

'What stuff?'

'All these adrenalin sports – coasteering, parachute-jumping, firewalking, whatever – all these manufactured ways of taking risks.' Just a few months previously I had interviewed a man determined to 'inspire others' by setting a record for swimming the greatest distance under Arctic ice. He had drilled breathing holes at regular intervals in a frozen Swedish lake and done it, too – despite blacking out on a practice attempt and having to be rescued. It was, he assured me, *a buzz*.

Sam shrugged. 'Maybe people's home lives are too dull? Who cares, as long as they keep paying me for it.'

But Sam's dad knew what I was driving at. 'I spent a lot of my working life in the nuclear industry,' he said, peeling off his wetsuit in the car park. 'It always struck me as ironic: you could have guys making stringent risk assessments on radioactivity levels at power plants during the week – then going bungee-jumping at the weekend.'

There was a name for this phenomenon, I later discovered: risk homeostasis, or risk compensation. In the same way that the body regulates itself by sweating or increasing blood circulation to keep its temperature constant, it has been suggested that each of us has an optimum level of risk that we maintain, often subconsciously, through day-to-day decisions. A famous experiment has shown how the introduction of anti-lock braking systems in cars has not reduced the overall risk of traffic accidents, because drivers tend to drive faster or more confidently in the belief that they will have more immediate control in an emergency. Or, less scientific but closer to home, bored youths contemplating a joyless future might 'joyride' or 'tombstone' to attain the elusive sense of personal risk and challenge. Clearly, I wasn't the only one trying to let go. In a society obsessed with the elimination of physical risk, danger sports were a release valve.

'I'd say it's mainly a guy thing,' said Ali on the train up to Scotland.

'What is?'

'This extreme sports malarkey. Men find it harder to take the risk of intimacy, so they buddy up and leap off a cliff together instead.'

'Oh, come on!'

Ali chuckled. 'Don't be so defensive! You said yourself that sailing across the Pacific was basically a way of forcing yourself into a bit of male bonding. Whereas women just go out for a coffee together and achieve the same thing.'

Her remark made me think. From an evolutionary point of view, you could see why a certain desire for heightened physical risk-taking might be hard-wired into men. After all, the caveman who never left his cave for fear of meeting a sabre-toothed tiger would never catch any food. But millennia later, with sabre-toothed tiger attacks unlikely, we were still plagued with an insidious, low-level anxiety whose source was unclear. The media fed off it, surrounding us with disasters and worst-case scenarios we were statistically unlikely to experience ourselves.

But was Ali right, that the important risks were now emotional ones – daring to trust others, lay oneself bare? Or had the daily encounter with stark bodily risk given our ancestors something beneficial we had lost? A physical resolution of the stress cycle, perhaps, a purging that was as important as breathing and excreting? I simply didn't know.

It seemed harder than ever before to judge which risks were worth taking and which weren't. Though of course, some risks were always there, lurking in the background, whether you chose them or not.

A few weeks later, for instance, sitting on a train from Paddington Station, I found myself pondering two very different scenarios of impending danger:

a) The recent news that my mother had breast cancer.
b) The fact that I was about to be strapped on top of a biplane and flown at 150 miles per hour over rural Gloucestershire.

The first of these was too difficult to face directly. It had come out of the blue – as my brother Dan had said, a 'punch in the face' from a routine check-up – on our return from Cornwall, and I had been determinedly pushing it to the bottom of my mental in-tray ever since. My mum was putting a brave face on it – they had caught it relatively early, and there was a good chance her forth-coming operation and bout of radiotherapy would be successful. But, either way, it was a risk I could do nothing to influence. Unlike my decision to go wing walking.

After the mild euphoria of my cliff-jump, I had been bragging to friends for days about my forthcoming gravity-defying step back into the golden age of flight. I had given my mother a slightly more economical version of the truth: I was down in London to do an article about biplanes, I told her, neglecting to mention that I would be standing on top of one. Thinking about it as my train approached its destination, I could hardly finish my sandwich for shaking.

'Actually, fear is an asset,' soothed Vic Norman, leader of Britain's only formation wing-walking team, sitting in the club-house of his private airfield half-an-hour later. 'If someone writes to me for a job saying they have no fear, I throw the letter straight in the bin. We need people who are at least nervous – because they'll look after themselves up there.'

We were calming our nerves with a pre-flight cuppa, along with Lucy and Danielle, two svelte young wing walkers decked out like superheroes in coordinating pink Lycra jump suits. They gave the lie to the idea that physical risk-taking was merely a male preoc-cupation. Lucy had wanted to be an air hostess before she found a job working *outside* the plane instead. 'It's strange,' she said. 'I get vertigo on the steps of old castles – but I feel right at home stand-ing on top of a plane. And it's impossible to be sick when you're travelling at a hundred and fifty miles an hour: with all that wind in your face, how would anything come out?'

Lucy was the older of the two women at twenty-one and there-fore my tutor for the day. Danielle had only just done her A-levels. She was spending her gap year flying with Lucy to air shows across

Europe, performing stunts ranging from handstands to a loop-the-loop that put their bodies through 4G as they went from momentary weightlessness to a 160 m.p.h. hurtle towards Earth. Their favourite stunt was called 'the mirror'. 'One plane flies along upside down above the other, five hundred feet up, so that we're hanging there between them, trying to join hands,' said Lucy. 'That really gets the crowd going. We try and shout things at each other, stick our tongues out ... it's an incredible rush.'

Wing walking originally emerged at the end of the First World War, when a generation of demobbed flying aces found themselves with too much excess adrenalin simply to go back to work at the factory or the family farm. Instead, the more enterprising bought up surplus aircraft and tried to fly themselves a living.

'The Americans called it barnstorming,' Vic explained. 'They'd fly any direction the wind was blowing, buzz over a settlement, land in a field and just charge people for rides. But that soon became old hat, so they thought: "Let's send the engineer out along the wing. That'll grab their attention."'

What emerged was a sort of snuff aerobatics, as competing wing walkers vied to outdo each other with increasingly insane stunts – leaping between two planes flying in parallel, or hanging by their teeth from a ladder attached to the undercarriage. As one promoter bluntly explained to his aerial stuntman: 'Don't ever forget that we're both capitalising on the chance of your sudden death.' Many dramatically obliged, each fatal plunge only swelling the crowds.

'They were huge heroes,' said Vic, whose own speed freakery was further evidenced by a collection of vintage motorcycles and his Harley-Davidson T-shirt. 'They were like rock stars, earning their keep from their flying, sleeping under the aircraft at night with a girlfriend. That carefree 1920s stuff!' A spate of particularly spectacular deaths finally pushed both US and British aviation authorities to ban wing walking shortly before the Second World War – when high-risk flying promptly became a patriotic duty all over again.

Vic's narrative was interrupted by a steadily growing roar on the airfield outside. 'That'll be your ride,' he grinned. Two magnificent pink-and-white Team Guinot biplanes were waiting on the grass airstrip – both originally crop dusters, one old enough to have been used for wartime pilot training. 'They're all in their third incarnation, totally rebuilt,' he added quickly, as my knuckles whitened. 'The engine power has been doubled, and the fuel intake modified to allow them to fly upside down.'

This failed to calm my nerves. It was still an enigma to me how a dangerous sport banned in the freewheeling 1930s was now permitted in an era of almost religious health-and-safety observance. 'It was the American Gypsy Moth pilots who eventually found the loophole,' recalled Vic, relishing the story. 'They looked through the rule book and noticed that it specified that any seat in an aircraft had to be designed to withstand certain loads and conform to particular safety standards – so they designed a seat to those specifications that just happened to be on top of the wing of the biplane. And the aviation authorities couldn't stop it!'

The piece of apparatus that awaited me stretched the definition of 'seat' in much the same way that a trapeze might stretch the definition of a handrail. It was basically an upright, waist-level frame with a leather harness and a padded ledge to rest your buttocks on. 'Welcome to my office!' said Lucy as I zipped up my fleece, strapped on some flying goggles and stepped gingerly onto the upper wing. 'Make sure you've emptied your pockets and double-tied your shoelaces – at a hundred and fifty m.p.h. they'll hurt if they whip loose.'

I nodded compliance, noting that the brightly coloured 'skin' of the plane was stretched over what looked like a scaled-up version of the fragile balsawood gliders I made as a child. In fact, these wings *were* made of wood. The only reason I wasn't putting my foot through was that the harness was mounted on the fuel tank. Evidently designed for petite showgirls rather than lanky writers, the harness would only go over my shoulders when I was semi-squatting. 'Don't worry,' said Lucy, tightening the straps. 'Just don't pull out the rotating pin, or you'll find yourself upside down.'

In the midst of this insanity, I thought suddenly of my great-uncle George. His was the other face – apart from my mother's – that I had been trying to keep out of my mind all morning. He had been flying at an airfield not unlike this one, back in 1927, when his RAF training plane clipped wings with another and crashed in a field. Rushing to the scene, reported the newspapers of the time, a bystander had found him 'beyond all human help' – a haunting euphemism.

I had decided not to mention this to Vic and the girls, just in case anyone was superstitious. I tried to fix my attention elsewhere. It was bothering me that a stiff breeze was whipping the trees around the airfield. 'You'll probably find it a bit bumpy up there, and you can expect some steep dives,' agreed Lucy, clambering down to watch. 'But you should be okay for bugs today – I've had to smile to the audience while they burst all over my lips.'

'You'll really know about it if it rains, though,' said Danielle, eyeing the stacked clouds above us.

'It feels like being sandblasted,' agreed my pilot, known locally as Dangerous Dave. He looked disconcertingly like my great-uncle George in his leather flying jacket in the cockpit below me. Lucy noticed the expression on my face. 'One emergency signal you might need is both hands out, thumbs down,' she shouted up. 'That means you've had enough.'

With that, the engines spluttered and growled as the propeller thrummed into a blur a few feet in front of my trembling legs. There was no runway as such – only a large field pocked with little clusters of mushrooms and the occasional startled rabbit. The two planes jolted across it into take-off position – the other bearing a photographer as passenger to mark the occasion – and Dangerous Dave checked his wing flaps, instruments and puff of stunt smoke. I savoured that flutter of the heart that signals the point of no return: speak now or for ever hold your peace.

Suddenly the engine noise rose several decibels and we were accelerating across the field. The wind resistance was fierce, and by the time we left the ground, I was finding it hard to open my mouth without the sense that my lips were going to peel back over my scalp. We soared and banked away from the airfield into a fabulous emptiness, and quite suddenly, all fear left me. In its place came a rush of insane energy. I stuck my fist out in front like Superman and attempted a triumphant whoop, but got a mouthful of wind instead. Below me the girls were pink dots waving from the side of the airfield, and I decided I'd better do something other than just stand there. I tried to lift a leg off the wing with the balletic poise of a true wing walker, but found it forced backwards so violently that I had to wedge it on the other knee, as if sitting cross-legged at a bus stop. I stuck my arms out experimentally like a human plane, and almost lost them to wind drag. They jerked backwards as if pulled by lead weights, my straining muscles showing through the flattened, flapping tube of my sleeves.

It was like one of my favourite flying dreams, soaring over farmland and country piles and little blue lozenges of swimming pools. We flew along the canyon created by two rain clouds, banking and soaring, mirroring the other plane, as a herd of tiny deer galloped across a field like wild steers in the days when this was a crop duster. I became conscious of my idiot grin, my quivering facial muscles, my hair whipping and snapping at my scalp. Then, after about three minutes, the critic piped up: *Are you actually enjoying this? Is it what you expected?* I was just about to launch a counterattack when, with a sudden lurch, the plane began to dive.

I opened my mouth to curse, but the wind snatched the words as they emerged, flung them back and out, a mist of jumbled letters scattered in the tail smoke. Then I was weightless and falling and aware of nothing but the ground rising to meet us, the roar of the engine and the distant high-pitched keening of my own terror as we hurtled towards Earth . . .

And it happened. For one intense, head-emptying moment, there was nothing but the ground and the sky and the screaming and the joy. A blessed glittering seam of pure consciousness untainted by past or future. Timeless like an orgasm or a blow to the head. Something almost like stillness.

And then Dave pulled up and skimmed low over the hedgerows, tearing a scream from my mouth like ticker tape as we whipped past the aerodrome: 'Yeeeeeeeeeeeeeaaaaagggh!' My stomach, AWOL for some time, returned, lead-heavy, as we made a final circuit and lined up for landing. Never had I felt so high on adrenalin, so utterly invincible. But by the time we'd bumped down and bounced across the field, I was back in my body, flexing my aching arms. The grin congealing, the breathing slowing. The moment past.

I wanted to do it all over again.

'I've always liked roller coasters,' said Lucy over another cuppa in the mess hut after a few celebratory photos. 'But I went to a theme park recently and it didn't do anything for me, there was no feeling in the tummy any more. It was like, Is that it?'

Adrenalin is like any other drug, requiring steadily increasing amounts for the same effect. Even 500 feet above the ground there is a limit to how long it lasts. Clambering out of their cockpits above the blur of another show crowd, the girls had taken to hyping themselves up with imagined action-movie theme tunes ('Eye of the Tiger' and the 007 theme tune, respectively), but sometimes the turbulence bruised them like a circus whip, and they ached for a lie down. Most of their predecessors had given up wing walking when they started a family. In fact, it wasn't even particularly useful as a conversation-starter with eligible men. 'To be honest, I think guys are a bit intimidated by it,' said Danielle. 'But we still look across at each other as we soar past in the sky and think, How lucky are we?'

Yet I was curious to discover whether high-adrenalin sports actually helped them to relax a little more in everyday life. Did it affect the way they assessed risk? 'Funny you should say that,' said Lucy. 'But I've got a lot more nervous about driving since I started this job.'

'Driving?'

'Yes. I'm a lot more aware of the risks you take every time you get in a car.'

This baffled me at the time, along with the idea that Lucy could happily step onto the wings of a biplane, yet suffer vertigo on the steps of a castle. But as I thought about it on the train home, I realised there was a perfect logic at work. For all its appearance of extreme danger, modern wing walking was, statistically, very safe. Unlike their forebears, whose probable deaths drew the crowd in the first place, Team Guinot had a 100 per cent safety record – a statistic I had logged from their website before committing myself to the flight. In a clear sky there was only the ground or each other to crash into. The variables took the form of two experienced pilots and a harness that was tested every day.

Down here on the ground, however, every second involved trusting hundreds of people you had never met. On a train you had to trust that nobody had put a log on the line. And on the road it was even worse. Every single metre travelled relied on cars passing only feet from you at high velocity but not veering into your path – or a pedestrian remembering to look before stepping off the kerb.

And compare the statistics on wing walking and cancer. My mother would have been safer strapped to the wings of a plane than at the mercy of a disease whose *raison d'être* was to multiply and destroy all other cells. What was fascinating was not that we took risks, but that we learned almost instinctively that in order to live a functional life, there were many risks it was better simply to ignore.

Danger sports were a fake form of letting go, I reluctantly concluded. A highly calculated risk taken within fixed parameters and supervised by experts. Good for a momentary thrill and the illusion of weightlessness, but essentially a distraction from the more difficult quest for real change.

It all begged an uncomfortable question: which as yet untaken risks was I trying to avoid?

3

Pure Clown

Perthshire and Edinburgh

'The secret of genius is to carry the spirit of childhood into maturity.'

THOMAS HENRY HUXLEY

'I'm afraid my breasts are disintegrating a bit,' said the woman in the queue in front of me. 'Someone got a bit carried away and rolled on them last time, but I've patched them up and brought them along again anyway.'

Ever since I announced that I wanted to learn to relax more, certain friends had been bombarding me – a little overenthusiastically, I felt – with flyers for workshops. Not the sort of workshop a mechanic might recognise, of course. This one was titled Spring Fool Workshop, and I had a feeling the only tangible thing it would manufacture was heavy blushing. Its daffodil-yellow publicity pamphlet depicted a barefoot loon in a state of unhinged abandon, wearing what looked like a hospital gown, his arms akimbo. 'This weekend is for anyone needing a burst of new life and those curious to explore the preciousness of the present moment' read the blurb. Coming a week or two after my wing walking, and only an hour's drive north of Edinburgh, it had sounded more like the kind of risk-taking Ali might respect: a kind of adrenalin sport for the emotions. On impulse, I had phoned the number and secured a last-minute place.

Which was how I came to be standing in a sort of dance studio cum retreat centre in rural Perthshire with seven mainly middle-aged women, queuing behind the one with disintegrating breasts. They did indeed look a little battered as she brought them out of her shopping bag – the sort of fake plastic strap-on variety favoured by stag parties. She dropped them onto a large pile in front of her, along with a feather boa and a bright-red ball gown. The leaflet had requested that we raid our wardrobes for dressing-up stuff, and the other participants had already deposited an impressive collection of coloured wigs, bunches of plastic flowers, hats, shawls, dresses, waistcoats and a Viking helmet.

My own offerings seemed a little run-of-the-mill by comparison. Searching vainly for something even primary coloured in the earth-toned wasteland of my wardrobe the previous evening, I had been struck afresh by how serious my adult life had become while my back was turned. Where were those Guatemalan patchwork trousers I once bought at a festival? Or the student-era jester's hat and juggling balls I used to divert myself from finals revision? All gone the way of the Oxfam shop, I feared. Instead, I had scraped together a paper sunflower, a long grey journalist's mac, and an unconvincing party beard.

This sorry selection only reinforced my conviction that it was high time I recovered a little communal *joie de vivre*. But was this really the way to do it? Not for the first time, I was amazed at my ability to high dive into situations that I would clearly regret later. *What were you thinking?* muttered the familiar voice from within. *You don't belong here! These people are all drama types or workshop junkies — you're a lanky bloke in spectacles. You're going to look like a prat!*

I nodded nervously at the small huddle of would-be clowns. It was true that they were mostly women of the dangly earring and silk scarf variety, while the only other man was currently doing yoga stretches. I steeled myself by gazing out of the window at a couple of peacocks strutting back and forth. The Orchard Conference Centre was set in a lush green valley near the village of Bridge of Allen, a short drive across the Forth Road Bridge from Edinburgh. It was early May, and the spring sunshine had already conjured up a flurry of apple blossom on the trees. Perhaps it could also coax some fun from a reluctant clown?

Behind us, the workshop leader was carefully tying elastic to red clown noses and placing one under each chair in the circle. 'You won't need these just yet,' she said, calling us together to begin. According to the pamphlet, Angela Knowles had been 'exploring fool and clown archetypes since 1985', whatever that meant. She had wavy auburn hair, intense blue eyes and smiled with a knowing mischief as we sat down and introduced ourselves in turn: Jess, Emma, Fay, Brenda, Shirley, Peter and me. Nobody gave any further clues — no occupations, no ages. We were just a group of apprentice clowns sitting in a circle.

I had always felt a little ambivalent about clowns, with their sinister grinning faces and greasepaint. They were epitomised for me by the Joker, who laughed maniacally through my childhood as he tied Batman and Robin to a conveyor belt that would send them to their doom. Even the circus variety were usually either derelict or near psychotic, attacking each other with giant mallets or ladders or paper plates wobbling with shaving foam. I had recently heard it was possible to have a phobia of clowns. I could well understand it.

'What we're doing here is called "pure clown",' said Angela. 'But I stopped calling it a clowning workshop because people have strange ideas about clowns – they think it's about performance and disguise when actually it's just about giving yourself permission to be yourself. So I focus on the figure of the fool instead.'

Despite the cap and bells, fools and jesters had a significant social role, I seemed to remember from my days studying Shakespeare. Scuttling around the feet of his great, flawed heroes, they combined physical slapstick and bawdy gags with profound and often slightly insulting truths about their supposedly wise masters. They were the only ones who got away with it because their low status meant their masters could dismiss anything they didn't like as the witterings of the insane. By dwelling at the bottom of the strict medieval hierarchy, they had a freedom of expression arguably greater than that of those at the top.

But Angela's fool was a more archetypal one. She pulled out a picture on a laminated tarot card. 'I don't know much about tarot, but this is the best representation I've seen of the fool.' We all peered at the figure in the picture, who was sauntering along a cliff edge carrying a small bundle on a stick, Dick Whittington-style. 'Blithe is the word I'd use,' she said. 'Head up, very little baggage, he's utterly at one with himself, travelling light. And of course he's about to step off a cliff.'

It was amazing how often cliffs were coming up. I was interested to hear someone else explain the apparent attraction. 'The next moment is always an abyss,' said Angela simply. 'We usually try and protect ourselves by pretending we can control the future, but in a sense we're just insulating ourselves from the present. When you're a fool you're always in the present moment. In fact, it's the only place worth being.'

She paused for a moment to let that sink in, then clapped her

hands and got up. 'Right, that's enough theory – let's play a game!'
She beckoned us to our feet, had us push back our chairs and
began scattering props and clothes across the room. 'I want you
each to find a partner.'

I was standing next to Emma, a friendly, vaguely hippyish
woman about my age, who recognised the look of a rabbit caught
in headlights and raised an enquiring eyebrow. 'Now, without
saying anything,' said Angela, 'I want you to hold hands with your
partner and go and find something to play with together.'

Oh God. What is this? muttered an Eeyore-ish voice somewhere
inside. *You're about to be humiliated and it's your own fault.* But Emma had
already taken my hand, and pulled me out into the middle of the
room. Evidently a drama type and used to this kind of thing, she
lead me over to a grass skirt that lay splayed across the wooden
floor.

'Now, have a little fun playing with your object,' said Angela.
'We're talking two-year-olds here – but no talking!'

There was no dignified way to do it ... with a hiccup of adrenalin, I decided to throw myself into it. I just had to think like a
toddler – which, from my experience of toddlers, meant combin-
ing borderline mobility skills with being the centre of the universe.
Feeling suddenly mischievous, I grabbed the grass skirt and put it
round my neck. That got a grin from Emma, so I spun around fast
enough for the fibres to fly outwards. Emma stifled a chuckle.
Brilliant.

'Remember you're not here to entertain the other person, only
to play,' said Angela, like a clown headmistress. I took the skirt off
my head and gave it to Emma. She threw it over her shoulder and
grabbed a fairy wand instead, and looked as if she were about to
stab me with it. Then she had a better idea and picked up an old-
fashioned brass car horn. Putting her nose and mouth in the horn

end, she began to squeeze the rubber bulb gently. This was going to be hilarious! 'Don't forget to breathe!' said Angela, just as it came – a strange, farty honk which instantly brought the house down. Everybody collapsed and howled with laughter, all of us rolling around the floor in huge, helpless gasps.

'How was that?' said Angela, finally calling us together. 'Any observations?'

There were a few sheepish chuckles as the spell was broken, and we all tried to compose ourselves as adults again. 'To start with I kept thinking, Don't make a fool of yourself!' said Jess, who had made a play-tent from a Palestinian scarf. 'Then I remembered that's what we were supposed to be doing.'

Angela nodded. 'Everything in society trains us to fit in and obey rules, so as soon as you start to break out of that, you'll find a huge resistance from inside – some call it the inner critic – telling you to behave. I want you to notice that voice.'

This was interesting. It confirmed that I was not the only one with an inner running commentary. Others just used different names: a censor, a perfectionist, a critic, a killjoy, an adult. 'Don't try to control it,' said Angela. 'Just watch what the voice says, like you might watch the weather.'

Emma admitted to a strong temptation to poke me with a flower. 'It felt like it would be crossing a boundary,' she grinned. 'But I wish I had.' For some reason I wished she had too. 'But aren't rules sometimes necessary to prevent something inappropriate?' asked Jess, her responsible adult self now back in charge. 'If we just did what we wanted, where would it all end?'

We all looked at Angela for her answer. It was a good question. 'You mean, what would happen if we all followed our impulses in life? Would there be total anarchy? Would we all kill each other like in *Lord of the Flies*?' She shrugged and let the question dangle.

'I'm not going to answer that one for you – I don't know ... I just know I love the feeling of being in the present, and not in charge. It sounds a foolish way to be in the world – and of course it is. But it's extremely freeing.'

I thought about this as I lay on my back on the floor for the next exercise, breathing through my nostrils. There was a heady hit of adrenalin in taking risks with other people, even when it was only the risk of seeming a fool. As I gave in to the sensations of the body, my inner critic gave up too, as if outvoted. In a world that evidently rewarded mischief and letting go instead of sobriety and control, I discovered I was only too happy to oblige – delighted in fact, as if this part of me had been waiting to come forth.

Next it was time for our first proper taste of clowning. 'People think of red noses as a disguise,' said Angela, handing them round like plums. 'But actually they're a sort of permission to be real.'

Greeted by a row of blank faces, she got us to pull up a line of chairs and try it out. One by one, we had to go outside the room, put on our red nose, and then walk back through the room in silence. The first time it wasn't even slightly funny – just a bit odd, like a sort of blank clown canvas – but next we had to choose a trait from someone we'd seen. 'Don't tell us who it is,' said Angela. 'Just exaggerate it slightly.' It was the deadpan expressions that did it – within moments we were all chuckling at familiar rounded shoulders, or an air-head peering into the sky. I threw in a flat-footed trot. Each time we did it, the walk seemed a little easier. The nose was important – when I put it on, out of sight, and re-entered the room, it was as if normal social customs were suspended.

Only after a few turns did we finally attempt eye contact: standing before our co-clowns, looking at them each in turn. The absurdity of this silent limelight terrified me. I watched the row of spectators smirking or empathising or blushing at me, and felt myself growing rigid with tension. For some reason I was holding my breath, and my eyes were beginning to water. When the tension eventually exploded out of me, it was in a ridiculous falsetto of schoolboy laughter.

'Sorry, but what am I supposed to be?'

'No words!' said Angela sternly.

It was both intimate and threatening. With no means of verbally clarifying what was passing between us, making it okay, there was just the vertigo of a bottomless gaze. After what seemed like twenty minutes, but was probably about two, Angela led polite applause. I bowed stiffly and walked off to rip off my nose, blushing heavily. *You utter fool*, muttered the critic. Which was accurate at least.

It got easier as each of my classmates attempted the same thing. It was always excruciating for the first few seconds – eyes creased with laughter, faces strained with the impossible attempt to be whatever it was they were supposed to be – then the humour subsided and gradually the red noses became an excuse simply to look at one another. It made me realise how rarely humans use the sustained power of eye contact. Do the same on the average high street, and it would be interpreted as a come-on either for a sexual encounter or a punch in the face. Here, staring for up to a minute at a stranger, you saw everything – the initial guardedness, mischief or bravado, followed by short intakes of breath, the sighs, the little flickers of bewilderment, the shy smiles, the nerves.

'I want you just to observe the different emotions you go through, like weather that comes and goes,' said Angela. 'Don't try to make it into something, or get into deciding if it's good or bad.'

Soon I ceased even to notice the red nose and saw instead the individuality and beauty of the people in front of me – their fatigue, pain, fears, sometimes even tears. Some flicked their eyes away, moved on for safety. Others seemed to stop time. I conducted an experiment to see what I could communicate through eye contact: when Fay was before us, I focused all my thoughts on compassion and understanding, saw her extreme bravery simply in standing there and tried to acknowledge it in a strong but gentle gaze. She gazed back transfixed, trying to read me – and then her eyes brimmed. I forgot almost where I was, how long I had been making this absurd, dangerous connection with a stranger in a clown nose. With no words available to make it jocular or funny or unthreatening, it was simply what it was, outside category or rationalisation.

'I found that strangely moving,' said Fay in our feedback session, looking at me again. I nodded.

'What you're seeing in other people's faces is in some ways your own face,' said Angela. 'We mirror one another. We all share this vulnerability.'

Lunch was my first opportunity to find out what my co-fools did outside this little cocoon of lunacy. Emma ran a theatre project for people with learning difficulties, Fay was a primary-school teacher, Jess ran a country retreat, Brenda was a herbalist, Shirley a student of Mandarin. Not exactly a cross section of society, then. A distinct lack of alpha males – or any other males, for that matter. Peter, it turned out, was Angela's partner and there to make up the numbers – and he left early, suffering from a heavy cold.

Angela herself told me she had begun her lifelong love affair with drama and improvisation as a difficult fourteen-year-old schoolgirl in Leeds. 'It kept me out of trouble for four years,' she said, munching on a breadstick. 'Then in my twenties I did a clown

workshop and one in circus skills, and I've been hooked ever since.'
She was now in demand at workshops and conferences around the
world. The joy of clowning wasn't so much its entertainment value,
she said, but the way it taught you to have a playful, loose relationship with yourself.

'The older I get, the less I know who I really am,' she said happily. 'It's a constant surprise to me, and such a relief. We go
through life telling these stories about ourselves, enacting little
dramas to bolster our self-image – *I'm a survivor, I'm a mother, I'm a
workshop leader* – but the joy of clowning is you learn to drop the
story any time you want. It's kind of like adventure travel, but inner
adventure: which abyss am I going to leap into today?'

After lunch we fell on the dressing-up box like inquisitive toddlers,
ready for the acid test of our ability to 'stay in the moment': one
by one we were ushered in front of our co-fools and required to
improvise a routine with the mystery contents of a cardboard box.

Fay found a voluminous blue IKEA holdall and folded herself
gamely into it; Shirley crammed three stale Ryvita into her mouth
with the hilarious intensity of a martyr. Brenda was attacked by a
swarm of clothes pegs. In each case it was the unpremeditated buf-
foonery that had us laughing – the seat-of-your-pants-ness of it.
And then it was my turn. I was feeling witty and confident until I
opened the box and discovered that it was completely empty.
Everyone laughed at me as I stared abjectly at Angela. 'Good,' she
said. 'You're learning how to fail. Keep eye contact. Now what are
you going to do?'

There was a long silence in which I had the brilliant idea of
inventing an invisible pet. I mimed stroking something inside the
box, getting bitten by it, grinning inanely at it ... all in deafening
silence. Someone yawned.

'Look at our eyes,' said Angela flatly after a few seconds. 'Is this working?' I stared out at six pairs of bored, apologetic eyes, and shook my head gloomily. 'Try something more obvious.' I took a deep breath, looked inside the box again, then realised what I was missing: the box itself! I lay it on the floor and was just bending down to pick it up when Angela commented: 'We can see your breasts.'

Instinctively I stood bolt upright in panic. I had forgotten I was wearing Jess's fake boobs. They were now hanging out of the front of the tailored tweed jacket I had chosen to complement my grass skirt and Russian Cossack's hat. It had seemed a gutsy, bohemian ensemble at the time, a new-mannish, nicely ironic way of playing with gender. But suddenly I saw myself as I really was: a trembling, bespectacled writer in false breasts standing mutely before a row of female hecklers.

Never had I felt so drained of ego. The women were cackling and hooting hysterically, and my miserable expression seemed only to increase the joke. I stood there for what felt like years, lamely holding my empty cardboard box, trying to cover myself with the feather boa. I was vaguely aware that my lungs were about to burst.

'Breathe!' yelled Angela, noticing too. I took a long gulp of air, as if surfacing at sea. 'Clowning is about learning to fail repeatedly. Every clown is born, dies and is resurrected many times every day. So pick it up!'

There was nowhere to go but onward. Somewhere deep down I made the decision to let go, as recklessly as if shoving my own ego off a cliff. Keeping my eyes on the women before me, I punched through the bottom of the box, creating a sort of frame to look through, like a TV set. I inadvertently framed my breasts as if in some bawdy seaside peepshow, triggering another explosion of mirth. Feeling suddenly energised, I began simply to follow each new impulse: sliding the box down over my head, my hand poked out of the top and became a character in its own right. 'I want to see an evil puppet,' said Angela. 'Whispering indecent things in your ear – now do whatever it says.'

I conducted a protracted silent debate with my own beaked fist, ruling out several things I feared even Angela might baulk at, before sliding the box down over my midriff like a sheepish Victorian bather.

'Give us the dying swan!' yelled Angela. 'We want the dying swan in a cardboard tutu.' I gave it my all, stretching out willowy arms above my head, standing on one leg and trying a couple of jetés, then accidentally ripping my cardboard tutu during my pirouette. I fell to the floor and gave tragic dying glances to women now crying with laughter.

'Now a finale,' said Angela, as I stood to bow. Did the woman never give up? I paused, smiled innocently at my audience and dropped my tutu like a bath towel to appreciative shrieks.

Who exactly was this person standing in front of these cackling women? A sort of wonder spread through me as they applauded and wolf-whistled: did I even recognise myself? And yet who was I to say this improvisation was any less real than the dramas perpetually enacted inside my head? What made Nick as workaholic, or journalist, or even husband any truer than Nick as transvestite clown – other than the fact that I acted these parts more regularly? At that moment, all felt equally plausible, just stories I dropped and picked up at will. I wandered back to my seat wrapped in my feather boa and a sense of infinite possibility.

'A masterful combination of Nureyev and Fonteyn,' drawled Jess with a smile. 'Now, can I have my breasts back, please?'

*

The afternoon wore on with dozens of costume changes as we paired up for ludicrous improvised jigs, each of us vying to outdo the other in flamboyance: Jess in a chef's hat and a granny shawl, me in a feather boa and blood-red wig. It was always the spontaneous moments that worked best, never the premeditated 'gags' or pratfalls. Slowly, we lost all fear and simply played together while Angela looked on, laughing. The peacocks shivering haughtily outside the window looked conservative by comparison.

Finally, at the end of the afternoon, Angela herded us into a line facing the back wall and ceremonially pulled back a long curtain to reveal a full-length dance-studio mirror. It took me a moment to recognise myself in the ludicrous family portrait that presented itself – a grinning loon peering out from behind thick Woody Allen spectacles and a bulbous red nose, framed in livid red hair and a boa.

'Have a good long look,' said Angela. 'Who do you see?' There were nervous chuckles, then a hushed awe as each of us took in our own transformation. I waited for the recriminating inner voice of scorn to kick in and tell me to grow up, get home, tell nobody. But, actually, I quite liked the man I saw in the mirror. It was his eyes – they had a sparkle and a mischief in them that I didn't often see staring back from my bathroom cabinet. An outrageous truth presented itself: that this grinning loon was just as much a part of me as the furrowed, responsible adult.

In the days after the workshop, the magic lingered a little. I found myself singing operatically in the car at traffic lights, grinning back at the frowning people on the bus. Walking Charlie, I played more. With both of us off the leash, the usual tug of war became a companionable stroll in the park. Apparently I was more playful at home too.

'What happened to you?' asked Ali, immediately noticing the difference. I wasn't exactly sure. There was just a sense of imminence, an expectation of something fun. It lasted a couple of days before the fool began to fade. *Okay,* said the critic, *you've had your fun.*

But I hadn't quite finished. It was all very well to let rip in a Perthshire conference centre – but, according to Angela, the ultimate test was to take our new-found folly onto the streets. So, before the lunacy had a chance to fade completely, she had extracted a promise that we would meet in a week's time, and hit the Edinburgh rush hour.

At around 5 p.m. on Friday, a slightly reduced group of five of us assembled bravely in a café on the Royal Mile, laden with costumes, crayons, buckets, wigs and plenty of reservations. The idea was to earn some money for charity as clown portrait painters, wandering around the city centre doing crayon sketches of shoppers and commuters in return for their loose change. Even with this fig leaf of motivation, the idea was terrifying. Supposing I bumped into a journalist colleague? I disguised myself as heavily as possible in the Woody Allen specs and explosive bright-red wig, and hoped to get away with shrouding the rest of my body in a long trench coat. Not a chance. 'Where's the rest of your costume?' said Angela. She threw a crimson ball gown at me. 'That's about your size, isn't it?'

A chill wind was blowing litter and grit down the Royal Mile as we jostled our way out of the café toilets and went in search of our first victims. I glimpsed the bistro where my brother Dan had challenged me the previous summer and thought, If you could see me now ... I kept to the back of the group, intent on staying as inconspicuous as a six-foot two-inch man in drag can reasonably expect, while Angela waved cheerily at a businessman coming up the street and pointed to her sketch pad. He hurried across the road and disappeared down a close before Jess could even get her crayons out.

It was uncanny how the street was emptying. It was going to be even harder than I thought. Nobody wanted to look at us, let alone laugh. I chased a couple of lawyers down Jeffrey Street, but they just wanted to get home, and jokingly told me where to stick my crayons – an understandable response to a guy in a ball gown at the end of a long week. But I was realising that Joe Public was far more intimidated by us than we were by him, which helped my nerves. Emboldened, I began to do things I would not dream of doing in my usual garb – impersonating the piper busking at the intersection, or peering through restaurant windows at people until they looked up. I enjoyed showing them my sketch pad and watching them grin at the stick-figure travesty I had drawn of their romantic meal, while Jess nipped in with the charity bucket for a donation.

All the same, it was hard work. We got ourselves thrown out of Waverley Station, the epicentre of busyness and seriousness, and ended up sitting on a wall outside a nearby shopping centre. Why was it so difficult to engage people? Emma had a theory. She had done a stint at the G8 protests with the Rebel Clown Army – an anarchist collective often seen sporting luminous wigs and camouflage gear at political demonstrations, to unsettling effect. 'People fear the lack of normality,' she said, picking her nose off the pavement after a particularly savage gust. 'Sometimes you can make connections you wouldn't make in civvies, but I guess we all rely on being able to predict fairly well what our fellow humans are going to do – and you never know what a clown is going to do.'

We were less mocked than feared – anarchic emissaries in the ancient tradition of the fool, out to disrupt society's Friday-night rituals. And, like the fool, we were not always well received, trying to tickle a smile onto the serious face of business and commerce. Angela suggested we tone it down a bit and stop using our voices: to attract interested people to us by staging spontaneous acts of human kindness. When she pointed to a random passer-by we applauded them rapturously, as if they had just performed a concerto. This provoked a variety of reactions. A little old lady with a wheely trolley tut-tutted us; a businessman took a bow and blew a kiss; and a group of bored teenagers came to sit next to us, asking to try on our hats and wigs.

It turned out that there were three sorts of people who could consistently be relied upon to respond warmly to unwarranted attention from a gang of clowns. The first was children and teenagers, who seemed to like the fact that we were disturbing the grey uniformity of the street, and wanted to join us. This made sense to me – for the young are still experimenting with disguises and masks of their own, and instinctively understand the playfulness of the fool. The second group was headed by a man with cerebral palsy, pushed in his wheelchair by his carer and delighted with our lavishing of attention and drawings. He, like us, was used to being stared at or avoided. We were probably the first strangers that day who simply smiled and waved at him.

The third group was tourists, who always came to have their picture taken with us and thanked us profusely for our execrable scrawlings, often putting folded fivers in our bucket. This, too, had a sort of logic to it: I thought how often as a traveller I had ventured abroad in order to escape the masks that habit had imposed – to try out a different me.

But even ordinary Edinburghers became a little more unbuttoned as rush hour gave way to happy hour. Grinning through a pub window at the top of Cockburn Street, we distracted the audience from a live guitarist who at first struggled to understand why his love songs were suddenly provoking laughter. Finally looking round, he dropped his guitar and dragged Angela inside to sing a duet with him. Naturally, we all had to go and rescue her – and the bucket came out a lot heavier than it went in.

In that sense, a red nose was like an extra pint of beer. It was permission to be yourself, to let down your guard and be silly for a while, without having to police yourself for shame. Clowning was like getting tipsy together and saying that unguarded, truthful thing you'd never say when sober. Thankfully, both drinking and clowning had their get-out clauses: in the pub 'it was the booze that made me do it' and here it was Angela who made us do it.

But what if we didn't need permission to be different, or simply ourselves?

4

As If

Edinburgh

'The only real voyage of discovery consists not in seeking new landscapes, but in having new eyes.'

MARCEL PROUST

The days after my clowning were strange and light, as if I were tethered almost arbitrarily to my personality. Sometimes I would stand in front of the bathroom mirror, looking into my own eyes, and find myself thinking, Who is this person? Perhaps it was my imagination, but the almost permanent vertical creases between my eyebrows seemed to have softened somewhat recently. And this time it wasn't Botox.

As spring turned into summer, I began to smile at myself as a kind of daily experiment. I had read somewhere that such habits could genuinely influence one's mood. In the past, nothing would have made me more irritable than the exhortation to cheer up – as if it were that easy! But after a couple of sessions grinning at myself like a paralysed hamster in the privacy of my own bathroom, I was amazed to find that my emotions did indeed have a tendency to follow the lead set by my face. On days when I woke feeling low or sad, the forced grin had a sort of manic quality to start with, but it soon gave way to a healthy sense of absurdity, and I found myself chuckling. And once I was chuckling, it was impossible to maintain any kind of clenched moodiness.

The implications of this were truly disturbing for a habitual worrier. Having afforded my emotional states the utmost importance all my life, as some kind of spiritual barometer to the truth of the human condition – or, at least, my own – I was suddenly discovering they were, in fact, as arbitrary and changeable as the clothes I put on each morning. If I could fool myself into feeling happier simply by pulling a happy face, what other possibilities might await me in my quest to live a more relaxed life?

'So, Nick,' said the social worker, pen poised above her notebook. 'How would you describe your personality? Are there any particular strengths you feel would help you in being a good father?'

It was a warm Friday afternoon in June and Ali and I were sitting nervously on our sofa for another session of what was known as 'home study'. Avril was a friendly but thorough social worker from the adoption agency. She had been assigned to spend six months collecting information about us for a report to be presented to a panel of experts at the end of the year. It had come as something of a jolt to be reminded that her primary job was not to find us a suitable child, but to check that we were suitable parents.

Having attended a series of introductory meetings, we were now required to spill the beans on our relationships with each other, with our parents, with our friends; we apparently needed to stump up bank statements and payslips to demonstrate that we could afford to bring up kids; we needed criminal record checks and chronological timelines for every period of our lives since birth. Even Charlie had been introduced to Avril in case he was a possible danger to young children. (Thankfully, he had refrained from disembowelling her handbag, preferring to sit reverently at her feet in the hope of food.) At some point we would need to attend detailed medical examinations to show that we were fit to take on the challenges of parenting, then we'd need three separate references of good character, copies of our marriage certificate, and statements on our understanding of nationality and ethnic identity. So far we had not been asked to hand over our teenage diaries, provide DNA swabs or itemise the contents of our bedside drawers, but it would not have surprised me.

Being adult about it, you could see how it was all both understandable and necessary: most children available for adoption had already suffered from one set of problematic parents and certainly did not need another. But on an emotional level it only emphasised the gulf we felt between our situation and that of an 'ordinary couple', for whom there was no interview process for parenthood except perhaps a bottle of Rioja over a romantic meal.

And what did any of it have to do with learning to loosen up? In some respects it was harder to think of anything less conducive to a spirit of contentment than being grilled by a social worker for the right to parent a child. It was like any other interview – unless I ticked the boxes on Avril's ideal parent list, I might not get the job. And yet if the clowning workshop had taught me anything, it was that the carefully constructed story I had learned to call my 'self' was less rigid or permanent than I thought.

So, what were the qualities I might bring to being a dad? As I began to talk to Avril, I found myself instinctively settling on the lighter, more contented me. Instead of a journalist with a perfectionist streak and a tendency to overwork, I described a freelance writer with lots of flexibility to arrange his day around childcare. Bored with the cliché of a worrier who was far too anxious for approval, I found I could identify instead a sensitivity to the emotional landscape of others. Likewise, I could have rehearsed my loss of faith and direction, but instead I told Avril how my inner journeyings had given me an openness and fascination with all kinds of ethnic and religious backgrounds.

Avril nodded vigorously and scribbled away in her notebook, evidently encouraged by what she heard. I'd never had much time for 'positive thinking', smacking as it did of Pollyanna-ish desperation, a sort of rewriting of reality to shut out all the difficult bits. But now it occurred to me that positivity was not so much a distortion as a decision about what you gave your attention to.

And what surprised me as I spoke was not simply my ability to summon up this positive, capable me, but my realisation, even as I spoke, that it was all true. Instead of my usual self-deprecation, I heard myself described faithfully from my own lips as hard working, honest, playful and empathic. It was like dropping one story and picking up another, and the new clothes fitted as I tried them on. Stepping into the void, I found the road rose up to meet my feet.

Out of the corner of my eye I could see Ali watching me with a thinly veiled amazement. '*That's* the Nick I married,' she said, kissing me happily after Avril had left. 'I'd like to see a bit more of him, please.'

5

The Garden of Eden

Cornwall

'Being naked approaches being revolutionary.'

JOHN UPDIKE

Camping has never struck me as an inherently relaxing activity. But on Midsummer's Day, in a deserted corner of a campsite in Cornwall, the process of pitching our two-man tent felt even more anxiety-inducing than usual. Perhaps it was the fact that one of the fibreglass poles had split, forcing me to botch a repair with duct tape. Or was it the ominous rain cloud hovering nearby, which threatened to baptise us before we'd got our fly sheet on?

Or perhaps it was the fact that I was stark naked. Yes, that was probably it.

'I wouldn't mind if we were the only ones here,' I muttered to Ali, as I rummaged in the car boot for the spare guy rope. 'It's meeting the other five hundred naturists that worries me.'

Nudefest had seemed like a great idea on paper. Remembering my furtive attempts at skinny-dipping on continental beaches over

the years, Ali had hit on the perfect birthday present for my year
of letting go: a ticket to the country's biggest gathering of naturists. Veterans and first-timers alike were invited to shed their
clothes in an outdoor festival of nakedness. After a day in the
great outdoors, the event would culminate in a Midsummer's
Night opportunity to eat, drink and roam *au naturel* around the
vast tropical biomes of the nearby Eden Project – temporarily
renamed, of course, the Garden of Eden.

Simultaneously terrified and intrigued by the idea, I had
accepted on one strict condition – that Ali came along too. My
early experiences of communal nudity had not been encouraging.
As a squeaky late developer, I experienced school showers as a
form of purgatory inhabited by sniggering, gorilla-like classmates.
A lot had happened since then – not least puberty, and the affir-
mations of Ali – but I had never really shaken off the sense of
deep shame instilled in adolescence. I wasn't the only one. At the
gym I noticed several other men still employed a complex towel
screening system when changing. And, judging by the amount of
cheap Viagra or 'penis enlargement' on offer in the average pay-
load of computer spam, most of mankind was in need of
reassurance in one particular department. While women gained
statuesque beauty when naked, it seemed to me that men exposed
a kind of dangling absurdity, like the bit left over on an evolutionary assembly line. But I envied naturists their carefree attitude,
and increasingly I yearned to let go of this cloying shame and
simply inhabit my own body.

The reality of Nudefest, however, grew steadily more alarming
the nearer the date drew. My pulse quickened even as we boarded
the train in Edinburgh, trying to envisage the terrifying moment
of baring all in front of hundreds of others. Jumping off a
Cornish cliff seemed a cinch compared with what we were going

back there to do. Staying for a few nights beforehand in ordinary B & Bs, we'd found ourselves unable to admit to other guests where we were going next. It seemed such an odd and unacceptable thing to do. By the time we had navigated up the last country road towards the private campsite, we were both almost hyperventilating.

It had been overcast when we drove onsite, and the receptionist who gave us our site map and directions was fully clothed, with the only naturists in sight little more than fleshy silhouettes in the distance. 'Just to clarify, it is definitely okay to, um, you know ... ?' I had said haltingly to the woman.

'Yes, dear, it's just been a bit chilly this morning,' she said kindly. 'They're probably all in the marquee.' I looked over at the large white tent in the middle of the field, trying to imagine the scene inside: a naked committee meeting? A Bacchanalian orgy? A barn dance? I decided we should pitch our tent first. Our space was between two unoccupied tents, with parked cars acting as plot dividers and providing at least some privacy. Then, suddenly, our first sighting: a middle-aged couple crossed the grass in the distance each wearing nothing but shoes and a towel over the shoulder. Sure enough, scraps of blue sky soon heralded the arrival of the sun. Which was when we took the plunge.

We were just starting to enjoy our solitary naturist experience – grinning sheepishly across at each other in a 'can you believe we're doing this?' kind of way – and had almost finished putting the fly sheet on, when I became aware of a naked man coming towards us. He walked jerkily across the field, waving awkwardly, his head at an angle in a way that suggested mild cerebral palsy.

'Hello!' He smiled, extending his hand, as if welcoming us to a PTA meeting. 'I'm Jason. Have you come far?'

'Edinburgh,' I said, trying not to stare.

'Blimey,' he said. 'And I thought Yorkshire was a long drive.'

We all chuckled and talked politely about the weather, and established that Jason was a graphic designer. We stood farther apart than one might normally, and I found it difficult to know what to do with my hands: on the waist looked exhibitionist, at the sides seemed awkward, and down in front like a choirboy looked downright defensive. Ali had folded her arms, but Jason gesticulated freely, as if it didn't occur to him that there was anything to be embarrassed about. And perhaps there wasn't.

'So, how long have you been naturists?' he asked.

'About five minutes.'

'This is your first time?' He gave a thumbs up. 'Nice one!'

He really was very different from the idealised men who advertised aftershave in the Saturday magazines. Yet somehow his utter self-acceptance, his take-me-or-leave-me shamelessness in the face of what anyone might think, meant that neither his disability nor his nakedness mattered at all.

'Thank you, Jason,' said Ali, making the kind of fixed and unwavering eye contact that is essential when you're naked. 'It's nice to be welcomed.'

We all nodded, and ran out of things to say. A nervous silence ensued.

'Well, see you later maybe,' he said, turning to go back to his tent.

Emboldened, we decided to head up the field to meet the naked masses. The first problem was what to take, and how. I would usually take at least a notebook and pen with me, not to mention a mobile phone, but now I had nowhere to put them. I assembled a few things in a bumbag, tried it on, took it very quickly off again, and carried it up the field by hand.

'I think I could learn to enjoy this,' I murmured as we strolled along together in the sunshine, our towels draped over our shoulders. There was the kiss of sun on skin, the glistening wet grass between the toes, the light breeze in unfamiliar places. And the farther we walked from our clothes, the harder it was to turn back. I shivered, not from cold but from a long-lost frisson of childhood innocence. We passed a couple of men with a friendly nod. No problem. We were all wearing the emperor's new clothes, but nobody was going to point that out.

The sun had gone in again by the time we reached the marquee, however. With a sudden chill in the air, we were perhaps less circumspect than we might have been about ducking through the opening. It was set up as a sort of exhibition tent with tables selling videos, books, T-shirts and so on around the sides, and an open space for milling around in the middle. We were in the midst of a couple of dozen other people before we had a chance to take them in properly.

'OhmyGod!' whispered Ali. 'Everybody else is wearing clothes!'

Have you ever had one of those humiliating dreams in which you find yourself exposed in front of your school class or work colleagues? This was it. But it was too late to retreat. Already a couple of friendly people wearing shorts and T-shirts were smiling and nodding at us. There was nothing for it but to nod back and pretend that all was normal. Ali steered me over to a table where a woman was selling tickets for the bus to that evening's event at the Eden Project.

'Hello there,' I said, dangling my towel strategically over my arm. 'We'd like two tickets please.'

'Gosh you young 'uns are brave!' said a grey-haired lady admiringly. 'It's still too cold for me!' She was wearing a T-shirt and, I suddenly noticed, nothing else.

'Well, actually, we're pretty new to this ...'

'It's your first time?' said the woman. 'Good for you! Hear that everyone?' Ali giggled, mortified, while I surpressed an urge to run screaming from the marquee.

'We can always tell first-timers,' said a younger man, appearing at my elbow in shorts and shirt. 'When you've been here a bit longer you know it's okay to put a T-shirt on when it's cold. We call it clothing optional.'

After bolting back to the tent to get dressed again, we were disconcerted to find that cold-weather rules did not apply to most of those lunching at the onsite café. In ambiance Abigail's Kitchen resembled an English country pantry, minus pants – at least for most of the men, who munched naked or with only a shirt on. Female partners, I noticed, tended to be fully dressed.

'Do me a favour,' whispered Ali as we waited for our jacket potatoes. 'Whatever else you do, don't get into the weird shirt-but-no-pants thing. What's that about?'

It was hard to tell. Nobody seemed to be talking except the cook, presumably Abigail, who bustled among the tables fully dressed and shouted: 'Two sausages and an egg butty?' A few men lunched alone, including a peevish civil servant type wearing nothing but polished brogues and a slightly bored expression, and a man with tattoos and a copy of the *Sun*. They were united only by their nakedness and the fact that they sat on neat squares of towel.

'That's the cardinal rule of naturism,' explained a man called Andrew, who introduced himself to us on the way out. 'Sit on a towel – don't put your bare bum on a chair. But that's about the only rule. And of course we don't want anybody staring or making untoward comments like, "You haven't taken your top off yet." You'll find naturists are very respectful.'

It is only relatively recently that nakedness became a lifestyle with its own rules. First gaining popularity in Germany in the early 1900s, naturism in prudish Britain has been a rather more secretive affair. The first club quietly established itself in Wickford, Essex in 1924, and other 'sun societies' restricted themselves to members-only arrangements on private plots of land – particularly after 1930, when naturists sunbathing by a reservoir in north-west London were attacked by an outraged mob. The free-and-easy sixties brought a slightly wider accept-ance to public nudity, but with only 150 clubs in the whole of Britain, the modern movement could still hardly be called main-stream.

Andrew Welch was its public face. As commercial manager of British Naturism, he was the only 'professional' naturist onsite, he joked, as we all wandered into the pub next door. 'I'm being paid to be here, but I'd do this anyway,' he said, though he was wearing shorts and T-shirt. We joined an awkward, clothed little gather-ing by the bar, while on the other side of the room a belly-dancing workshop was in progress, involving a group of ample ladies wobbling around wearing only sequins. Andrew sensed our discomfort.

'I'm finally warming up a bit now,' he said cheerily. 'And the great thing about naturism is that if I decide to take my shorts off now, I'm just going to do it. If I stood in a normal pub and did that I'd be arrested.' He didn't do it, though, at least not in the pub. Instead he waited till the sun broke through again, as we were walking across the car park half-an-hour later, then dropped his shorts casually without even pausing for breath.

'There, that's better,' he said, removing his T-shirt too, and striding over to a patch of grass to lay out his towel. Disconcerted but emboldened, I did likewise, trying to emulate his no-fuss single-movement method while leaning against a hedge. It wasn't the nakedness or clothes that were the problem, I reflected, tripping on my underpants – but how you got from one to the other. Ali exercised her right to stay warm and rubbed some sun-screen on my back.

'There are a lot of misconceptions about naturism,' said Andrew, sitting on the grass beside us. 'It's not about sex or shag-ging in the bushes. In fact there's nothing sexy about it. People talk as if the human body is an abomination: "God, what would you do if you saw a pair of boobs or a willy!"' He grinned like Benny Hill, then chuckled, shaking his head. 'But we all know that it's just ridiculous. I mean, there's nothing unnatural or awkward about this, is there?'

Ali, lying fully clothed in the sun, chose to ignore the question. I found myself oddly divided. Part of me shuddered with the sheer ludicrousness of what I was doing. But in a deeper place I felt relief, almost contentment – a return to the purity of child-hood, the days before judgement. 'At the risk of sounding flaky, there's almost a kind of spirituality about it,' said Andrew. 'We don't know our bodies very well. We keep them wrapped up twenty-four hours a day. But after a day naked in the sun, some-thing about going to work the next day is not nearly as bad as it might have been. People say you strip off your worries when you strip off your clothes.'

As if to demonstrate, a rather large lady walked up wearing only Velcro sandals and a necklace. 'Sorry to interrupt,' she smiled, a mighty statue of flesh, soft and pillowy and utterly unabashed. 'Andrew, you're needed in the marquee in about quar-ter of an hour – we need to go over to the Eden Project to help set up.' She wasn't conventionally beautiful, certainly – nothing like the idealised shapes draped across billboards. But there was something very attractive about her relaxed demeanour, her total self-acceptance, that bestowed a beauty of its own. She smiled at us, and walked away.

'You find naturists who are missing limbs, women who have had mastectomies – it's all just normal,' said Andrew. 'A lot of people, particularly larger women, will have spent much of their lives worrying about what an ideal size is and then discover that it doesn't matter.'

The sun had come out again, and a mixed volleyball match was in progress. Nearby, a family of four were enjoying the sandpit together. We wandered back into the marquee, where a naked woman was lying on a massage table having her lower back rubbed by a clothed therapist in front of a queue of waiting customers. There was t'ai chi later, promised Andrew – but a 'hotly anticipated body painter' had sadly dropped out due to a transport glitch. I peered at the photographic display, a record of the annual British Naturism trip to Alton Towers amusement park. Little white bodies draped over black rubber rings going down the flumes – people with triumphant, exhilarated expressions in their eyes.

'There's definitely a barrier the first time,' Andrew was saying. 'But once you've taken your clothes off, it seems no big deal – you must have experienced that yourself now, yes? For men the main worry is: Will I get a stiffy? But I've never seen it in all my eighteen years of naturism. We're self-regulating creatures, and when you come to a place like this you know that's not the kind of thing you should do.'

It was a markedly optimistic take on human nature, let alone human biology. Since when had the male member done exactly what it was supposed to do? Yet I liked the idea that nakedness could still be as wholesome and rich and unproblematic as it was when we used to run through the garden sprinkler as kids. Sitting here chatting in the sun, it was possible to forget for, oh, whole seconds that I was utterly exposed. I thought of the ancient myth of the Garden of Eden, and wondered, not for the first time, what exactly was symbolised by the eating of that apple from the tree of knowledge of good and evil. 'Who told you that you were naked?' asks God, as Adam and Eve stitch together their first fig leaves in a flurry of new-found shame. What exactly changed for us in that loss of innocence, some time before puberty? Did it have to change? Andrew didn't think so.

'What's sad is that naturism has been linked erroneously with sauciness and pornography over the years, so that people can't tell the difference. Victorian prudery and modern-day media titillation are really two sides of the same coin – both had a problem with the naked body. The Victorians said: "Retain your modesty, your dignity" – but for God's sake, you were *born* naked. I get people ringing me about doing TV documentaries promising it will all be "tasteful, nothing visible", but I'd rather they showed the human body in all its ordinariness. Instead, the media shows the nude form as provocative by hiding it.'

He was right. There was nothing provocative here precisely *because* nothing was hidden. It was a glorious festival of the body. Men sinewy or full-bellied, simian or balding, hung like gorillas or unashamedly compact. Women casually bulging with the voluptuous curves of Rubens paintings or leaping sylph-like across the volleyball court. Nipples and scars, muscles and stretch-marks, all unveiled, free of the tyranny of Simon-says fashionistas selling 'must-have' disguises. I saw no preening narcissists here – these were mutineers. Suddenly I loved them all for their happy abandonment to the mixed physical legacy of genes, easy living and the laws of gravity.

'All of human life is here!' proclaimed Andrew as we took in the scene around us.

'Then why are there more men than women?' asked Ali pointedly. It seemed a fair question, if naturism was really so innocent and family oriented.

For the first time Andrew looked uncertain. 'I don't know why that is,' he admitted. 'We do have a lot of single men in naturism. I guess some may come here looking for partners, viewing it as a kind of nude dating agency. But a lot of men have realised it's not really about that . . .'

He looked at his watch and gathered up his shirt to go. 'You should ask some people yourself – they'll tell you what it's all about. Birds of no feather flock together.'

It had turned into a perfect sunny afternoon, and, after the strangeness of our arrival, we were both feeling sufficiently uninhibited to spend an hour or two by the pool. Lying there listening to the sound of children's squeals and a game of pool volleyball, I felt a deep contentment. Ali seemed to be enjoying herself, too. We joined in the game, then got talking to a couple of the male players at the edge of the pool.

'We're first-timers,' I said. 'I'm curious: how did you take the plunge?'

'I do life modelling all round the country, and I didn't even have to think about it,' breezed the taller and balder of the two. By contrast, his rotund friend was a social worker who had spent several months working up the courage to go to an isolated cliffside naturist beach near his home. 'The first time I was so nervous – in fact, I was more nervous at being seen by a woman than having a rock fall on my head. I took enough equipment to climb Mount Everest, what with the sunscreen, chairs, sun umbrella and Thermos flask. But it was worth it. I was much more overweight than I am now, a bit prone to depression, and I'd never felt good about myself. But when I took that step it was like shedding something I'd been carrying around for years.'

It was a story we heard many times that day. Some people told it like a religious testimony, wet-eyed, marking a line in the sand after which things were different. Others were more matter of fact, like the young Ph.D. student I met on the way back from the pool.

'I'm not a naturist – I just don't like wearing clothes much,' shrugged Ruth Brooker. 'In fact, my parents failed to make me wear clothes for most of my childhood. Then I met Andy and it was just another thing we had in common.'

Her noticeably older husband appeared at her shoulder and grinned. 'Naturists are by far the friendliest people we've met,' he said. 'On this site you can walk up to anyone and start chatting. You're a case in point. But if you go to a campervan site where there are textiles, you can go whole days without so much as making eye contact.' Textiles was the shorthand for people who preferred to keep their clothes on. They had inadvertently shocked textile friends on a recent French holiday by setting off to the beach on their tandem wearing only trainers and sunglasses.

Back home in London, they'd found friends disappointingly censorious about their penchant for naked gardening and house-work. 'A lot of people think it's got something to do with sex,' said Andy. 'But I can't think of anything less sexy.' I could see what he meant. 'Still, we've found it's best to get net curtains if you want to hoover in the nude.'

'We don't want to upset the textiles, do we?' smirked Ruth. 'They're very sensitive. You have to look after them, poor things.'

I liked them a lot, envied their cheery disregard for convention. 'Well, I was a textile till now,' I grinned. 'And I almost didn't take the risk.'

Ruth looked at me, amused. 'What's the risk? The only thing you really risk here is sunstroke.'

'Or possibly being talked to death,' said Andy.

It was almost time for the evening party at the Eden Project, and we'd been asked to get dressed again for the twenty-mile bus trip, to avoid distracting other motorists. It felt a shame to be back in our clothes.

'I've cheated!' said a mischievous granny, pulling up her track-suit top to show her bellybutton. 'Nothing underneath! So I can get 'em off quick at the other end!'

The Eden Project appeared seemingly from nowhere as we breasted a hilltop, a series of vast geometric glass domes set in a quarry like some alien colony. I was intrigued by the logistics of getting several hundred people out of their clothes and into the biomes. Would we all strip in the car park? What would we do with our clothes? And how would we carry our wallets?

My most pressing concern was answered by a sign stuck to the doors as we queued outside the admissions hall: 'No cameras or mobile phones allowed.' It was a profound relief to know we wouldn't be turning up on YouTube. It took a while to check all our tickets and issue goodie bags, including an apple for the Garden of Eden. A nice touch. Then staff directed us along a walkway to the changing room and issued us with black bin bags. With an impatient sort of joy, hundreds of people were stripping off and stuffing their clothes into the bags, which were labelled with our ticket numbers. It was a measure of how much inhibition we had lost that we just went ahead and did likewise, handing our last vestige of propriety to a woman standing behind the counter. *In uniform.*

It hadn't occurred to me that not everyone would be naked. For the second time that day, I felt a lurch of horror. The staff were all clothed! Having spent all afternoon settling into a protected world of acceptance, we were suddenly facing people from the real world. There were dozens of them, all dressed in red polo shirts, and looking fixedly into the middle distance.

'We need to be easy to identify!' explained a young usher, awkwardly, as he held a door open for me. His averted eyes reminded me of the expressions of commuters in Edinburgh when confronted by clowns. But at least then we had the benefit of a disguise.

There was a buzz of nervous excitement in the air as we all trooped into the entrance hall for the biomes, clutching our meal vouchers. The elegant tinkling of a clothed harpist somehow failed to soothe. Ali made an urgent beeline for the wine-tasting stand. The place was quivering with flesh of all description: substantial bodies, soft bodies, lanky bodies, damaged bodies. A very large woman was being pushed around entirely naked in her wheelchair by a man wearing only a leather Stetson, while others made their way around on crutches. I waved to Ruth and Andy, who could be seen disappearing along an upper walkway towards one of the biomes – clearly veterans, they needed nobody's approval, and I envied them. By contrast, I was once again the naked emperor in the children's fairytale – this time feeling much as he must have done approximately one second after the kid in the crowd pointed out the obvious.

'Shall we get some supper before we do the tour?' I said, faking a business-as-usual tone to quell the rising panic.

Beside me, Ali downed an emergency glass of Chardonnay. 'I'm not sure I can do this,' she said, surveying an echoing canteen in which naked people were queuing with trays and towels, while uniformed staff tried to keep their eyes on the pork curry. 'All these people wearing clothes!' But we had come this far, and neither of us could think of a dignified way to make an exit.

After the chilly clatter of the food hall, the tropical biome was, thankfully, another world entirely. A vast temperature-controlled bubble of jungle, its warm, damp heat embraced us from the moment we walked through the automatic doors. It explained why naturism in Britain could seem such a nerdy affair. We just didn't have the climate for it, whereas in the tropics you glowed with the mist of water on skin, and your muscles relaxed automatically. It was getting dark outside, and ahead of us naked silhouettes moved along the shadowy walkways overhung by palm fronds. Instinctively, I slipped off my shoes and carried them, feeling the warm pathway beneath my bare feet.

'This is more like it!' whispered Ali. 'This I can do.'

If there were a collective noun for naturists, it should surely be a 'vulnerability': a gaggle of geese; an obstinacy of buffalos; a vulnerability of naturists. Yet each time I successfully brazened it out past a clothed staff member, the vulnerability felt less of a problem. Here, as in my Edinburgh clown excursion, the power imbalance was not necessarily in the direction I had first assumed. Increasingly, we made eye contact with others in the biome, exchanged conspiratorial smiles. Walking around Eden in front of 'textiles' felt both more risky and more rewarding than simply blending in on a naturist campsite. There was an unspoken solidarity in it which I found oddly moving. Unlike a solitary leap off a cliff, this was a shared risk. Rather like a group of twelve-step alcoholics standing up one by one to confess all, we found a kind of strength in dropping any semblance of disguise. It was a joyous graduation into the freedom of nothing left to lose.

We took a tour with a rather flustered-looking Eden guide in a sweat-sodden safari shirt, who seemed to bring out the group's playful streak. 'I suppose he needs somewhere to pin his badge, poor man,' whispered someone, as he tried to marshal us all through the biome. It was an extraordinary place, made all the more magical by the fact that the dark roof panels 55 metres above us now reflected the floor lighting like stars. A waterfall plunged from the highest rock, sending a warm, wet wind down over the jungle canopy. A few people looked like they were resisting the impulse to take an *al fresco* shower.

At that moment, however, a haunting sound issued from the jungle below us – a sort of strangled trumpet call. 'That's the next part of your tour,' said our guide, with some relief. 'Something a little different from my colleague, I think you'll find.'

A minute later we arrived in a clearing to find Eden's resident storyteller waiting for us. On his head he wore a velvet top hat with feathers stuck in its rim. In one hand he carried a long wooden staff with a snake carved round its upper portion. In the other was the ram's horn he had just blown. A kilt lay discarded at his feet. 'So, here we are in the Eden Project and we're all naked,' he proclaimed in a theatrical Scottish brogue, throwing his arms wide with an accepting grin.

At last, an Eden Project employee brave enough to shed his uniform – and for good reason. Because tonight he was retelling the story of Adam and Eve – how they gave in to the serpent's tempting, ate from the forbidden tree, and were thrown out of paradise. It was strange standing there in a naked huddle, listening to a story I'd last heard in church.

'I have a theory that many of our seven million visitors come here because they'd like to be let back in to Eden,' he said to his hushed audience. 'They're looking for peace and innocence – and trust. So, let me ask you a question: which of you told your colleagues you were coming here this weekend?'

There were a few guilty chuckles in the uncomfortable pause that followed. Five or six hands were raised in the group of fifty. Ours were not among them. The storyteller nodded gravely. 'There's nothing shameful about the human body – I take it you all believe that?' He looked around at us all, standing goose-pimpled in our birthday suits. 'And yet there must still be a shard of that first shamefulness – am I right?' The silence was charged, guilty. *Who told you that you were naked?*

He held up his staff with its carved serpent. 'Well, there are many creation stories, but in the Moroccan creation story, there's a great extra part that we don't often get told. Do you want to hear it?'

'Yes!' we all shouted.

Adam and Eve were cast out of Eden much as we had all heard as children, it transpired, but in this version of the story, God gave his rebellious couple a kind of divine get-out-of-jail-free card. 'This was God's promise,' shouted the storyteller. 'If you are able to look at your own reflection without shame, then you can come back to Eden!'

He looked around at us with what looked like pride, a naked prophet surveying his naked flock. 'Do you understand?' he grinned. 'We should be celebrating here! Because maybe in the future a new story will be born where there isn't guilt and shame and fear – and you're all part of that story! You're the first people that have walked around Eden naked!'

He ended grandly with a flourish of his wooden staff, as if signalling a naked revolution in which people of all shapes and sizes would surge voluptuously into the streets, offering sunscreen and self-acceptance to our poor rag-shrouded compatriots. Instead, a few people whooped and chuckled, and we followed him down towards the sound of drums and guitar in the vast foyer.

If not quite paradise, the scene that greeted us was a cheering one. On the dance floor, naked people were jiving happily to the African rhythms of a fully clothed band, while up on the balconies, people were having official photos taken as mementos.

Neither of us felt that brave. But, just occasionally, among the turbulent sea of flesh reflected in the plate glass of the foyer doors, I caught sight of a me I barely recognised.

And I grinned.

6

The Tragic Flaw

Edinburgh

'Man is the only animal that laughs and weeps, for he is the
only animal that is struck with the difference between what
things are and what they ought to be.'

WILLIAM HAZLITT

Every month, two plain envelopes drop through our door bearing
magazines with stark titles: *Be My Parent* and *Children Who Wait*.
Their faces smile out bravely at us, page after page of kids who
have been neglected or abused or abandoned by their birth parents
and are now desperately in need of loving new families. We are in
no position to help any of them until we've been approved by an
adoption panel at the end of the year – but I still find it impossible to browse for any length of time without being left with a
gnawing anxiety. Suddenly, instead of the general concept of adoption, here are actual children with names and very real needs.

My background reading, and the adoptive parents who spoke at
our adoption classes, leave us under no illusion about the level of
commitment required. In the old days, the taboo of unmarried

motherhood pushed thousands of women into handing over their babies in the delivery room, regardless of their competence as mothers. Thankfully, this is now a rarity – but it means that children needing adoption now tend to be older, with often tangled histories and complex emotional needs.

I fear for what we might be letting ourselves in for, and yet I'm also curious about that fear. A stark realism is evidently essential if we are to take on the daunting task of reparenting a vulnerable child, but how much is my apprehension governed by the simple habit of my essential outlook on life? After all, another person might look at the same little faces and feel a completely different set of responses, based on their predisposition to optimism or pessimism. Where do those default attitudes come from? Can we change them?

And why does so much in life encourage us to think the worst?

Reactions to last week's brief dabble with naturism are an interesting case in point. Having failed to admit where we were going beforehand, we lost no time telling friends and family all about it once we got back. But while a few seemed genuinely delighted to hear about it – and one or two even admitted to their own fondness for baring all on holiday – the majority were embarrassed, as if we had done something morally hazardous by allowing ourselves to be both naked and unashamed.

And the body is only the most obvious symbol of humanity's deep-seated mistrust of itself. You don't need to be religious to believe that there is something fundamentally tainted about us. It's at the heart of all human drama – from the tragic flaw in Shakespearean or Greek tragedies to the catalogue of violence or political wrangling in the average newspaper. Why so much suffering in the world? How to explain the famines and tsunamis and wars? We may no longer subscribe to the literal belief that we're all cursed by the actions of Adam and Eve, but many of us still hold to secular variants. The second law of thermodynamics, about as empirical and non-religious as you can get, apparently enshrines a universal principle of decay that's as observable as a rusting car or the slackening jawline in the bathroom mirror. Because, let's face it, things fall apart rather than together (the reason why we're so enchanted by those reversed films of demolished rubble leaping back up into perfect buildings, or shattered china reconstituting itself into a vase). Creating order takes effort, whereas chaos seems to thrive by itself. Shit happens.

And yet so do unexpected miracles, flowerings from the compost. Balancing the second law of thermodynamics is the first: that energy may change forms but is never ultimately lost – a burning forest becomes heat and light. A rotting body fertilises the growth of new life. Everything comes round again. For every Hitler there's a Gandhi. For every selfishness, an unexpected act of kindness. So you can choose how you view the same data – is the glass half full or half empty?

Increasingly, it all boils down to one existential, practical six-million-dollar question: Can I trust myself? The answer to that question, it seems to me, will determine many things, not least whether I can ever truly learn to let go. After all, if humans really are essentially flawed, then why on earth would anyone want to relax enough to risk walking blithely into the abyss? Surely the only sane action in such a world is to increase our vigilance and exert control over our own and others' actions wherever possible, in order to avert disaster. And yet my experiments so far hold out hope for another way of looking at the world. It seems to me no coincidence that those I know with a generally trusting outlook tend to foster much closer relationships, and live much happier lives.

Since we were first married, Ali has undergone a change in out-look akin to a conversion. We come from more or less the same psychological stock – both raised as Christians, both influenced by faith's more liberal fringes, both generally disillusioned with dogma. I still remember the moment I first saw her standing at the back of a church, campaigning for disability rights – a vision of loveliness from her Irish curls to her black suede Doc Martens. She exuded a passion for helping others, and yet as we got closer I also noticed that this often caused her to sideline her own needs. By the time we had been married for three years, she had more or less burned out in the bottomless pit of need that is social work, and was looking for a better way to live.

She found it, after our year of travelling in South America, on a counselling course. Almost immediately I noticed some domes-tic weight shifting back onto my shoulders, as Ali gave a little more priority to her own needs. Household tasks she had taken on almost without thinking were now shared equally, and she made a regular habit of heading for a coffee shop with a novel to recharge, away from the demands of others. In her old life there would always have been a suspicion that such needs were essentially self-ish – we had both been well schooled in original sin, and the need to keep a constant check on our desires. Now, under the influence of Carl Rogers, the humanist founder of her particular school of psychotherapy, she seemed to have converted to a belief that human nature, if not exactly good, was at least essentially con-structive. Accordingly, I watched her grow more trusting of herself, and less critical. Happy, even. One of her goals as a therapist, it seemed, was to offer the same unconditional acceptance to her clients.

'But I thought you were trying to help people change,' I said, puzzled. 'What if a client tells you he's attacked someone? Are you going to accept that, too?' Surely we needed to find some way of restraining or renouncing our darker impulses before we could truly grow into bigger people?

'Actually, I think it often happens the other way round,' said Ali, carefully. In her experience, when people could truly accept themselves as they were, then real growth came naturally. It seemed to me as much a change of creed as a change of profession: a kind of 'original goodness'.

Years on, I yearn to make the same leap of faith. It seems to me that what was once a matter of philosophical preference has acquired a new urgency, as we contemplate the very real challenges of adopting a child. It feels more important than ever that I learn, like Ali, to trust that there's potential for healing and a natural impulse to grow towards the light.

But if we are going to be ready to make this leap of trust as adoptive parents – or to see clearly that we shouldn't – I need more than an arbitrary change of philosophical stance. What began as a quest for a balanced, stress-free life is growing daily in significance. I need not only a gentler vision of humanity, but also a method for rooting this in the gritty reality of everyday life.

I need a full-blown conversion.

7

Drop the Story

London

'Hell is just resistance to life.'

PEMA CHÖDRÖN

'Einstein said there's really only one important question to ask yourself, and that is: Is the universe friendly?' The silver-haired woman standing at the front of the stage had the flawless coiffure and elegant scarf of a day-time television presenter, but her eyes had an extraordinary aqueous intensity, rippled with laughter lines. 'I don't know if Einstein found the answer to that question, but I invite you to test it for yourself today – to find that the universe is friendly.'

Byron Katie had not always been so radiant. At forty-three, a depressed divorcee from a small desert town in southern California, she had become so paranoid and suicidal that she was afraid even to venture outside her bedroom. But, twenty years later, she was touring the world giving seminars to thousands, and hailed by *Time* magazine as 'a spiritual innovator for the twenty-first century'. I was curious to know what had made the difference.

It was Angela, at the clown workshop, who had first aroused my interest in Byron Katie, talking about the often arbitrary way we had all experimented with different identities – the way it was possible to 'drop the story' and discover who we were without one. It was a phrase of Katie's, apparently, born of her extraordinary experience of waking up on the attic floor of a halfway house one morning without any concept of who or what she was. 'There was no me,' she had written. 'All my rage, all the thoughts that had been troubling me, my whole world, the whole world, was gone. At the same time, laughter welled up from the depths and just poured out. Everything was unrecognisable. It was as if something else had woken up.'

For a while she wandered around her town, befriending strangers and arousing curiosity among her family and neighbours, who began to hanker after whatever it was she was on. Her explanation had been stark and bewildering: 'I discovered that when I believed my thoughts, I suffered, but that when I didn't believe them, I didn't suffer ... Freedom is as simple as that. I found that suffering is optional. I found a joy within me that has never disappeared, not for a single moment.'

Since her transforming experience, she had devised a simple, four-step method to teach others how to experience the world in the same way. She called it 'The Work'™. Two decades later I found it hard not to be sceptical. If there was one thing the world didn't need, it was surely another trademarked US self-help franchise. And yet the more I read about it, the more curious I became. Which was how I came to be in the packed auditorium of Kensington Town Hall one Sunday morning in early July, listening to Katie herself (her fans used her second name as if it was her first). On the stage, a couple of armchairs were arranged by a little table with a vase of flowers, in the manner of a chat show. Stewards were quietly handing out work sheets for us all to fill in with thoughts that habitually troubled us.

'The Work is a way to investigate and question all the thoughts that cause all the suffering and violence in the world,' she explained, like a school teacher addressing her favourite class. 'It's not a little thing we're going to do here, so I'd invite you to get what you came for. We're dealing with *stressful* thoughts today. The other ones, thoughts that bring a smile, that bring balance and reassurance, they don't need work: they're tied to our nature. Today we're dealing with the thoughts that cost us that awareness and that balance, which at its highest level is what we describe as enlightenment.'

There was nothing particularly new about Katie's basic philosophy. It had a lot in common with Taoism and Buddhism, and could be summed up by the saying of the first-century slave-philosopher, Epictetus: 'We are not disturbed by what happens to us, but by our thoughts about what happens.'

From what I had read of her work, Katie's particular system for applying such truisms was a kind of Socratic inquiry for the emotions, winkling out inbuilt assumptions and habitual thoughts of the sort that had plagued me all my life. I watched with interest as one of the keener members of the audience walked up onto the stage so she could demonstrate how it worked.

He uncrumpled his piece of paper and read out his most painful thought in a voice that cracked and wavered. 'I . . . I need my father to be alive.'

Katie looked at him. 'Is that true?' Her tone was gentle but it was a stark question – the first of a series she routinely applied to any statement.

'Yes,' said the man flatly.

'And is he?'

'No'. There was something tired but solid about his disappointment, resting like a scuffed piece of luggage on the stage between them.

'And can you absolutely know you need him to be alive?'

The man looked a little puzzled, then pensive. Finally he said quietly: 'No.'

Katie nodded silently and moved on to another of her routine questions. 'And how do you feel when you believe this thought: I need my father to be alive?'

Interesting. Totally sidestepping any discussion of whether it was natural for a man in his mid-forties to be grieving his long-dead father, she was looking practically at the effects of the thought. 'I feel angry,' said the man. 'I feel sad. I miss him.'

Katie nodded empathically but persisted – as if trying to prise the man like a limpet from his rock of emotional certainty. 'Now, how would you be without that thought: I need him to be alive?'

He sighed. 'I guess I'd feel peaceful; I wouldn't be so serious.'

Katie's aim, it seemed to me, was not to invalidate the man's grief, but offer a number of possible alternative realities. She did so by inviting him to swap around the basic components of his original statement. 'So, try turning your sentence around.'

'I *don't* need my father to be alive?' We all watched him trying that one on for size. It seemed not to fit particularly well, so he tried another. 'I need *myself* to be alive?' He swallowed and nodded, grinning nervously.

'Yes,' said Katie simply. 'It's your argument with reality that costs you your peace, not your father's death. So turn it around again.'

'I need him to be *dead*?'

'Absolutely. It seemed an outrageous statement, heedless of all the taboos surrounding death and grieving. And yet there was a slow dawning in the man's eyes.

'How do you know you need your father to be dead?' persisted Katie.

'Because ... I have to find my independence?'

Katie nodded. 'Isn't that what the perfect father would want for you?'

The man sighed, getting the hang of what was going on. 'It's true, I had to learn to find my own way, support myself.'

'And can you find another way in which "I need him to be dead" is equally true?'

'I spent a lot of time with my mother, became much closer to her.' There was little hesitation now, and a lightness was creeping into the man's heavy demeanour.

Katie went on methodically, as if unpicking knots in tangled string. 'So what does it mean to your father, if the opposite is true?'

'He was quite old, quite ill, quite tired. He had a lot of difficulties.'

'And you need him to be alive? Is that true?'

The man smiled sadly. 'No, it's not true.'

'Welcome to reality. Another statement?'

The man looked back at his paper. 'I don't ever want to lose anyone again.'

'Who are you afraid to lose?'

'My mother ...'

'So if the inevitable happens, how would that be a good thing?'

The man took a deep breath. 'Because it would be time for her to die, time for me to move on and experience another time in life.'

'And for her? Why would it be better for her?'

The man's eyes welled up again. 'Freedom from pain.'

Katie nodded and looked out at the audience. 'We live. We die.

It's life. We teach our children to be sad ... but all suffering is confusion.'

The man gazed at her wonderingly as he got up to leave the stage. 'So, I look forward to losing my mother?'

She gave him a sad, enigmatic smile. 'Life happens. And everything that happens, without exception, happens for our enlightenment.'

I watched, intrigued, as others followed him up onto the stage, one by one, to subject their dearly held thoughts to this unortho-dox scrutiny. A woman was convinced that her husband should be better at voicing his emotions; a man was furious at what he felt was a betrayal by his best friend. These long-standing stories were clearly causing great emotional pain to their bearers – and doing nothing to resolve the situations in question. On one level, there seemed a pragmatic, humane generosity in helping them to loosen their grip, to find alternative stories that were less corrosive to their peace of mind. Yet there remained something deeply unsettling about the idea that one could simply 'drop the story' and find another that might be equally true or truer. Could it really be that some of our most passionate convictions were in fact arbitrary?

Mainstream brain science seemed to suggest so. I had been doing a bit of reading around the subject, and the evidence was not comforting. While most of us like to believe that we weigh the facts and make informed decisions to adopt the opinions we do, the truth is that our conscious minds are simply not capable of processing the vast amount of data that enters through our senses. In fact, 98 per cent of everything we do as humans is governed subconsciously. This presents a challenge to the conscious self, which seems to need some kind of coherent inner narrative.

In order to solve this problem, the human brain has evolved a very sophisticated piece of kit which amounts to a kind of inner spin doctor. Constantly bombarded with information, this busy but skilled device in the left brain does the best it can to weave a believable story from sometimes questionable and confusing information, both past and present. Called the 'interpreter' by neuroscientist Michael Gazzaniga, its task is to create that important identity we call our self. If there are significant gaps in what's coming in, it is not averse to a spot of embroidering – much like a pressured editor in a busy newsroom. Better to have over-egged stories than blank spaces. We have to believe our own propaganda because without it the whole operation might grind to a halt.

When I thought about it, I could see examples of it everywhere. We had learned about it in adoption classes: when a child was abandoned or failed by his birth mother, for example, he often blamed himself, constructing a fantasy in which his abandonment was directly triggered by something that he did. To a child subconsciously trying to make sense of the world, it was better to hold oneself responsible for such a disaster than to believe that such things 'simply happened' outside one's control – and could therefore happen at any time.

I found it somewhat humiliating to accept that the cobbled-together story of my life – even my very sense of self – was probably about as reliable as the average tabloid newspaper. But that was, apparently, how it was. It wasn't a deliberate unreliability – indeed, it wasn't even conscious. Like the over-helpful stranger who gives incorrect street directions rather than admit he doesn't know them, the brain is trying to protect us from the things we find hardest to deal with: chaos and uncertainty.

Over the centuries, of course, the most popular stories had taken on lives of their own and entered the mythic or religious realm. The Eden narrative was a good example, explaining why the world was always beset with suffering – and putting the blame squarely at our own door, much like a child's abandonment fantasy. Another was the Flood narrative, known in Abrahamic faiths as the story of Noah's Ark but common to many cultures, and quite likely to have arisen in response to an actual tsunami that flooded coastal regions many thousands of years ago.

Watching documentary footage of the Asian tsunami of 2004, I had looked on in fascination as new flood narratives were born, each religion or culture finding its own explanations for the sudden onset of death and disaster. A Buddhist blamed bad karma, a Christian leader claimed his church and congregation had miraculously been saved by prayer, a Muslim sobbed that Allah had obviously summoned his family 'home'. But most interesting to me were some tribespeople of the Andaman Islands. Asked how they had survived the wave on one of the lowest-lying pieces of land in the region, they shrugged and explained that according to their ancestral stories, the world should be expected to shake sometimes, since it was balanced in the topmost branches of a tree. 'We know from our ancestors that the sea and the land sometimes fight,' an elder had told the reporter. 'And when we listened to the sea that day, we knew that it was going to fight the land, so we went inland and climbed trees, as our ancestors told us. And when the fighting had finished, we came back.' In such situations stories seemed to be more useful if they incorporated and explained the chaos – but they couldn't all be 'true'.

Which was why the age-old process of inquiry was so important, be it Socrates' patient interrogation of assumptions, Byron Katie's questions and turnarounds, or a trainee clown's attempt to 'drop the story'. It was like a truth commission set up in my own skull to cross-examine my most ingrained narratives – whether that meant my favourite personal gripes, my default tendency to see glasses as half empty, or the personality I subconsciously projected into the world.

Once Katie had peeled back the particular grievances of those on stage, it was the underlying beliefs that were most interesting, perhaps because they were also the most universal – like the idea that death was always to be feared, rather than befriended as a part of every life. Or that really caring about someone meant feeling his/her pain – was that even possible, let alone useful? Or that we should always know what to do in life – instead of embracing its uncertainty. When you looked carefully there were unexamined assumptions everywhere.

According to Katie, there was nothing in our lives that wasn't open to cross-examination. Suffering was optional, she had said – or, at least, her own suffering was. She had for some time experienced an acute degenerative condition called Fuchs' dystrophy, which rendered her almost blind.

'It's extremely painful,' she told us. But physical pain was not the same as suffering, which was caused by our response to pain.

So she had accepted the condition, wore an eye patch, tripped over things for a while, learned how to compensate with her other senses – and then accepted a corneal transplant when one was offered. 'Now I can see you as a result of wearing other people's lenses – amazing!' But would she really have retained that acceptance if the operation had failed, I wondered? Surely some life events were unequivocally bad news?

'I haven't met a problem in twenty years,' insisted Katie. It's like you're walking through the desert, it's an amazingly beautiful day, and you happen to look down and see a poisonous snake – you jump back and are paralysed with fear, your heart is beating, then you look again and it's a rope. You know what happens, you laugh, the adrenalin starts to drain away, you've just realised what's true for you. That's all we're doing here today. You can stare at that rope for a thousand years but you won't make yourself afraid of it again. I invite you to test it for yourself and see that, without exception, every problem is a rope.'

At lunchtime I wandered out onto Kensington High Street to buy a sandwich. I'm not a fan of London, having grown up on its outskirts, and I had felt the usual frenetic undertow of its overcrowded sprawl as I stepped off the train at King's Cross the previous evening. But leafy Kensington on a slow-moving Sunday morning was a different matter entirely, which exposed yet another assumption. (*London is an overcrowded sprawl: can you absolutely know that's true?*) I looked around at the people in the queue at Boots and imagined all the arbitrary thoughts choking our brains like bindweed that we kept on watering. There was something attractive about the idea of pulling them up in fistfuls. I was willing to believe that if Katie's method could be applied to ordinary anxieties, life would seem much clearer. But there seemed also a way in which, by internalising the whole world, she was contributing to a dangerous complacency. What, for example, of the real injustices and atrocities suffered by many around the world? Surely they weren't simply a matter of perspective. Even if I had not grown up believing in original sin, I had only to turn on the television to see a mass of evidence that the universe was fundamentally unfriendly. But I yearned to think differently.

Searching for a place to eat my lunch, I tentatively sat down on a bench beside a thirty-something couple. She was peroxide blonde, while he wore oblong specs. They smoked silently, exhaling disillusionment, and made no comment when I joined them.

'Are you at the Byron Katie thing?' I asked, feeling awkward.

'Oh God, does it show?' asked the man. His name badge read 'Nathan'.

'No, I was just thinking you didn't look the type.' I calculated correctly that he would take this as a compliment. 'How are you finding it?'

'I have my doubts that we're in a friendly universe,' he said.

'Me too,' I agreed, feeling suddenly vindicated in my scepticism. 'If you fully accept *what is*, how do you ever change the world? Mandela would never have defeated apartheid if he'd just shrugged and said "life happens", would he?'

Nathan was smiling faintly at me. 'So you're busy changing the world, are you? How's it going?'

I felt suddenly foolish. It was a fair point. What tangible difference had my angst about the state of the world ever made to it? 'You can't change other people, only yourself, right?' I conceded grudgingly. 'But surely it's a recipe for anarchy if we all focus only on our own experience.'

'Is that true?' said Nathan, deploying Katie's opening question. 'What other kind of experience is there?'

'But you can't live like that, can you? I mean, sure, ultimately we have only our own experience of the world, but if you punched me in the face, I'd know objectively that something happened – and we could both verify it.'

He raised his eyebrows. 'Can you absolutely know that's true?'

The smirk was starting to irritate me. 'No, obviously not *absolutely* – but in practice how do you live with that kind of uncertainty?'

Nathan shrugged. 'Just like most people do – with cigarettes and a bit of chaos.'

His partner shot him a look. 'You're always hiding behind your bloody sense of humour. No wonder people don't know whether to take you seriously.' Her name was Jane, and her exasperation suggested that her attempt to cultivate a New Age openness in her sceptical partner had so far been unsuccessful. She got up and poked him in the chest. 'I'd like to see you up on that stage. Katie would take you down like a wildebeest.'

'I'd like that too,' said Nathan in a tone which suggested the opposite. 'My sentence would be: I hate people.'

'Is that true?' I said, enjoying the opportunity to turn the spotlight back on him. I had a suspicion that his carapace of cynicism masked a craving for authenticity, if only you could get under it.

'Sort of true,' he said, smiling thinly as we walked back inside. 'I hate *some* people . . .'

I decided to drop the subject.

Katie began the afternoon with a few more questions from the audience. A woman who suffered from poor self-esteem and 'weight problems' – *is that true?* – ended up crying with relief as Katie affirmed her beauty from the stage. I thought of the large women I had met at Nudefest and the radiance that came from self-acceptance. Perhaps beauty was all in the mind. But could you really say the same of all suffering?

'What if someone is being badly beaten by their husband?' challenged a questioner.

'Well, it's either true or it's not true,' said Katie. She didn't ask whether the question was hypothetical or from experience. 'I may walk into the house and he beats me. But if I keep on walking into the house, who is beating me? The prison is the prison of the mind.'

Amazingly, the woman questioner seemed happy with this answer. It seemed to me dangerously simplistic. I put up my hand.

'But can you really accept reality as it is *and* fight for a better world?'

'Of course,' she responded. 'But as long as my thoughts are an enemy to me, they're going to project life as an enemy. You can free a country through war and violence but the people are not free. Ultimately, nobody is free until the mind is free. But learn to love yourself, and then you're available to help from where you are.'

It reminded me of that disconcerting sentence in an aircraft emergency drill: 'Please secure your own oxygen mask before attempting to help those around you.' I always winced trying to imagine myself ignoring the old lady or child gasping for air beside me and putting the mask on myself. And yet it was a logical instruction: how could you be a heroic parent or friend if you were slowly asphyxiating?

But this had practical implications in my life just now. 'Can I come back with a personal example?' I asked. 'One of the things I wrote in my list was: "I shouldn't be afraid to adopt a child." Now, if I look after my own needs first, and accept my limitations, the result might be that I never feel ready to be a parent.'

Katie cocked her head a little and looked at me. 'How can you accept your limitations when you don't even know what they are? You're afraid to adopt a child. True?'

'A little, I guess.'

'You're afraid to adopt a child: can you absolutely know that that's true? Have you adopted one yet?'

'No.'

'You're creating your own reality: "I'm the man who's afraid to adopt a child." As though that's you! How do you react when you think, I'm afraid to adopt a child?'

The audience around me listened, poised for a resolution. There was no going back. 'I guess I create different imaginary scenarios ahead of time: things that might go wrong, ways I might not cope ...'

Katie nodded and cut in. 'You see, honey, our thoughts are not enemies. It's just a matter of whether you believe them. So as they appear, meet them with enquiry, meet them with understanding. So, who would you be without the thought, I'm afraid to adopt a child?'

'I'd be a little more open, I guess.'

'Yes, sweetheart,' said Katie. 'Now look again. There's a child in front of you – in front of your face. Visualise a child there, drop the thought, take a look. I dare you to look into those eyes and into that face.'

In the expectant silence I tried to imagine one of the children I had seen in *Be My Parent*. But it was no good. The face wouldn't come.

'Now, who would you be if you weren't a father who was afraid to adopt a child?'

I sighed. 'I guess ... we'd be a family?'

'Wow!' said Katie, and suddenly everyone was clapping and teary-eyed and sentimental. I felt intense shame, and anger that my well-intentioned pondering of the issues around adoption had been hi-jacked by an emotional chatshow audience.

Interestingly, Katie seemed to sense this too. 'You would be free to make intelligent decisions,' she said, moderating it carefully. 'It's just that you have blocked the opportunity to love, to connect. I'm afraid to adopt a child – turn it around, what's the opposite?'

'I'm *not* afraid to adopt a child.' Interestingly, I felt something shift as I spoke the words. I was trying out a different me, a different narrative.

'So, give me an example of why that's true or truer.'

'The same stretching that might have broken us might also be the making of us. We'll discover things about ourselves we never knew.'

She beamed at me. 'Yeah. You see how our thoughts can keep us from these precious things? Now we can look forward to them.'

If only it were that easy. And, in fact, I still felt a little cheated. If parenting was really as simple as an instinctive connection with the eyes of a child, why did so many families run into problems? Wasn't that why adoptive parents were needed in the first place — because people acted on impulse, in the heat of the embrace, without thinking properly about their parenting capacity?

The next woman on stage presented a less hypothetical take on child-rearing.

'My daughter has lost herself,' she said with a quiet, desperate dignity. 'She is on drugs. She's ruining her health.'

The woman was only slightly younger than Katie, but Katie didn't miss a beat. '"My daughter has lost herself": is that true? Whose business is it if you lose yourself?'

'Mine.'

'Whose business is it if your daughter loses herself?'

The woman looked exasperated. 'She's only sixteen! I have a sense of responsibility!'

'But how do you feel when you think that thought: "She has lost herself on drugs"?'

'I feel lost.'

'So you're both users. She's on drugs and you're on her. Who would you be without that thought, My daughter has lost herself?'

'I would be free . . . I would let her be free.'

'She's free already, have you noticed? So you're not *letting* her be anything. My daughter has lost herself: turn it around.'

'*I* have lost *myself*.'

'How often are you in her business?'

'Ninety-eight per cent of the time.'

'So mentally you're out on the streets with her!' said Katie. 'How responsible is that? So you'll have her raped and murdered in your mind! You're lost in a world that doesn't exist.'

I thought of my own mother, and every mother's prerogative to worry herself sick about her children – and my own equally vivid fears for those I loved. Wasn't this, essentially, empathy that Katie was attacking? The ability to think oneself into another's shoes?

The woman sighed and read another sentence: 'I need her to be a responsible person who calms down and cares for others.'

'She's busy being sixteen! Turn it around ...'

The woman looked thoughtful. '*I* need to calm down, be a responsible person and stop fooling myself and others.'

Katie nodded and pushed on through. '"She should not ruin her health." Can you absolutely know that's true? How do you react?'

'I see her dead at twenty-one.' There were tears in the woman's eyes.

'Even though she's alive, yes. So who would you be without the thought that she's ruining her health?'

The woman paused, thought for a moment. 'I would imagine the moments of fun, when she's enjoying herself.'

'You'd see her as she really is – strong, beautiful ...'

Here again, it seemed to me that sentimentality was clouding the issue. Not knowing the teenager in question, Katie could, in reality, have no idea whether she was really 'strong and beautiful' or on the edge of drug-addled breakdown. Yet leaving aside such leaps of assumption, there remained something important in the exchange. For even if the mother was right, and her daughter really was in mortal danger, it seemed suddenly obvious to me that her maternal misery and projected fear were doing little to help. We were back to the idea of the emergency oxygen mask again – the woman scrabbling frantically to save her daughter's life before securing her own.

'"She should not ruin her health" – turn that around,' Katie was saying, methodically.

'*I* should not be ruining my health,' said the woman. Something in her seemed to settle, quieten at the self-evident truth of her words.

Something in me quietened, too. I thought how little my own fears and anxieties strengthened anything, apart from the drama of my own inner soap opera. But could you care deeply about life or other people without worrying about them? If so, I wanted to see how it worked in practice – how your average mystic combined 'letting go' with housework and teenage tantrums.

Katie plucked a new sentence from the woman's sheet: 'Next one: "She's violent/ugly with her language." Let's role-play this one out. I'll be you, you be your daughter ... How are you?'

The woman adopted a face of comic sullenness. It was obvious to anyone looking that this was now a teenager sitting in front of us. 'Fine. Where's my mobile?'

'I don't know where it is.'

The teenage face flared into anger. 'You're always moving things! It's always the same, you fucking bitch!'

Katie didn't blink. 'You know, I *am* always moving things around, that must be difficult for you. You put your mobile somewhere, and I move it, and you can't find it, that must be very frustrating! Let's try to find it together ...'

'You're suffering from compulsive cleaning behaviour.'

Katie nodded cheerfully. 'I *love* these conversations. What do you suggest?'

'I just want you to leave things as they are!'

'Do you realise how hard that would be?'

'That's your problem.'

'I had no idea you were so wise,' said Katie, still closer to sincerity than sarcasm. 'It *is* my problem and I keep making it worse. Can I at least make up your bed?'

'If you have to.'

'Oh, I do. I love the idea of you climbing into clean sheets. Is there anything else I could do that wouldn't be so disturbing?'

The woman looked like she was enjoying playing her daughter. 'Give me more money,' she grunted. There was a ripple of uneasy laughter through the audience.

'Well, you know me, I usually say yes, that's just how I am,' said Katie, refusing to be knocked off balance. 'If I give you more money can I run a vacuum in your room?'

There was a pause. 'Yes.'

'Is there anything else you'd be comfortable with?'

'I'll think about it . . .'

It was this exchange that stayed with me as I got on the tube for the journey back to my parents' house in the suburbs. It was only the briefest insight into how Katie's philosophy might play itself out in a normal domestic conversation, and for the most part it seemed crazy. My dad's reaction was probably typical. 'Sounds like a recipe for being a doormat,' he said when I told him and Mum about it over supper that night. He had been a tolerant and playful father, but went unequivocally ballistic when pushed too far, leaving us in no doubt who was in charge.

'Then again, those teenage arguments only ever ended with slammed doors,' sighed Mum, spooning out some apple crumble. 'I sometimes wish we'd managed to keep talking to you all a bit more in your difficult phases . . .'

'You both did a great job, Mum,' I said, giving her a squeeze round the shoulders. Mum was always castigating herself for imagined failings, despite an unstinting generosity to her children. It was easy to see where I inherited my worrier's genes. The two of us often ended up playing a kind of conversational ping-pong, trying to deflect perceived anxieties from one another. Mum was currently awaiting test results from her recent lumpectomy, for instance, but waved aside my enquiry.

'Mustn't grumble,' she breezed, not wanting to worry me. 'And how are your adoption plans coming along?'

'Fine, thanks,' I said, not wanting to worry her.

Dad rescued us from the stalemate. 'It's all very well taking verbal abuse from a teenager in a role-playing exercise,' he ruminated, still obviously thinking about Byron Katie. 'But does this woman honestly think it would work in practice?'

It was a good question. In principle I still wanted to believe that, despite all the signs to the contrary, children could be trusted to know what they needed, and grow in the right direction. But I wanted to see it happening with my own eyes. I could think of only one place where such a liberal code had been properly tested. Where children were put on an equal footing with their elders, given the freedom to set their own rules, and positively encouraged to answer back. Where ideas about how children should behave were abandoned in favour of allowing them to find their own way.

Its name was Summerhill School.

8

Original Goodness

Summerhill School, Suffolk

'The absence of fear is the finest thing that can happen to a child.'

A. S. NEILL

Getting into Britain's freest school proved trickier than I expected. It was early July, only days from the end of term, and Summerhill was not exactly on the beaten track. I drove for hours into the East Anglian countryside in my mother's car, only to find myself at a dead end on a deserted beach overlooked by Sizewell B nuclear power station. When I finally found the school down a back road in the market village of Leiston, I was greeted at the main gate by a small battalion of heavily armed ten-year-old boys.

'Where are you going?' asked the leader, a stocky child wielding a plastic M16 at my driver's-side window. Behind him, a grubby-faced kid was peering inside, waving a hockey stick.

'Um, hopefully the visitor's day. Do you have a car park?' He pointed to my left and saluted.

Returning to the gate on foot, I nodded at a child manning a sandbagged machine gun post, then reported to the gang leader, who was sucking an ice lolly at an improvised sentry box covered in camouflage netting. 'Any chance of an escort to reception?'

A cheeky kid with a long fringe of sandy hair proudly walked me through. 'We've had a lot of visitors recently. Last week there were tons of Germans – we decided we had to stop the invasion. But you're all right.' He was cheerful, matter-of-fact, talkative. His name was Jacob.

'What time do your lessons start?'

'I don't go to any lessons,' he said, shooing a couple of hens out of the way as we walked towards a red-brick Victorian house adorned with skateboard ramps. 'At Summerhill you don't have to if you don't want to.'

'What do you do instead?'

He shrugged. 'Play in the woods and stuff like that. It's good here.'

Summerhill has always had a lot of visitors. Ever since its inception in 1921 by the radical Scottish educationalist A.S. Neill, it has roused curiosity, hostility and praise in varying measures as a significant crucible of ideas almost unthinkable to the establishment. A product of a harsh Presbyterian upbringing near Forfar, Neill reacted by founding his own school on opposite principles.

> We set out to make a school in which we should allow children freedom to be themselves. In order to do this, we had to renounce all discipline, all direction, all suggestion, all moral training, all religious instruction. We have been called brave but it did not require courage. All it required was what we had – a complete belief in the child as a good, not an evil, being.

In this sense, Summerhill was the testbed of everything I dared to hope might be true: that as human beings we could be trusted to know what's good for us without being funnelled or moulded or bullied into submission. In this quiet little corner of England a risky and radical experiment in letting go was under way: what would happen if you allowed children to do as they liked?

The question, and the school, has sharply divided educationalists for more than eighty years — and not always down predictable lines. Dr John Culkin, one-time Jesuit priest and Harvard scholar, described it as 'a holy place', while Max Rafferty, the superintendent of the California schools system, famously declared: 'I would sooner send my children to a brothel!'

I feared he might not have been particularly reassured by the armed guard at the gate, but the well-groomed teenager who greeted me at reception augured much better. He grinned at the scruffy gang and sent them back to play. 'I didn't go to lessons for my first two years, either,' he said, when I asked him about them. 'I ran around in the woods and didn't wash and things like that. It was exactly what I needed to do.'

Like many of his classmates, Tim had come to Summerhill because no other school could cope with him. 'I guess I had a problem with authority,' he shrugged, as we waited for the rest of his group of visitors to arrive. 'I didn't fit in.' Diagnosed with attention deficit hyperactivity disorder (ADHD), he landed up in the headmaster's office within days of starting most conventional schools. But at Summerhill the headmistress put his Ritalin quietly in a drawer and sent him off to play for as long as he liked in twelve acres of woodland. He couldn't believe his luck.

Six years later he was a friendly and winning young man with more social skills than the average adolescent. What had happened? He shrugged. 'After two years I was getting bored and a little curious about what some of the other pupils were saying. I just decided I wanted to learn. So I went to my first lesson.'

A small group had gathered – a mix of curious educationalists, teachers, students and journalists – so we set off on Tim's tour of the school grounds. It was an idyllic setting, with mature trees bearing tree houses, swings and wooden climbing frames, and a number of single-storey classrooms clustered around the main red-brick building. A small boy flew past on a skateboard wearing only swimming trunks and a grin. A girl lay on the trampoline reading a book in the sun. Hens pecked in the grass.

From A.S. Neill's original roster of five pupils in 1921, there were now nearly one hundred, divided into three classes according to inclination for learning rather than age. 'Everyone matures at their own rate here,' explained Tim. 'People move up when they're ready.' In Class One's block, behind a six-foot cardboard replica of a Dalek, an attendance list of twelve children showed that only three had been to more than one lesson so far this term, and several had been to none. I noticed Jacob's name among them. In the Class Two block, a couple of boys were building a wooden scale model of the Bismarck, while another played a shoot-'em-up game on a computer. None showed much deference to visitors. They had a lot of them.

Over in the science block, the teacher was about to start his lesson – with one pupil. 'Jon here has come to learn about the amazing screaming jelly baby,' explained David Riebold. Jon, a small, dark-haired boy, looked mildly interested as his teacher pulled a white screw-top container of potassium chloride down from a shelf and instructed him to pour about an inch of the white powder into a test tube. 'Potassium chloride is normally used as a weedkiller,' he told Jon. 'But they're making it a bit harder to get as a weedkiller because you can also use it to make bombs.' Jon looked suddenly more interested, and followed his teacher across to the fumigation chamber, where David clamped the test tube above a Bunsen burner. Jon got out a lighter and set the tube heating, while his teacher produced a packet of jelly babies.

'Now, what have jelly babies got in them?'

Jon dug a green one out of the proferred packet. 'Sugar,' he said. 'And that stuff we get from bones.'

'Gelatin, yes,' said David. 'And a lot of sugar. So it's got lots and lots of energy.' He proceeded to explain the chemical reaction that was about to take place, all of which passed me by. I couldn't remember a single thing about school chemistry lessons. But I would have remembered screaming jelly babies.

'One jelly baby lasts you about four miles,' Jon was saying, trying to make it easy for his spectators.

'About an hour of energy, yes,' said David. 'Now put the jelly baby in the test tube and stand back – it's going to oxidise in quite an impressive way.'

With the white powder now liquefied, he dropped in his green jelly baby and watched as a pinkish flame shot out of the end of the test tube, accompanied by a noise like a malfunctioning coffee maker. The potassium made it purplish, explained Jon. His teacher smiled proudly.

Jon hadn't decided whether to sit GCSEs. Most people did a few to get into sixth-form college after they left Summerhill at seventeen, but it wasn't compulsory. He was just going to take as long as he needed to work out what he wanted to do. 'Much as I hate exams, I don't think GCSE coursework is much better,' said David. 'The pupils who have clever parents will do well in coursework, while the ones that don't are disadvantaged. We don't really care about the National Curriculum.'

There was something exhilarating but unsettling about such disdain for the system, and I wasn't surprised to learn that Ofsted inspectors had taken a rather less relaxed view in their 2000 report. The sticking point was the optional lessons – a case, the inspectors felt, of 'mistaking idleness for personal liberty'. The Department for Education duly tried to have the school closed. But they reckoned without the fighting spirit of hundreds of angry supporters and Summerhillians old and new, who raised £120,000 and took the government to court, winning a landmark case and the right of the school to be judged on its own terms.

The subsequent Ofsted report, in 2007, could not have been more different. 'Pupils' personal development, including their spiritual, moral, social and cultural development, is outstanding,' the inspectors concluded. Students were 'courteous, polite and considerate', made 'good progress' and were 'well-rounded, confident and mature' when they left. The only actual criticisms concerned a bit of worn carpet in the porch, an area of dodgy flooring in the corridor and the absence of a disability policy.

What most impressed the inspectors was that, far from being anarchic, Summerhill embodied a sort of child democracy. In meetings held three times a week after lunch, each of the ninety-five pupils and seventeen staff had the opportunity to vote on the day-to-day running of the school – which of course meant that the children could easily outvote their teachers, and frequently did. We were going to see how a meeting worked later on. In the meantime, I was intrigued to see the famous and ever-changing book of school rules, a battered-looking ring binder hanging on the dining-room wall.

Its first page set the tone:

In Summerhill, 'freedom' means individual freedom. This means that you can do what you like, so long as it does not interfere with the freedom of somebody else. So you can wear no clothes if you want to, dye your hair bright pink, and never attend any classes at all, because that is your own business – but you cannot play your music at 3 a.m., pee on the lounge floor or skateboard in the corridor, because it affects other people.

The Summerhill laws generally define the difference between freedom and licence, though some are there to protect particular people, or things. Just because there is no law against it does not necessarily mean that you can do it! And if there is a law you don't think is good, bring it up in the meeting!

The successive pages outlined nearly two hundred individual laws that decades of student meetings had wrought. Some were run-of-the-mill indictments against wearing rollerblades indoors, throwing cushions in the café or forgetting to bring down laundry. But a few caught my attention:

- No throwing knives at trees
- You can't go back to bed before lunchtime
- Alfie can have his spear made with nails but has to use it outside only and has a strong reminder to be careful and not frighten people
- When playing dodgeball outside back door – if window is broken all people playing pay for it
- Zoë [the headteacher] can stand on the dining room tables to sing
- You get sent home for four weeks if you drink

Whoever said kids didn't like rules? These kids seemed to love them – as long as they had agreed to them in the first place. 'Basically, in Summerhill, for every action there's a reaction,' said Tim proudly. 'Nobody is under any illusion that they can do whatever they want. It's a very fair system. It's very rare for people not to respect it.'

Punishments usually came in the form of fines – some of them standard, like five pounds for smoking or fifty pence for spitting on Tarmac, set by popular vote in the school meeting – or other sanctions. Bullies, in particular, were excluded from social events and trips, prevented from speaking or voting in the meeting, and forced to go to the back of all queues. Needless to say, there wasn't a huge problem with bullying. As a last resort, repeat offenders could be permanently excluded. 'I've only seen it once in six years,' said Tim. 'The whole community felt bad. It was a really sad thing, because nobody wants to get sent home. Personally, I get bored as hell when I get sent home. Here I wake up every morning and my friends are all around me.'

It was difficult to imagine this sociable, genteel young man as a disruptive influence in the classroom. The experience of being given a second chance had coloured his whole outlook. 'I'm definitely an optimist,' he said, cheerily. 'There's good in everybody.'

It was almost time for Tim's drumming lesson, so he led us into the dining room for our question-and-answer session with the headteacher. Zoë Readhead was the daughter of A.S. Neill and had assumed the mantle of authority in 1985 – if authority was the right word for the head of a democratic school. As if acknowledging the paradox, she was dressed in baggy jeans and a hoodie, but exuded raw charisma.

'Thank you, Tim,' she said, as he exited. Some of the visiting teachers were still clearly reeling from the news that this paragon of virtue was once like the hyperactive kids they taught.

'We don't *do* ADHD here,' explained Readhead, with a firmness that brooked no contradiction. 'We find people are just people and some are very lively and don't like to concentrate. Tim is Tim – over the years he's been a pain, sure, but that's not unusual. And he's fantastic. He's a great guy. We couldn't have wished for him to develop any better.'

Zoë Readhead was the living embodiment of Summerhill. 'I honestly feel like the luckiest person who has ever existed in the whole wide world,' she said. 'I was born here in the upstairs bedroom, where children sleep now. I have four children who came here. I feel that my whole life has been – for want of a better word – moulded by Summerhill.' It was an interesting slip of the tongue, given her father's famous insistence that 'what is wrong with our sick, neurotic world is that we have been moulded, and an adult generation that has seen two great wars and seems about to launch a third should not be trusted to mould the character of a rat'. Decades later, without specifically saying so, Readhead seemed to concede that, even at Summerhill, adults would always influence children one way or another. But she evidently believed her own 'moulding' to have been as benign as was humanly possible. On her wall she had a framed cover of the *Picture Post* from 1949, showing her as a grinning three-year-old, below the memorable headline 'The Child Who Never Gets Slapped'. Inside, an approving feature writer evidently believed that she, of all the children in Britain, had the best chance of being truly free – though she might have had a few qualms if she had returned a few years later.

'I was very good at stealing money,' reminisced Zoë of her early years at the school. 'I did it for a year or two when I felt I needed a bit of money. You can do that here: try being that person. But in meetings people told me it was out of order, that it wasn't okay to steal someone else's money, and after a while I just stopped. I didn't give it a lot of thought: I just grew up.'

You could understand why most press coverage created the impression that Summerhill was some sort of anarchic cross between St Trinian's and *Lord of the Flies*. But Zoë was particularly annoyed by one headline, 'School With No Rules'. 'For God's sake, there's a folder down there with about two hundred rules in it!' she said, raising her voice. 'And there's a big difference between this and *Lord of the Flies*. If our pupils crashed on a plane on an island the first thing they'd do is have a meeting, then they'd get a committee together to explore. I don't suppose it would be that much different from being here.'

But surely child democracy sometimes produced undesirable results? Zoë looked unconvinced. School meeting had never yet dissolved itself – and although it did once vote to eject her father while he was headmaster, Neill had simply tinkered happily in his workshop for a fortnight, until he was voted back in. 'I've been here all my life, and there's really nothing new under the sun,' said Zoë. 'We have to abide by UK law, of course. They can't vote to smoke dope because it's illegal, and when we have a fire practice at the beginning of term they have to do that because it's health and safety. But there are no real surprises. This is a very well-oiled machine.'

One enduring hallmark of freedom, of recurring interest both to newspaper reporters and Ofsted inspectors, was the Summerhill tradition of permitting nude swimming and sunbathing – and the fact that toilets were mixed. A source of surprise to some visitors – and that surprise a source of amusement to others. 'It's so English it's painful,' laughed Readhead. 'Visitors from Germany or France just burst out laughing and say, "What's the problem? You English are obsessed with toilets and nudity. Just grow up!"'

Having tried naturism myself so recently, I rather liked the idea that its healthy normalising of ordinary bodies could be a force for good in the usually cripplingly self-conscious teenage years. We had asked Tim about it earlier and he'd just shrugged like a mature adult and said, 'Everyone's cool with it.' Though I noticed that the school had found it necessary to invent a standard fine to protect it: 'Harassing naked swimmers – five swimming sessions banned'.

But never mind nude swimming – how did the usual teenage preoccupation with sex work itself out at a 'free' school? The question was raised tentatively by a visiting teacher. Zoë chose her words carefully.

'We abide by the law of the land, which means they're not allowed to have sex. But I'm not naive enough to think that they *don't* have sex. We give them information about sexually transmitted diseases and protection. And because there's still a relationship with us, they're very outspoken, so they don't have any problem coming to talk to us about these things. We've got three couples at the moment and it's lovely. They're just having a happy time together. But they're not allowed to sleep in the same room.' She paused for a moment. 'Our basic philosophy is the same as Neill's: that sexuality should be able to be expressed when you want to, how you want to and with whom you want to. But we don't have promiscuity here. There's none of the bravado of the outside world. These are loving relationships, even if they're short term.'

The other question was Summerhill's abundance of guns – on computer screens, in carpentry workshops, in the hands of the kids guarding the gate.

'Ah, yes, I expect you were all frisked when you came in,' smiled Zoë drily. 'That's been going on for about three days, and every day I arrive I get escorted from my car by heavily armed boys. One visitor had to show a bus pass.' She smiled indulgently. 'It's not very PC in the outside world, but we're actually fine about people playing soldiers. It seems to be something a lot of boys do.' She was adamant that there was no link with the constant stream of newspaper stories about stabbings and shootings in urban Britain.

'People have got it the wrong way round when they think it's the guns making people violent. If you stop kids buying knives, they'll just sharpen pencils. But those guys at the gate are just doing what kids have been doing for thousands of years – and when they grow up they'll be the most peaceful, law-abiding people you could meet.'

She pointed out of the window at a small boy wandering happily past in the sunshine ... wearing pyjamas. 'Take Ed, for instance. He's only been here about a year, and he spent the whole first term in his room playing computer games. Even we began to worry. But this term Ed is around all the time. And he's so relaxed that he always wears his pyjamas. He even goes down town in them. How individual is that? That's what I call personal freedom. I think he's absolutely wonderful.'

The more I saw, the more I wanted to believe in Summerhill's philosophy. I felt a little envious of these children, left to blossom in their own time instead of being tested constantly against attainment targets. I loved the idea that if you allowed the supposedly prohibited emotions to emerge, you would self-regulate. Having retained almost nothing of my state grammar school education except the piece of paper I received at the end of it, I wished that at least something of this ethic of freedom had been a feature of my youth. Funnelled urgently through successive examinations from the age of eleven to eighteen, I had learned not to question this Darwinian game of winners and losers, perhaps because I turned out to be good at it. So I had been stunned, on finally reaching Oxford University, to be exhorted by my unusually free-range English tutor to stop boning up on critics and exam questions and instead 'write simply about what you love, and *why!*' This unfamiliar act of listening, tentatively at first, to my own heart was what subsequently sparked my creative awakening (and admittedly I perhaps could not have been there to receive it without all the academic hoop-jumping beforehand). But why so late in my youth? I wondered now how my childhood might have been different if, instead of termly academic rankings in each subject, I had enjoyed Summerhill's organic freedom to explore and work out my own direction in life. Would the small boy in the paddling pool have continued to daydream instead of anxiously measuring himself against others? And would I thereby have missed my potential, or found it? Might some relaxed experimentation have saved me from workaholism and the fear of falling? Who would I be now with a Summerhill education? It was a tantalising thought.

And what about our own future child? Perhaps something similarly free-range might be possible closer to home – but without the necessity of boarding and fees? And yet I already knew no such school existed. But why not? If it was such an unbeatable recipe, why did Summerhill remain an anomaly in Britain?

Zoë sighed. 'Because people are afraid. Summerhill turns the whole thing upside down. It frightens people. Everybody is brought up to believe that adults know best, that children have to be made to behave. Here we just let them get on with it.'

But did it work in the longer term? The most common critique was that even if such a system was psychologically in the best interests of the child, it prepared them badly for a life of hoop-jumping and competition in the big, bad world outside. And of course, despite the availability of a limited number of bursaries, it remained a private school whose fees were about twelve thousand pounds a year full board – a lot to stake on an educational experiment. Readhead could point to a handful of famous alumni – including journalists, actors, a maths professor and the lead dancer at Sadler's Wells – but baulked at the question of whether pupils in general were 'successful'.

'Success is a funny word,' she said carefully. 'But peaceful, sociable and loving? To a man. And don't forget some of these kids should have ended up in jail. We're every prime minister's dream. We're not rebels, we're not angry, we're happy to go and live our lives. We're not difficult customers. Our pupils are pretty robust – they've all lived in the outside world, they know what's coming.'

Zoë wrapped up the session and we broke for our packed lunch on the lawn. The kids had voted not to let the visitors into the dining hall, presumably a little weary of being a sort of zoo for inquisitive liberals. But we were promised that they usually allowed visitors to watch the school meeting that afternoon. Wandering towards the back door, I paused for a while in front of the wall set aside for graffiti. 'If Japanese whaling is scientific research, I hope I never meet a Japanese sociologist' read one comment amid declarations of love and scored-out romantic pairings. Another read simply: 'Life! Live it to the FULL!'

On the dot of 2 p.m., a senior pupil appeared at the main door and beckoned us in. The meeting room was a wide, high-ceilinged atrium with a scuffed linoleum dance floor in the middle and a flight of stairs winding up one side, its banisters dented and worn by decades of use. There were perhaps thirty children and a couple of teachers scattered around the edges, seated on blocks or steps or the floor. The rest were away on a hike – meetings being no more compulsory than anything else. The children eyed us neutrally as we found spaces and sat ourselves on the floor. 'Can you be quiet please?' said a teenage girl standing at the front. There was a frisson of apology as the visitors realised she was talking to us – we settled ourselves with a rustling of bags. The girl allowed the ghost of a smile to cross her face, and called the meeting to order.

The well-oiled democratic machine was running almost before we'd had a chance to register the fact. One of the first to speak was Jon, the young boy who'd incinerated his jelly baby earlier on. 'Someone stole three quid off me, so I propose I get three quid compensation from funds.'

'Where was the money?' asked the chair, whose name was Annie.

'In my locker – but I lost my key and when I found it again the money was just gone.'

There was a short pause while everyone considered the plausibility and fairness of Jon's story. Then a teacher called William – who was the son of Zoë and now ran the woodwork lessons – said: 'I want to propose he gets one pound fifty back from funds.'

'Votes to give Jon three pounds from funds?' said the chair. There were no hands. Evidently Jon's story had failed to pull his classmates' heart strings.

'Votes for one pound fifty from funds?' A scattering in favour carried the motion. Apparently the reduced reimbursement carried a standard message of shared responsibility on the part of Jon for not looking after his possessions well enough. Everyone seemed to accept it.

Next up was Jacob, the boy I'd met at the front gate, evidently off guard duty just now, and sitting up behind the stair banister. 'I want to bring up Harvey for using my Warhammer without asking and then leaving it out overnight. I think he should get a strong warning to ask if he uses it and make sure he puts it back.'

'Is it broken again?' asked an older girl.

'Not broken exactly, but there's a bit missing.'

'I want to propose he has to pay you fifty pence back.'

The chair efficiently tabled two proposals: firstly that Harvey should get a strong warning – carried unanimously – and secondly that he should pay a fifty-pence fine. This was carried by a margin of about five hands. I was struck by the innate instinct of children for fairness – and how smoothly and unfussily the process ran. Nobody questioned the result – though, if justice had not been done, it could be appealed against, as in any other courtroom.

The final motion came from David, the science teacher, who proposed that people stopped feeding the seagulls to prevent them growing more aggressive. It was carried by about ten votes to one – the only dissenter being a small, disconsolate boy with ragamuffin hair, who looked just the sort of child who might have enjoyed a bit of wild interaction with seagulls. And the meeting was over.

'That was miraculously short,' said William the woodwork teacher afterwards, as the pupils dispersed for more important activities like swimming and rollerblading. 'Sometimes you get a very long one and you lose the will to live. But it's always interesting. The little guys learn how to be older kids in a community like this. They see the responsibility they have to take.'

A chiselled, relaxed man in T-shirt and jeans, William had been a pupil as well as a teacher in the school his grandfather had started. He'd seen bedtimes abolished and reinstated enough times to know that each generation of kids got it right in the end.

'Governing freedom is actually very complicated,' he said thoughtfully. 'And it's very practical. It has to be. Obviously we've got a book full of rules, which is a lot more than other schools. But here you're free to do something about it if you don't like it – you're an active part of the process. Which is what gives freedom in the first place.'

Out at the gates, Jacob was back on guard. I stopped to chat. He was a friendly child whose directness seemed to have been a little overpowering for the teachers at his last school.

'My brother had been chucked out and I decided to start a rebellion there,' he recalled. 'We started trying to get kids to express what they liked so that when the teachers told them to do something, they wouldn't feel they had to do it. It wasn't totally successful, but I changed a few things before I left.'

Like what, I wondered?

'Well, it used to be a healthy school, but now they're allowed muffins.' He shrugged modestly. 'It's not much, but it's something.'

At Summerhill, needless to say, an entrepreneurial soul had already set up a junk-food café serving fizzy drinks and crisps for those wishing to rebel against the three healthy alternatives offered at school meals. Indeed, the only problem with Summerhill, it seemed to me, was that there was nothing very much left to kick against. One sensed that even playing soldiers in the woods might lose its allure before long.

'This is the best school I've been to,' said Jacob as he escorted me to my car. 'I think I'm definitely staying here.' He fiddled thoughtfully with his gun. 'And next term I might even go to some lessons . . .'

In the days after my visit, I talked endlessly and evangelically about Summerhill, bending the ears of friends and strangers alike – anyone who would listen. Most seemed interested in its radical vision, but rather sceptical about any claims of success on behalf of its pupils.

'What do these people actually do when they leave the place?' said a high-flying young diplomat who had been to a leading public school. 'Are any of them making a difference? Doesn't it just produce children who are content with what they have?'

'Is that such a terrible thing?' I retorted.

'Maybe not,' he conceded, stroking his chin. 'My old school

famously produces fucked-up but phenomenally driven children who achieve a lot as adults.'

His response struck me as annoyingly true. Was this form of letting go not dangerously passive, leaving the way clear for all the pathologically driven people at the helm of society? I wanted to believe that happy, contented pupils could change something more than their own souls. I wanted them to be reformers and world-changers, spurring the rest of us on to a more sustainable and peaceful way of life.

But in the few informal surveys of former pupils, the consensus seemed to be that a Summerhill education equipped people with none of the grinding angst or ambition necessary for climbing greasy poles or fighting corners. Almost none had gone into politics, though plenty had gone into the caring professions, trying to make a difference at an individual level.

Hylda Sims, an old Summerhillian I contacted in London, was typical – if there can be anything typical about a woman who describes herself as a skiffle player, teacher, single mother and Elizabethan minstrel. 'I haven't had to let go because I haven't been hung up in the first place,' she said, when I explained my own quest. 'When I first left Summerhill, I did feel different, but after a while I was just glad I didn't seem to fall prey to the same kind of worries as other people. I'm aware that if I had been pushed like other children I might have succeeded in getting my novels published. But I'm not overly worried by it.'

'And do you trust people?' I asked her.

'I trust myself,' she said simply. 'What I've always done is follow my heart's desire, and it's never let me down. A.S. Neill was once asked if he trusted people and his answer was, "I don't trust adults much, but I trust children."'

I thought back to the touchstone of my cherished childhood

moment in the paddling pool, and once again felt a wave of yearning to recapture that innocent joy. It was what fired me up so much about Summerhill. It was more than just a successful social experiment. It seemed to me to get to the heart of the big questions about being human: the sense that, after all the self-inflicted prohibitions, all the life-hating edicts, the original sin, the fear of perpetual failure, there is something at our unmolested core which, when given unconditional love and acceptance, will flower in a beautiful and uncomplicated way.

Was it possible to rediscover that simple part of myself? It was clearly too late to go back to school and undo everything I had learned. But my clowning had taught me there were ways of recapturing something of that innocence, even as an adult.

Recently, I had learned of a place where such experiments were the norm. A kind of playground for adults, sheltered from the collateral damage of a competitive society. A place where all were encouraged to still the critic and see what arose in the space where all that ambition and fear and worry normally lived.

It was easy enough to find on the internet. My Google search picked it up with just two words: No mind.

9

The No Mind Festival

Ängsbacka, Sweden

'Minds are like parachutes. They only function when they
are open.'

SIR JAMES DEWAR

'What you're doing here is real!' shouted the woman, as her assistants raked hot coals into a glowing carpet. 'Real fire, real feet, real spirit! I challenge you with these fires to make a commitment to the divine in your life. This is not a party trick.'

Nor was it even slightly rational, it struck me, watching with something approaching culture shock. Only that morning I had been in safe, familiar old Edinburgh. Now I was in a forest in Sweden, just about to witness hundreds of New Age hippies hotfooting their way to enlightenment. They called it the No Mind Festival.

'Take a moment to feel your body,' shouted the woman, an American with long blonde hair. 'Now take a moment to feel the earth underneath your feet.' In the broad circle that surrounded her, people were taking off their sandals, some of them bouncing on the spot, as a row of musicians pounded out a beat on samba drums. It built steadily, reverberating through the ribcage. 'Take a moment to feel the infinite above you! And the human heart in you, the heart that brought us together here! Now let that heart expand ... and start any time you want!'

The red heat fluttered in strange mesmerising patterns through the carpet of coals as the first two people strode calmly forwards, their eyes fixed as if on some distant point. I craned my neck to see over the crowd as a long-legged Nordic brunette in cut-off jeans and a spaghetti-strap top made first contact. There was no sizzling sound, no yelp, only a flaring of the nostrils and a breathy 'yes' of accomplishment as she trod one-two-three-four steps to the other side. Teenagers whooped and high-fived each other and followed her through, then old women. The drumming was hypnotic, drawing me in.

I mentally reshuffled what I thought I knew of Sweden: eco-friendly, militarily neutral; birthplace of ABBA and IKEA; high taxes, enlightened social policies, generous welfare system. It had seemed as good a place as any to look for a working utopia. After the flight from Edinburgh that afternoon, I had picked up a hire car at Stockholm airport and driven west for four hours, through seemingly endless forest interspersed with glittering lakes and occasional settlements of quaint wooden houses. Feeling tired but peaceful as I approached the little village of Ängsbacka, I had imagined relaxing in a traditional Swedish sauna, the steam rising from the hot coals. But walking on them was another matter entirely. It seemed to demand a pitch of spiritual intensity I didn't possess — not to mention asbestos feet. I kept my shoes on, and retreated in search of refreshment.

'Any idea how it works, this firewalking thing?' I asked the man in front of me, while queuing for a cup of herbal tea.

He was a short, bespectacled fellow from the Netherlands, who introduced himself as Alexander. 'I think it's basically mind over matter,' he said, his brow furrowing earnestly at my question. 'But I haven't done it myself.'

'I did!' said a woman behind us. 'I got two blisters from it because the coal stuck to my feet. But I still feel like I achieved it – I did it!' She grinned triumphantly, but I couldn't help noticing her slight limp.

'Did you have to do any mental preparation?'

'No, I just felt like joining in.'

Alexander coughed disapprovingly. 'You need the preparation, I think.'

The woman looked at him levelly. 'Are you saying the coal wouldn't have stuck to my feet if I had been more spiritually enlightened?'

It was an interesting question. We both ducked it and retreated outside onto the veranda to watch the last of the firewalkers straggle up the field. The timber coffee shop sat at the centre of the community, which looked a little like an Amish village, thanks to various barns, and even the odd horse-drawn buggy gathered around a more stately looking house. Ängsbacka was a year-round commune with a core of about twenty people. For the summer No Mind Festival there were hundreds of visitors, little clusters of Bohemian-looking Scandinavians lying around in various postures of complete relaxation in the grassy orchard. It was an alcohol-free festival, so most of them were sipping mugs of tea or coffee in the evening sunshine.

Alexander was an orchestral conductor planning a career break and searching for some kind of guidance. He had an air of bewilderment that was familiar to me. Together we finished our teas and wandered over to an awning, below which a large whiteboard displayed the daily schedule of workshops offered in the ever-changing festival programme. Tomorrow we could choose between Primordial Chi Kung, Body Reading, Manifesting your Dreams, Spiritual Revolution, Dynamic Meditation, Contact Improvisation, Drum Circle, Zen Coaching, Radical Honesty, Breathwork and a Women's Sweat Lodge. I stared at it for several minutes, as one might ponder a menu in a foreign language.

'What would you recommend?'

Alexander looked very carefully and wrinkled his nose. 'Perhaps Breathwork?'

After a refreshing night's sleep in a nearby boarding school, we gathered in a barn to learn how to breathe. 'Most of us breathe only in the upper part of our lungs,' explained a long-haired American called Peggy Dylan, addressing around sixty of us sitting cross-legged on the floor. Proper deep breathing should massage the heart, liver and digestive system, she claimed, as well as exponentially increasing the efficiency of the body. But it was a sign of humanity's perpetual state of anxiety that most of us habitually adopted the sort of shallow breathing intended only for moments of fight or flight.

'The one thought that creates more stress for the human race than any other is "not enough",' said Peggy. 'Not enough money, not enough sex, not enough oil, not enough time, not enough things. But what's *really* going on is that the body is not relaxed because there's not enough air! Of course there's not – you're getting one tenth the amount of oxygen you're supposed to be getting!'

It was a little depressing to be told we were screwing up something as basic as breathing. Quite how the species progressed to astrophysics or nanotechnology was beyond me. But the good news, according to Peggy, was that you could turn panicked breathing to your advantage. The idea of that morning's session, as far as I could make out, was to hyperventilate ourselves into a state of heightened arousal and purge ourselves of the stressful emotions that plagued us. As a first step, we were asked to share our 'issues' with one another in groups of three.

Alexander looked even more nervous than I was about this, but luckily our group was completed by a Scandinavian called Stig, who plunged into the emotional surf with the vigour of a cross-Channel swimmer.

'My problem is with intimacy,' he told us immediately, amid the low murmur of other voices. 'It's a recurring problem. It's like I'm either choosing women I don't really love so that I'm not risking anything if it doesn't work — or I go very quickly into a relationship and then quickly get out of it.'

Alexander confessed to similar yearnings for emotional stability in his love life, as well as anxiety about his future, while I told them that I wanted to learn to let go. It was relatively painless so far. We all nodded respectfully at each other.

'Now I want you to take it in turns to lie on your back and breathe,' said Peggy from the front. Alexander blinked and took off his spectacles. 'Okay, so keep it at the top of the lungs and through the mouth only,' said Peggy, as he lay down between us. 'We're trying to bring the subconscious out here. Let the breathing bring it all to the surface, and use the other two to support you.'

I watched a tiny dimple of a frown form on Alexander's forehead. He tried very hard, rasping through his mouth, trying not to make his belly wobble. He reminded me a little of a fish expiring out of water.

'Can you put your hand on my chest?' he said suddenly, his eyes still shut. Stig nodded sagely at me, so gingerly I laid my hand on Alexander's heaving chest. I was starting to feel a little uncomfortable. All around us, people were breathing frantically over the tinkling of calming flute music. It sounded like a low-budget porn movie. Across the room, a woman was straddling a man's chest to 'support' him, as he groaned his emotions. Someone somewhere was weeping softly. A bearded man screamed suddenly like a Bond villain being thrown off a cliff.

'Good!' said Peggy, cheerily. 'Now change places.' Alexander's eyelids flickered open. He was wheezing like a man at the end of a marathon, wearing a puzzled frown. Stig was clasping his socked feet like furry animals. 'I just intuitively wanted to hold them,' he explained.

'Thanks,' said Alexander weakly, feeling around for his spectacles. He looked at other people sobbing, lying in each other's arms like exhausted lovers, and scratched his nose. 'I think maybe I wasn't breathing from high enough in my chest?'

My heterosexual discomfort index was getting dangerously high, but I decided to get my turn over as soon as possible – there was a fug of male sweat and intimacy I hadn't experienced since the school locker room. It didn't take much breathing to turn me light-headed, so I concentrated on pushing out with my stomach. Disconcertingly, somebody had laid his hand on it. Worse still, a pair of hands began to massage my temples. I kept my eyes tightly closed. 'Keep breathing from the top of the lungs,' said Alexander, evidently convinced that this was where he went wrong. I panted harder and harder, while trying to make it sound more like a brisk jog than a marathon sex session. I was just starting to get a headache with the tension and performance anxiety when the full absurdity of the situation struck me: the clasping hands, the gasping and howling noises from around me, and all because I wanted to let go! The thought forced an involuntarily grin, and I found myself chuckling aloud.

'Good!' murmured Stig intensely, massaging harder, which only made me guffaw more heartily, my belly pushing Alexander's hand up and down. Soon I was gasping with laughter, tears rolling down my cheeks. I had certainly let go of something – quite possibly my marbles.

'Okay, it's time to come back to normal breathing,' I heard Peggy say.

'I don't want to come back!' I croaked, laughing even harder.

But it was Stig's turn on the floor – the grand finale, as it turned out. Feeling duty-bound to perform some reciprocal massaging of his temples, I was startled witless when he suddenly arched his back, pushed his head into my stomach and roared like a werewolf. 'Good!' I said, in the absence of any other obvious response. He roared again, and I rubbed harder, trying to soothe the veins that were standing out alarmingly on his temples. By the end of his five minutes, Stig was lying limply in my arms, unable to do anything else. 'Thanks, guys,' he groaned.

'Glad it helped,' I said. The three of us hugged awkwardly.

Peggy looked out over the carpet of interlocked bodies and said: 'I'm impressed by how quickly and deeply you have entered into this.'

Sitting out on the veranda during tea break with Alexander, I just kept chuckling. I felt purged, but also a little wobbly and bewildered. 'What *was* that?' I asked him. Alexander shrugged. I got the impression he was still disappointed that he hadn't enjoyed the emotional climax he was hoping for. But I was distracted from further analysis by the sound of English voices nearby.

I traced the source to a man and a woman I knew, though it

took me a few seconds to place them. As our eyes met, I realised where I'd seen them before: it was Nathan and Jane – the lunchtime cynic and his partner from the Byron Katie seminar.

'Bloody hell!' said Nathan, a slow smirk spreading over his face. 'Are you stalking us?'

'What are you doing here?' I was flabbergasted at the coincidence.

'I fancied a spot of guru-baiting,' shrugged Nathan, bagging the role of the dragged-along partner. 'Half of these people think they're enlightened, but I'm not impressed so far. Enlightenment is like A-levels these days – they give it out too easily.'

I saw Alexander's frown deepening. Jane jumped in, glancing at her watch.

'Have you signed up for sharing group?'

Sharing group, it turned out, was an important component of the festival, which took place every day before lunch. Alexander, Jane and Nathan had all been randomly assigned to separate groups that had been meeting for a couple of days. Late arrivals like me were invited to join a new group, hastily convened by a middle-aged Swede in the dappled shade of a tree.

'No spectators – everyone participates,' he said, evidently in a hurry to get off to his own group. 'We suggest giving each person six minutes to say whatever they want. Whatever's on your mind – or maybe you just want a massage or a hug. But there's to be no advice or comeback on what's said – you're just there to listen, unless the person specifically asks for feedback. And everything said inside the group stays inside the group – unless you have permission from a person to talk outside. Everybody understand?'

There were nods from around the circle, and the man left us to look at each other. I was encouraged to find that three months on from the clowning workshop, I was still able to hold eye contact without flinching. There were seven of us, all strangers to one another, though it turned out that two had been there the previous week and found themselves unwilling to go home. One of them, a Danish twentysomething called Rosie, had an expression of the most profound placidity I'd ever seen without the use of pharmaceuticals. The other was Mikael, a Swedish IT specialist with intense blue eyes, who volunteered to take the first six-minute slot.

'You're going to love this place,' he said. 'I was here last week and only just got home when I decided I needed to be here for another week!' He grinned and paused to look at each of us in turn. The done thing seemed to be to nod back wisely with a half-smile. 'So instead of talking, I want to try out this game I heard about. Has anybody heard of raccoons?'

'Like the animal?' said Bengt, an impressively muscular blond with a passing resemblance to Dolph Lundgren.

'Exactly. And you know how raccoons lie around on their backs and warm themselves in the sun? They all lie around in a big heap, feed off each other's energy, wriggle and change position till they get comfortable.'

We all nodded slowly, wondering where this was going.

'Well, that's what I'd like to do in my last three minutes.'

There was a pause. 'So,' said one of the women slowly, 'you want us all to lie around on top of each other ...'

'Yes,' said Mikael. 'Is that okay?'

Nobody could think of a sufficiently persuasive reason why not, so, with a rustling of yoga mats and some polite giggling, we clambered into one another's personal space. I politely pulled myself across Bengt's legs and positioned my hand on a patch of grass I could see between two more legs. A contented grunting was coming from somewhere in the pile as Mikael moved around to get himself comfortable. I realised a little too late that I was at risk of lying across the breasts of a complete stranger — though it was impossible to tell whose. I ended up holding myself in a sort of contorted press-up for two minutes, trying not to make actual contact. Everyone else seemed thoroughly relaxed by the time the three minutes were up.

'Thank you!' said Mikael with a simple smile. I couldn't help wondering what other six-minute activities one could request — and at what point this open-minded place would reach a sticking point.

'I'm Nick,' I said, jumping in next. 'I only got here last night, and I'm still trying to work out what's going on. I'm a writer, and to be honest I came with the idea that I'd get some great material for my book on letting go, get a few laughs out of describing some blissed-out hippies . . .' A few eyebrows lifted, but nobody said anything. 'But now that I'm here, I'm surprised to find I just want to dump the cynicism and dive in.'

A few people smiled at me, so I carried on, rambling about my search and the things I had learned — and my fluctuating emotions about parenthood. 'Sometimes I feel this amazing sense of excitement — other times I wonder if I'm up to it.' It was good to be able to say this stuff and not have someone immediately try and give me advice. The eyes were enough: open, encouraging, deep. I ended by assuring them that I wouldn't be using anyone's story or real name unless given explicit permission. 'But mainly I want to say I'm finding this surprisingly enjoyable, just sitting here.' And it was. The rustling of leaves above us, the dance of sunlight, the gentle intensity of eye contact and smiles. And then six minutes were up.

'Am I allowed to comment?' said Bengt, waiting for my nod. 'I just want to say I don't mind at all if you write about my story. I've spent too much of my life being secret already.'

Bengt was about my age, nearing his late thirties, but his face was somehow older, wiser, with an impressive set of laughter lines. It seemed he had already suffered enough for one lifetime.

'I was married for five years before my wife died,' he said, looking up forlornly. 'She had leukaemia, and I had to speak to her inside a sterilised space in case I gave her any infection. In the end she didn't die of cancer, she died of pneumonia.' He paused and looked down at his feet. 'The hardest day of my life was taking my two daughters to say goodbye to their mother. I thought I had cried all the tears I could cry about it, but yesterday in a workshop I just wept and wept again. It was good to let it out.' He looked up and smiled at us all, his eyes wet. 'But in many ways this tragedy has been the making of me. It has given me the impetus to search for meaning and love every moment. And to be open rather than secretive. And every time I tell my story it gets a little bit less painful.' He smiled at me. 'So, thank you for listening!'

Everyone seemed transfixed by this strong and vulnerable man. It was hard not being able to respond with anything more than a nod and a 'thank you', and others, visibly moved, extended their hands, palms down, and waggled their spread fingers in his direction, making a quiet shushing noise with their mouths. This, I would later learn, was a 'love shower' – an eccentric Ängsbacka way of signalling that you were 'sending positivity and blessings'. Bengt grinned and nodded and made the same gesture in return, chuckling to himself.

We continued round the circle, others coming forward with stories of disappointments in love, dreams of career changes. Most were in creative industries like music or interior decoration, and everyone seemed poised and expectant, hoping that they would find meaning or peace. None of them appeared to mind sharing their innermost struggles with strangers. After an hour I felt a curious closeness to them all.

But then suddenly it was all over for the day. Everyone drifted away.

Lunch was an unexpectedly lonely affair – the sort of loneliness that is only exacerbated by a crowd. Perhaps it was the impact of all this touchy-feely right-brain experience, but I found myself getting maudlin as I munched my veggie stir-fry alone beneath a tree. I spotted several members of my sharing group, each deeply involved in conversation with a partner, or laughing with a group, and felt a stab of envy. I retreated to the sanctuary of the toilet, where the flowery Post-it on the inside of the door failed to improve my mood: 'Do not seek perfection in a changing world. Instead, perfect your love.'

I'm fourteen years old, and waking from the fog of migraine. There's relief – the pain has gone – but also confusion. Where am I? As sleep evaporates, I find myself alone in the cabin of a yacht. I'm on a youth sailing holiday, but where is everybody else? Clambering groggily out onto deck, I discover that the other teens and leaders have left me aboard the anchored yacht and rowed ashore for a game of rounders. I sit stranded, watching them running and shouting in the distance, as I try unsuccessfully to be outraged that they have left me behind. Nobody waves. I will never find out if I have been accidentally forgotten, or if a leader has taken a calculated risk that I will sleep until they get back. Because deep down, I know this is what I should expect. Nobody, not even my parents, can help me with this illness, which leaves me writhing and vomiting until I'm delivered into the blessed oblivion of sleep. So I must learn to cope alone. Sitting on that oddly peaceful boat, waiting for the world to return, I feel the settling of the matter.

This is how life is going to be. I feel not sadness but determination. It's just me — me and God. I will not be a whiner. I will endure it and recover, and continue as normal. I don't need to ask for help.

But that was then. A quarter of a century later at Ängsbacka, remembering that moment on the yacht, I realised I was mistaken. That despite all my efforts to be independent, I needed other people on a level I had not acknowledged. I was not a self-contained artist but a lonely man, pining for people who understood me. That morning's brief taste had been enough to reawaken a primal hunger that startled me. And now I was alone again, with no way to reach the shore.

I should simply have phoned Ali, the one who knows me best, but I couldn't bring myself to admit how frustrated I felt. Instead I spent the afternoon wandering moodily through a sort of open-air New Age supermarket, bolstering my scepticism by looking at books on angels and 'cosmic ordering', a shop selling crystals, yoga mats, tarot cards, and CDs promising ever-more relaxing ways to meditate. Browsing through a little encampment of therapy booths, I experienced, in close succession, a blood-curdling scream from a man regressing to a former life (presumably not a very nice one) and the unexpected sight of Nathan hanging upside down from a tree. A man holding one end of the rope was turning him occasionally, and laying a hand on his stomach. With his eyes closed and his long arms dangling below him, Nathan resembled an incompetent fruit bat.

'Nathan tends to find most alternative treatments a bit mild,' explained Jane, watching with interest. 'They generally don't get through to him. But he thought hanging upside down for an hour and a half might do the trick.'

Inversion therapy was apparently supposed to relieve pressure on joints, promote 'whole body wellness' and even help depression or writer's block. I tried to suppress a grin. 'He certainly looks a bit more vulnerable than usual.'

'Do you think so?' said Jane dubiously. 'I was hoping for some screaming – or at least a groan.'

I grabbed half an hour's kip at the back of a seminar on dynamic meditation, and returned to witness the results. Nathan was now the right way up, but seemed to be walking tentatively in an extremely upright manner, as if clenching a fifty-pence piece between his buttocks.

'You look taller!' I said, failing to hide a smile.

Nathan didn't smile back. 'Six foot five inches – nothing new there,' he said curtly. 'I just try and slump whenever possible.'

'So, how was it?'

A twitch of annoyance flickered across Nathan's face. 'The man said my pain threshold was high . . .'

'You see! You're totally invulnerable!' said Jane, exasperated.

Nathan pretended to be hurt. 'Jane thinks that nothing touches me!'

'It doesn't!'

'I'm as vulnerable as I need to be,' he smiled thinly, beginning to wander off. 'Think of me as a sort of alpha dog of vulnerability: pit me against the regular alpha dog and I'll always get the girl.' He threw Jane a knowing look and she punched him playfully.

What was it that bugged me about Nathan? His reflexive cynicism was nothing new – I'd traded in it myself for years as the default currency of journalism, a kind of emotional limitation masquerading as intellectual rigour. But what was a guy like Nathan doing in a place like this? I needed a sanctuary in which to expose my vulnerable underbelly, and his porcupine presence unnerved me. Then again, who had been smirking at whom during his bold and rather literal attempt to hang loose? I felt suddenly ashamed. Maybe he was more like me than I cared to admit.

I was back on the café veranda with Alexander, watching the sun go down. A man dressed as a tree was weaving his way among the beautiful Nordic gods and goddesses lying on the grass. Kids with painted faces were running across the fields with kites. It was an idyllic scene and yet, as I was telling Alexander, I still seemed to be having trouble relaxing into it. Even my Ayurvedic massage had been spoiled by incessant brain chatter: in a little white tent in the forest, a beefy Israeli had oiled my limbs and pulled my joints gently while I chastised myself alternately for being too cynical and too gullible.

'Maybe it's possible to let go too much,' I said. Alexander looked thoughtful and nodded slowly. We were quite similar – both of us simultaneously craving and dreading the dismantling of our defences. It should have drawn us together.

'Yes, I think letting go is only part of the answer,' he said, finally. 'In music, for example, you have to learn both freedom *and* control.' He put down his drink and held up a finger like his conductor's baton, waving it absently against the reddening sky, then putting it down again. 'In fact, conducting an orchestra is like riding a horse. You have to let the horse know that you are in charge, but also you must not hold the reins so tight that you break his spirit, or he will not take the fences.'

I nodded sadly. I felt like that horse. But I was also the rider.

It was sharing group again, and this time Mikael wanted a six-minute massage. All of us gathered round him, massaging different bits of his body as he lay on his front and groaned in pleasure. 'A little gentler on the legs, please,' he mumbled. I had to hand it to him. He knew what he wanted. But I found myself wondering if New Age therapies were quite as spiritual as they claimed to be. Apparently Mikael enjoyed spending time in one of the therapy teepees, trading massages with female strangers. Another group member spent her six minutes telling how she had 'gained some clarity' that it might be time to leave her husband. I tried very hard to stay open-minded, but couldn't deny that my judgements were there, waiting in the shadows.

'I had a bit of a weird day yesterday,' I confessed, when my turn came. 'I enjoyed our session, and the level of openness in the group – but then everyone suddenly disappeared afterwards, as if nothing had happened. I felt a bit cheated, to be honest.' I looked up and all eyes were on me – not defensive, but sad. 'Maybe it was because I made myself a bit vulnerable, about adoption and so on, which is quite unusual for me. But anyway, when I realised that it was just a kind of exercise, and only for an hour, I just felt this kind of dark ... existential loneliness ...'

I stopped, mortified to realise I was welling up. I coughed and rubbed at my left eye, pretending to be adjusting my glasses, but it was hard to fool six people staring at me. Worse, three of them had brimming eyes too. A wave of emotion rose like nausea from within and I gasped and snuffled desperately for a moment. Someone handed me a tissue. 'Really sorry, this isn't normal for me,' I said hoarsely. 'I'll stop now.' I managed to regain control, but they were all doing the funny finger waves in my direction and I couldn't help but laugh. I remembered what it was I wanted from them. 'Actually, I have a favour to ask: does anyone fancy joining me for lunch after this?'

I felt a hand reach across my back and rub gently. 'Count me in,' said Bengt. 'Me too,' said Mikael.

'But don't forget the meditation!' said Freda. It turned out we were supposed to be joining a worldwide hour of meditation over lunch, in order to influence 'the vibrational energy of the planet'. The organisers of this strange event had 'suggested' that we should all continue the 'spirit of meditation' by sitting in silence over lunch.

Mikael and Bengt winced apologetically as we all sat down at the same table and slurped our lentil soup wordlessly. 'I don't think it will disturb people if we talk quietly,' said Bengt presently. 'How are you feeling, Nick?'

'Oh, fine, thanks,' I said, reddening again. 'Nice of you to ask, but it's just ordinary existential angst – nothing like you've been through . . .'

'I thought you were brave for sharing it in the group,' shrugged Bengt. 'And anyway, my experience is that when you show vulner-ability, people step in and help. In fact, they welcome vulnerability, because it shows them their own soul.' He paused. 'I went back to work three days after my wife died, because I just wanted to throw myself into something. And I just sat at my desk and cried. But it was good to cry with other people, not on my own.'

Mikael nodded. 'A while ago I had a mission to be able to cry anywhere – on the subway if necessary – and not be ashamed of it.'

I looked at Mikael. I had pegged him as a bit of a New Age wide boy, playing the sensitive-man card in order to attract women. But now I wondered if there was something I didn't know.

'Why were you, um, crying?' I asked carefully.

He looked at me. 'It began as burn-out, then terrible muscle pain in my legs, neck. I've had problems since 1996, but it was only in 2003 when they diagnosed multiple sclerosis.'

Multiple sclerosis? We both gaped at him. It explained his craving for massage.

'My God, I'm so sorry,' I said, feeling terrible for having mis-judged him.

He shrugged. 'I don't know why it took them so long to diag-nose it, but in a way I'm glad about it, because I was working all that time – I was the product development manager for an inter-net firm. I earned a lot of money and luckily I was insured for ninety per cent of my salary – so I've been trying all kinds of new therapies. I've been off work since I was diagnosed.'

'Any success in treating it?'

He rubbed his neck absently. 'It comes and goes. Right now it's okay. People say with MS you can never be sure what will happen.' He looked round at us suddenly. 'But that's true of life, isn't it? How do any of us know we'll live to see tomorrow? It means I am always thinking of the present moment.'

I felt the hairs on the back of my neck stand up. I so rarely met men like this – able to look so unashamedly at the truth of their lives. A kind of strength in vulnerability. I thought of the blokeish jokes and music trivia that I so often allowed to pass for male friendship, and suddenly I wanted to talk to Mikael and Bengt for hours, days – sit at their feet and ask how they got where they were.

'Thank you so much for telling us,' I said. 'I—'

A large woman loomed suddenly in front of our table. 'Would you PLEASE respect the silence!' she hissed. 'You were told clearly that this was a time to meditate for world peace!'

I gaped at her. For a moment I was so furious I thought I might actually throw my soup dregs over her kaftan. I was groping for something sufficiently barbed to tell her about world peace, when Bengt and Mikael just nodded in apology and turned back to their soup. And the woman left, shaking her head.

'Later, maybe?' whispered Bengt. And the moment was over.

Charlie: my kind of guru (Nick Thorpe)

Afloat in the tidal impact zone (Sam Starkie)

'It's impossible to be sick when you're travelling at 150mph . . .' (Sam Furlong)

High-adrenalin options: strap your body to a bi-plane . . . (SWNS)

. . . or push your ego off a cliff (Nick Thorpe)

Child democracy at Summerhill School (Nick Thorpe)

New Age idyll: Sweden's No Mind Festival (Nick Thorpe)

One of life's more unusual crossroads (Nick Thorpe)

Hotfooting it: firewalking at Ängsbacka (Nick Thorpe)

Fraternal drifting on the River Klarälven in Sweden (Mark Thorpe)

Tom Hewitt with Durban streetkids (Nick Thorpe)

The Albuquerque International Balloon Fiesta (Nick Thorpe)

When Pigs Fly
(Nick Thorpe)

The road to silence (Nick Thorpe)

Monastic cell in New Mexico desert monastery (Nick Thorpe)

I retreated to the sanctuary of the toilet, where the sign on the inside of the door read: 'Did you know that you are the rain's teacher?'

I was tempted to kick the door off its hinges.

That afternoon, I took radical measures. I went dancing.

Back in the other universe, of course, I was about as likely to dance as, say, enrol on a flower-arranging course. It just wasn't something I did, except grudgingly at weddings, in that awkward, shuffling way some blokes have. Less hip-hop, more hip op. I rarely went clubbing due to a twin incapacity for late nights and alcohol, both of which seemed to be essential to the practice. Which was precisely why the Five Rhythms session caught my attention. Freda was helping to organise it: a kind of nightclub in the afternoon with no alcohol. Perfect.

In a vast barn lit only by a few coloured spotlights, a DJ from Stockholm led a pulsating mob of us through five different rhythms. I danced cautiously at first, only occasionally flicking my eyes up from the floor to check if anyone was laughing at me. Hearteningly, many had their eyes closed, so I began to expand my apelike shuffle with a few hand movements of the kind I'd proba-bly last seen on the Eurovision Song Contest. Still nobody batted an eyelid. In fact, we were all as unhinged as each other: young things in Lycra, hirsute flower children in baggy Indian trousers, old blokes with beards and piercings. Shining with sweat, I danced with all of them, moving through the room in complex fractals and chaotic couplings – making eye contact, then breaking it, copying someone, then taking the lead. You could dance any way you wanted, as long as you were roughly in the rhythm.

By the time we'd got to the third rhythm – chaos – I probably resembled a *Thunderbirds* puppet wired to the national grid, but nobody minded, least of all me. In fact, the mind didn't really come into it at all. I lost all sense of social inhibition, all words and explanations blown away by thudding bass riffs, as the body set its own agenda for once. Instead of brain chatter about how I looked, there was only sound and light and movement and the feeling of sweat and adrenalin – the raw sensual data of the right brain. And I loved it. By the time we got to the ambient, ethereal bit, moving gently as if in a breeze, I felt as if I were flying. It was like wing-walking, only better, as I stood with my eyes shut and every part of my body tingling with life.

Staggering out into the afternoon sunshine afterwards, I felt both knackered and exhilarated. Nothing objectively had changed since yesterday, but it was as if I were in a different world, no longer alone, but at one with those around me, yet also utterly present in my body. And the mind? As I had discovered in clowning, in Eden, and smiling at myself in front of my own bathroom mirror, the mind tended to follow what the body did. When I danced as if I were free, it was only a moment or two before I felt it for real. Strange to think I had got it the wrong way round all these years.

'So, what do you make of it all so far?' asked Nathan, puffing his cigarette down to the filter. He and Jane were sitting in the smoking enclosure, which was on the edge of the therapy area. 'Any pearls of wisdom to share with us poor, spiritually starved smokers? I was hoping that a journalist might help me dissect just what's going on here – or have you gone native?' He had regained his conspiratorial hunch after his bout of inversion therapy, and his humour was back, stretched thin over a well of impatience. A few of the gang craned their necks to hear, blowing smoke out and narrowing their eyes as if weighing me up. They seemed to have taken on some of Nathan's scepticism. I was tempted to do the same, to avoid looking like a gullible hippie.

'Well, I liked the Radical Honesty seminar,' I ventured. This was a workshop Bengt had recommended to me, in which a US psychotherapist called Brad Blanton called for a commitment to speaking the truth at all times to those around us in order to frustrate what he called the 'bullshit factory of the mind'. In some ways it sounded like a recipe for social pandemonium – especially when you applied it to questions like 'Does my bum look big in this?' But I had enjoyed the refreshing absence of calculation, the idea of a mind laid bare in all its petty contours, much as Eden had revealed the body.

'Really?' said Nathan. 'Tell me something radically honest, then.'

I looked at him and took a deep breath. 'Okay, if I'm honest, I don't feel very safe being honest with you.' I winced at how pathetic this sounded, but it was certainly true.

For a fraction of a second, he looked nonplussed, then put on a mock-caring voice: 'Reeeallly? Why's that, then?' His expression was one of amusement or perhaps pity, his head cocked to one side. But I noticed Jane was watching him intently.

'Because I can't tell where I am with you.' I had started so I would finish. 'One minute you're serious, the next you're cutting in with some witticism. I'm guessing it's just a defence.'

Nathan rolled his eyes and minced in camp abandon. 'Here I am, then, take me!' he lisped. 'I'm defenceless!' Jane rolled her eyes for different reasons.

'That's exactly what I mean. At the first threat of sincerity, you deflect it with humour.'

'Whereas you do *what*, exactly?' snapped back Nathan, suddenly livid.

'Fair point,' I persisted, reddening. 'But once you get past all the

New Age flakery, I think there might be something powerful and good at the heart of all this. I don't want to miss out on it . . .'

'It's a shame you didn't experience my cult of Eeyore,' he said, nodding back towards the smoking circle. 'I had them bowing at my feet, didn't I, Jane? None of these A-level gurus – I am the shining Ph.D. of enlightenment!'

I chuckled wearily and made my excuses. The moment had passed, and yet something had changed. I felt foolish and overearnest . . . and yet I also felt freer.

It was the last morning. After an emotional sharing group, all of us were preparing to re-enter the left-brained universe of jobs and timetables and sarcasm and snap judgements. But Bengt was no fragile dreamer. He believed in this stuff because traditional male defences – stoicism, jocularity, emotional containment – had done nothing for him when his wife died.

'My mother was a psychotherapist, and I used to think it was all bullshit,' he said as we sat in the sunshine, trying to delay our departure. 'But my wife's death changed me. Now I think it's fine to hold open your hands and show your emotion. Then everybody else has permission to do it, too.'

Recently he had been helping a friend whose wife had terminal breast cancer. 'I can see him going through all the same phases I did. In the last stages you have ninety-five per cent sadness and five per cent wishing she would die – you wish God would either take the knife out or get the job finished. My friend feels the same things – his wife is in a wheelchair and he feels he is in a prison. But he can't talk to her about that five per cent.'

Bengt's eyes grew watery as he looked into the distance. 'If it happened again, I would go for radical honesty. I would tell my wife the things I was feeling and trust that we could handle them together. When she was three days from death, and understood she was going to die, she tried to commit suicide in a bowl of water with an electrical cable connected to the mains. We didn't talk about it, but clearly she had the same urge to put an end to it. Both of us trying to protect each other from thoughts of the same thing! If we had talked about it maybe we could have given each other support.

'Then one day the hospital called and said there was no more to do. I went in with the kids – Carolyn and Johanna were five and six – they didn't really understand. My wife was the one who was supporting us all, even though it was she who was dying and in pain. I took the kids away and came back myself, but I still couldn't express myself. They turned on the morphine and I talked about our plans to go to Japan together – something we'd never got round to. She reached out and touched my cheek and consoled me as she died.'

Bengt's face was a mess of snot and tears as we knelt in the middle of the campsite with people casually drinking herbal tea around us. It didn't seem to matter – crying was routine here. Nobody panicked. Bengt looked up at me and grinned suddenly, as we both realised he had left snot on my shirt.

'Sorry, man!'

'No worries – the other shoulder has lentil stew on it.'

Bengt laughed and wiped his nose with his sleeve, as we sat back down side by side. 'A lot of positive things came out of her death. I learned to be more honest, to show my emotions more. When I think about the relationship we had, I sometimes wonder, if she hadn't got sick, would we still be together? That's the thing about death – you realise how irrelevant all the surface things were.'

He looked at me. 'But do we really have to wait until it's too late before the truth can come out?'

I thought of my own mother and the way I had learned to 'protect' her from difficult subjects by avoiding them. I had called her two nights ago, delighted to hear that her post-op tests showed all the cancerous tissue had been removed — but I was vague and upbeat in return, struggling to think what to tell her about Ängsbacka. She had joked that she only ever found out what was really going on by reading my books. I resolved to find a way to be more open before my parents' ruby wedding anniversary celebrations the following month. In the meantime, I had a more immediate way to practise — with my two brothers, who were meeting me later that afternoon for a rafting holiday. I felt both excited and uneasy just thinking about it.

'Why are families the hardest places to be totally honest?' I wondered now, as Bengt and I got up. 'I suppose there's just too much at stake.' More, at least, than in a transient group of strangers.

'Absolutely — but it's possible,' said Bengt. He hugged me one last time, turned away, then stopped. 'And for what it's worth,' he said, looking back over his shoulder. 'I think you'll make a great dad.'

I smiled back. From Bengt, it was worth a lot.

10

Don't Push the River

River Klarälven, Sweden

'You have been warned against letting the golden hours slip by. Yes, but some of them are golden only because we let them slip by.'

J. M. BARRIE

I had been fantasising about this moment for months. Three brothers, gathered in dappled sunshine on the forested banks of a river, preparing to build our own raft and drift back into a second boyhood.

Here in Sweden they offered it as a sort of wilderness package holiday. An enterprising ecotourism company was providing the logs, half a kilometre of rope and an icebox of provisions – all we had to do was put them together and push off into the current. A no-brainer, surely? The three of us had been virtually salivating at the thought ever since I picked them up at the train station in Karlstad. We'd driven an hour or so to a sort of adult Scout camp in the forest and collected our equipment – large wooden boxes full of cooking utensils, plates, a shovel and a large piece of roofing canvas for our floating home. I was checking and refolding this when Dan spotted an unnerving message. On the corner, in neat blue biro, someone had written three tiny words: 'It's a hell.'

We both stared at it, and then at each other, laughing nervously.

'What's that supposed to mean?' said Dan, cracking open a beer.

Sunny and idyllic as our surroundings were, the statement was hard to ignore. I tried to imagine what might have befallen the last person to use our equipment, to prompt such a stark verdict. Shipwreck? Splinters? An overbearing mother-in-law? Or perhaps it was the rather basic dig-your-own toilet facilities, using the shovel behind any available bush — already a deciding factor for my sister Hannah, who had been less than devastated to discover she had a wedding to go to instead.

'Or maybe it just rained a bit?' shrugged Dan, always the least flappable sibling. He stirred our pot of tomato pasta with his hunting knife. Mark, the exhausted escaped parent among us, was snoring contentedly from the tent. 'Come on, let's get some grub in us — it's almost time for orientation.'

Lars, our blond, muscled and unmistakably Swedish instructor, was waiting with a cluster of newly arrived fellow voyagers in front of an equipment store cluttered with buoyancy aids, camping stoves and boxes of rope. He could offer only the most cursory clues as to what might have gone wrong. 'Last year a few people complained about getting stuck on sandbanks,' he offered, as we practised tying logs together in the car park. 'But this year there's much more water in the river, so the more likely problem on a two-tonne raft will be working out how to stop.' He grinned encouragingly. 'If all else fails, you can swim ashore with a rope between your teeth.'

Two tonnes? The logistics solidified before us the following morning when a coach disgorged us fifty kilometres upstream in a field stacked high with logs. We tried not to look intimidated in front of our fellow drifters, who included a family from Yorkshire, a Swedish dad with three teenage sons, and what looked like an entire dynasty of Germans. Still, as a veteran of a cross-Pacific voyage, I liked to think this kind of package raft trip would be child's play – and perfect territory for the kind of relaxed attitude I was trying to cultivate. We put on our protective gardening gloves, unloaded our various crates from the coach, and bagged ourselves a sandy launching point between two clumps of trees on the bank.

'Timber is hard and humans are soft,' advised our safety-conscious Nordic hosts, sporting bright yellow polo shirts and muscles like Popeye. 'Please be careful and watch out in order to avoid crushed toes and lumbago.'

Scrambling gamely down to the river in the sunshine, we began hefting the requisite ten-foot logs around like telegraph poles. Overnight, Mark had transformed from an exhausted parent into a let-me-at-it grafter. 'What are we waiting for?' he said, shouldering the first coil of rope. The prescribed knots were tricky at first, a compromise between security and the necessity of untying them all again at the other end. It was tough, satisfying work, wading knee-deep in water with the sun on our backs, lining up the logs and reaching down under the water to catch loose ends. We laboured steadily but affected a certain nonchalance, trying to pretend we weren't racing to be the first to cast off.

'Are you taking regular breaks?' asked a motherly instructor called Jasmine, frowning at our Gordian knot-work. 'I think you need a break, or you will become angry and make a mistake.' We obediently boiled up a quick cuppa on the Trangia stove, then lashed timber double-quick to impress her. It was noon when we finally staggered ashore, proud architects of a floating three-layered square of nearly fifty logs. My body felt as if we had felled and stripped each one.

'Very good,' said Jasmine. 'Now do the same thing again.'

She was serious – it turned out that the full raft was *two* squares lashed together. I was sure I caught her smirking as we limped back to the woodpile. By the time we had secured the perimeter logs, erected our canopy and loaded our luggage boxes to double as seating, it was mid-afternoon. Gallingly, a super-fit young Dutch couple were already a speck in the distance, but we were well ahead of the German dynasty, who were adding a whole third section to create an eight-person nautical juggernaut.

'Now *that* could be a hell,' murmured Dan, levering us out into midstream using a twelve-foot-long staff. It was a good moment. We were a few inches above the surface, with only minor sagging at one corner, our luggage stacked under the tented section. All things considered, we were as proud as if we were launching the *Kon-Tiki*. We waved graciously at the six other groups still labouring in the shallows and watched them shrink slowly in the distance. Very slowly. Finally they disappeared around a bend and we were alone among forested slopes.

'It's a bit ... gentle, isn't it?' said Dan presently.

The Klarälven flowed at a stately, democratic two kilometres per hour, rising north of the Norwegian border and winding south in fattening curves until it eventually reached vast Lake Vänern. Of its 460 miles, we were rafting the most scenic and navigable fifty. We had been warned about a couple of rocky places, and a timber trap much farther down, but after wasting a lot of energy splashing around with paddles, it quickly became obvious that we didn't really need to steer. Even on the bends, the raft took its own course, following the deeper, faster water to each outside curve, then meandering across with each new swing of the river's broad hips. Standing redundantly at one corner, ready to pole off the bank, I felt the subtle change in the current beneath us, and watched the raft curve away in its own time, as if on invisible tramlines. I put down the pole and sat down in the vast silence. After all the hurry, there was nothing to do but surrender to the river's timescale, like the millions of logs that once took this route towards the sawmills.

'The river has its own wisdom,' intoned Mark, adopting the style of a kung fu movie guru as he headed for the food box. Dan chuckled. The pair of them had been ribbing me as a New Age flake ever since I told them about the No Mind Festival on the way there. 'You can't push the river.'

You could, however, push your siblings into it. Soon we were whooping and dive-bombing like the schoolkids we once were, taking it in turns to float and swim alongside in the chilled, sunlit water. It was impossible to see far below the surface, due to its tea-coloured tint, and we stayed well clear of the front of the raft after various gruesome scenarios painted by our instructors about the effect of getting caught between a rock and two tonnes of timber. But as long as we floated alongside, it seemed we were always in the deepest part of the river.

The limitations of going with the flow only emerged a few hours later when we had dried off and were thinking about pitching camp for the night. When the world's most perfect camping beach of pristine white sand slid into view on the inside bend, it was farthest from our natural trajectory along the outside curve. 'If we paddle like nutters we should make it across,' insisted Dan. There followed five entirely futile minutes of lung-bursting exercise as our vision of paradise scrolled steadily past. Swedish *allemansrätten* or 'everyman's rights' entitled us to a night's camping at any point along the river bank – but only if we could figure out how to get there.

Frustrated, but not yet ready to chomp on a rope and dive overboard, we untethered our secret weapon. Trailing behind us like a packhorse in a western was a red canoe – an optional extra we had hired shortly before departure. At the next glimpse of sand, Dan paddled quickly ashore with the end of a very long mooring rope, wrapped the end around a tree and let the current swing us effortlessly towards the beach. 'Result!' There was a gentle hiss of logs on sand as we ran aground for the night, near an oxbow lake at the foot of steep forested hillsides.

Our celebratory tinned meatballs tasted almost gourmet under the shell-pink sky. Soon a white mist crept from the reeds and the first mosquitoes sent us wading ashore to pitch our tent. Dan sat whittling kindling from branches he had collected, stacking them around his sandpit and coaxing them into flames. We warmed our wet toes, using smoke to keep the mosquitoes away.

'So, Nick,' said Mark, opening a can of lager with a sly smirk on his face. 'I'm impressed that you haven't brought your computer. This letting-go thing must be working for you. Or are you just embarrassed that you're not enlightened enough to buy a Mac?'

I grinned back, recognising the opportunity for some fraternal banter. Mark was evangelical about the benefits of his stylish, gently glowing Mac laptop versus my dull, corporate-looking PC. 'Ah, the familiar smugness of the fashion victim who believed all the shiny advertising . . .'

'Stop!' said Dan, uncharacteristically animated. 'I'm going to brain the next geek who mentions computers. We're supposed to be in the wilderness!' He poked the fire and looked at me with a faint grin. 'Though for the record, I'd say you're on thin ice talking about fashion victims, Eighties Man – from the guy who used to wear hairspray on his quiff?'

Mark guffawed from the other side of the fire. I pretended to be insulted. 'Hey, it was a superficial decade, okay? At least I didn't go for the unwashed hippie look . . .'

How easily the years fell away! We were all in our thirties with grown-up things like long-term partners and mortgages and even kids, and yet here we were throwing peanuts across the campfire at each other as if we were on youth camp. As the fire burned down, we mellowed into contented silence together, then turned in for the night. It was good to be out in this wild beauty, being our younger selves.

Wedged between my brothers in our three-man tent, I slept deeply, dreaming of sliding vistas of trees.

I woke earlier than the others, crept out to the moored raft, paddling through the cold shallows. The sun was slanting through the tops of the trees, burning off the last of the mist from among the reeds. I filled a kettle from the river and sat watching the fish rising in the stillness. Presently, Dan unzipped the tent and came out to join me. He stretched and surveyed our wild kingdom.

'This is the life! All we need now is some coffee.'

I watched Dan in his element, heating coffee in a pan on the Trangia stove, then a round of bacon and eggs.

'So how *is* your year of letting go?' he said, handing me a steaming mug. 'You seem happier than last time we met.'

'I'm definitely on the trail of something,' I said evasively, wary of a ribbing over something that still felt vulnerable and new. 'I guess I've learned to relax a bit more – just not quite as much as you . . .'

'You always say that, but it's bullshit,' said Dan, lighting a roll-up. 'You've got this idea of me that I don't even recognise. I'm the most anxious of all of us — why do you think I'm so fond of my beer?' I looked at him with interest. 'I worry about stuff all the time.'

'Like what?'

'Mum's cancer, for a start.' He sucked hard on his cigarette. 'After all the grief I gave her and Dad growing up ... I'd never really allowed myself to think about losing them one day. It does my head in, to be honest.' He looked into the distance, his brow furrowed. 'Anyway, thank God the operation went well ...'

'Right.' I sipped my coffee. My own approach had for once been more steady than Dan's — if only because I had somehow sealed off the darker possibilities in the back of my mind, until Mum got the all-clear.

But it was strange how inadequate those fixed childhood roles suddenly seemed. Who was the worrier, and who the rebel? Perhaps I had misjudged Dan. I smiled back sadly at him. 'Maybe we're not so different after all, eh?'

The day rippled past in delicious eddies of reading, cooking and skinny-dipping. Dan and Mark were determined to catch a fish, though they had only hooks and line, and cubes of tinned ham as bait. Knowing from bitter experience that I was to fishermen's luck what kryptonite is to Superman, I contented myself with gazing at the changing scenery. Amazing to think that this had been an industrial logging river until as recently as 1991; the towns and villages slipped past us almost unnoticed behind the trees, signalled only by the brief sigh of traffic and the occasional fisherman. Yet we were never quite alone. Dragonflies and house-martins flitted alongside, a solitary heron flapped overhead.

Sometimes, drifting quietly past thickets of pines, we heard the rustling of – what? Elks, bears and even wolves were possibilities, but most likely it was the resident beavers. The river echoed to the warning slap of their flat tails on the surface, and occasionally we glimpsed a retreating V-shaped ripple – but mostly we encountered only their felled trees, which occasionally threatened to poke our luggage overboard.

'So what's it like being a dad?' I asked Mark as we drifted along. 'Has it changed you?'

Mark put his book down, scratched his beard thoughtfully. 'Yes and no. You're never exactly ready for it, if that's what you mean. But you get the hang of it.' He looked pleased to be asked, if a little surprised. 'Why, have you got any news in that department?'

'Not yet,' I said, not elaborating. 'I just can't imagine how it feels – suddenly being totally responsible for a little person.'

'Yeah, well, you can read up on it, but it doesn't really prepare you for the reality, any more than reading an aircraft manual would equip you to fly. When Sammy arrived it was amazing and intense and a little bit terrifying – sort of like being harnessed in and pushed off a cliff. All that potential and vulnerability, and fists the size of your thumb ...' He looked at me, trying to read my expression. 'I mean, it's definitely the best thing I've ever done, and the hardest.'

'What's hard about it?'

He shrugged. 'Sometimes I miss all that freedom to travel and be spontaneous – but I'd miss being a dad much more ...'

I wondered if Mark knew how much I respected him – and whether I would ever find the humility to tell him. Although he was eighteen months younger than me, he had always been sportier, more effortlessly sociable – more mature in every sense, as I grudgingly noticed sometime in our teens. I would never have dreamed of admitting this to him, of course, but it seemed somehow entirely fitting that he was the first to be a parent. I thought of the cheeky grin of my nephew Sammy – born four years earlier, while I was trying to hitch a ride on a fishing boat out of Aberdeen harbour – and his little brother Ethan, two years younger, waving a toy boat at me, shouting: 'Uncle Nick's ship!' I had not been the most attentive of uncles, it occurred to me. But perhaps all that might change.

'Actually, babies are pretty straightforward, once you're used to the initial shock and wonder of it all,' Mark was saying, looking into the distance with a thoughtful expression that reminded me of Dad. 'They basically eat, sleep and fill nappies for a year or so, which gives you time to get the hang of things before they work out how to give you the run-around.'

'Not necessarily in our case,' I said. 'We're going for the full-immersion version – could have a hyperactive five-year-old on our hands from day one ...'

'Right, blimey – I forgot,' said Mark. 'Sorry.'

'Not a problem,' I chuckled.

And it really wasn't. Since the No Mind Festival, I had noticed a marked drop in my defensiveness and brain chatter, even a general contentment. It probably helped that I was dipping into the *Tao Te Ching*, that ancient manual for living, allowing its mysterious lines to drift through my mind like a fish-hook in the water.

Do you have the patience to wait
Till your mud settles and the water is clear?
Can you remain unmoving
Till the right action arises by itself?

It was the very opposite of the way I had begun the year – in a clenched fury of willpower, trying to wrestle myself into submission. And yet, when I thought about it, the best actions of my life had indeed arisen by themselves. Like meeting Ali, knowing in a deep, calm place that she was the one ... the way my best writing ideas emerged spontaneously, usually while I was doing something else ... the strange serendipities of hitching boat rides around Scotland. Going with the flow, as the hippie dictum had it, dropping your resistance and letting life happen. It was the common theme of so many of the activities I had sampled recently, from clowning to cliff jumping to dropping the story.

We were definitely in Tao territory here on the river. You could sit for hours just absorbing nature as it lapped at your senses. Living barefoot on this slowly turning stage, we found that sibling rivalry seemed to limit itself to important, primal things like fire-lighting and Travel Scrabble. Conversations surfaced naturally and spread like the ripples from rising trout, covering all the classic male themes: love, power, betrayal, female beauty and cult children's TV programmes of the 1970s. And that inevitable one about the existence/non-existence of God.

'This is going to sound a bit flaky,' I mused one afternoon as we drifted along. 'But at the moment "God" basically comes down to a sensation I get sometimes – a sort of energy.'

In the sceptical silence that followed, I felt suddenly vulnerable. Dan had angrily dumped the whole religion thing as soon as he was old enough to skip church, while Mark channelled what remained of his faith into his job in international development – always more interested in tangible action than philosophising. 'You know that feeling you get when you look at an amazing sunset?' I persisted. 'Or really connect with someone?' Music did it, too. I had only to listen to the 'Sanctus' of Fauré's *Requiem*, for example, to find myself ambushed by a tingling sensation that spread from the top of my head down the spine and to my fingertips. But that didn't really do it justice. 'It's like a feeling of awe, but also a deep sense that everything's going to be okay. Does any of that make any sense?'

'Yeah, sure,' said Dan, putting another cube of ham on his fish-hook and dropping it off the back of the raft. 'I get tingly feelings, too, watching the sun set or listening to music. But what makes you think that's got anything to do with God?'

I pondered this. I could still vividly remember the first time I felt it, as a twelve-year-old on Bible camp in Devon. I was kneeling in a tent with a few other kids, trying to think of sins to repent of, while the vicar prayed for 'Jesus to come into our hearts'. The fact that the feeling was entirely unexpected made it all the more powerful: like a warm wave breaking over me, flooding me with what I can only describe as joy. For most of my teenage years I followed that recurring sensation, using it as a kind of spiritual Geiger counter. Church leaders told me it was the Holy Spirit, but it bothered me a little that I also felt it at less predictable moments: cycling along a sunlit avenue, listening to 'Comfortably Numb' by Pink Floyd, or kissing a girlfriend after telling her how I really felt. Studying English literature at university, I found tremors and flickers coming at me from all directions. The bracing nihilism of Beckett's *Waiting for Godot* moved me as much as Wordsworth's *Intimations of Immortality*. What was going on? It was as if any fragment of poetry, any dying chord, any chance encounter could set off this connection between spirit and Earth. Everything seemed electrified, carrying current. There would be periods in my life when I lost track of it for a while – generally whenever I grew clenched and driven – but then it would break in again. I had felt it many times in recent months, most recently in the sharing group at the No Mind Festival. In fact, I was feeling it now, just thinking about it. 'It's basically all about a connection with something bigger – a sense that it's all good,' I said.

I stopped talking, and waited for a response. The raft brushed the riverbed briefly, turned ninety degrees, slipped onwards. Mark lay beneath the awning with his eyes closed, possibly asleep. But Dan looked thoughtful.

'I had what I'd call a spiritual experience, one of those connected moments,' he mused presently. 'I was in Sumatra, back in my stoner days, trekking with three other guys in the jungle. We got totally lost out there, it got dark and the jungle just came alive with all kinds of mad noises and luminous bugs. We had to get down river in pitch darkness to the village where we were staying – and a lot of the path was just a ledge with a thirty-foot drop into the rapids. I should have been scared shitless. But that night, not to sound too cosmic about it, I just had this deep sense that the Earth was our home, that everything was going to be okay. And it was. Even with these seriously wild noises coming out of the darkness, none of us freaked out. It was just one foot in front of the other, like the path was pulling our feet to meet it. I had this weird certainty that nothing that happened to us could change the basic truth that everything kind of ... belongs.' He paused and looked up with a self-conscious grin. 'Anyway, it felt profound at the time – probably something to do with the magic mushrooms.'

A chuckle issued from the shelter. 'You old hippie!' said Mark. 'Give me a mushroom and I'll have a spiritual experience too!' Dan threw his apple core at him instead.

Of course, Dan's drug-induced experience was probably quite

similar to those I might more piously have called 'spiritual'. For millennia, Native Americans and other ancient cultures had ignored the distinction by using natural hallucinogens in their religious rites. And neurologists and psychologists, long able to track the effects of drugs in the brain, were nowadays foraging into territory previously deemed unscientific in search of the so-called 'God Spot'. In fact we knew quite a lot about the mechanics of religious experiences – to the extent that they could be simulated or triggered using magnets or LSD, or monitored in the brains of meditating monks. But the question that remained unanswered, disputed even among scientists, was *why?* Why were our brains and bodies wired to feel these strange sensations in the first place?

Some scientists theorised that Homo sapiens had evolved this near-universal propensity for religious belief because it helped the species to endure suffering and thereby perpetuate itself. But you could say the same of our tendency to seek a mate – and few would argue that this disproved the existence of love. The sceptics, it seemed to me, were mixing up cause and effect. In one sense, of course, the question 'why?' was as irrelevant as it was unanswerable. The simple fact was that when we felt these sensations of serene oneness, we relaxed and opened a little more. So, regardless of whether they were self-generated or sent from beyond, they seemed crucially important to my quest to let go.

'Just because you can explain the brain chemistry doesn't mean the experience wasn't real,' I argued now. 'Does it?' I looked at Dan.

'I dunno,' he shrugged. 'It *felt* real.'

On the third day, as the hills subsided into pastureland, we took a brief trip ashore. I was starting to feel almost weightless, shorn of all the usual reference points that anchored me to the world.

We looked at our map and stopped at the village of Eskharad, scrambling up an embankment and through the back of a farm to see the local tourist draw: a seventeenth-century red timber church, an historic stop on an old pilgrim route. Outside, the burial ground was studded with strange wrought-iron grave decorations, their tinny leaves tinkling eerily in the breeze. There was distant rain on the wind, a sense of a change in the weather.

Within a few minutes of being back on the river, we were having to pole off from the bank, as the breeze caught the canopy and pushed us off the tramlines of the main current. The rain spat fitfully and then passed, but the wind remained. Late in the afternoon, we were right in the middle of a broad section of river enjoying some unexpected sun, when the raft scuffed the bottom, turned slightly, then hissed to a halt in sand.

'We're aground,' said Dan, peering over the front. Sure enough, the water was barely shin deep. We stepped off the raft and it freed itself for another few feet, then ran aground again.

'We can't go forward – it's getting shallower,' said Mark, scouting ahead of the raft. 'We'll need to push backwards.'

We grunted and heaved against the weakened current, watching the raft inch backwards and then get caught again. There was a solidity about its stuckness that was worrying. Twenty metres to the east, the light colour of the water disappeared into tannin blackness, marking the main current.

'How did we get so far off course?' said Dan. 'It's only a light wind.'

We resorted to trying to dig our own raft-width channel across the current, which proved predictably futile. Every scoop of sand was replaced by more swept downstream. Eventually, stumped and famished, we slopped back on board to look at the instruction pamphlet. 'Eat first then work your way free,' it advised, as practical as ever. 'All problems seem bigger when you are hungry.'

'Great idea,' muttered Dan, gorging on Pringles. 'If we eat all the food then jump overboard, the raft will float free.'

And with one major modification, it turned out to be a brilliant plan. Loading all the food and several bags into the canoe, we watched the raft inch forward once again, now buoyant enough for us to shove it painstakingly back to the deep channel again.

'Was that a hell?' wondered Mark.

'Not even close,' I said. 'That was just an initiative test.' In fact, it was a wonderful relief to have a purely physical problem to solve, rather than an existential one. It reminded me of a line I learnt studying Milton at school: 'The mind is its own place/ And in itself can make a Heaven of Hell, a Hell of Heaven.'

It seemed truer than ever. Perhaps hell and heaven were only ever in the mind – or, at least, the anticipation of either prevented one from living in the present moment. Determined to enjoy the final day of the trip, I tried to throw myself into the physical world as much as possible.

Obligingly, more sandy ambushes followed, requiring further teamwork, and a particularly sneaky row of submerged boulders succeeded in realigning several of our logs like Jack Straws. Mark and Dan seemed to relish the challenges as much as I did, welcoming the focus of muscle rather than intellect. And when the German loggernaut floated noisily past like a Thames party barge on our last night, bearing two guitarists, a gaggle of inebriates and a man gloating over his bucket of fish (we'd caught two tiddlers) – it seemed more surreal than irritating.

Finally, we dismantled our floating home and freed the logs to float downstream to their collection pen ready for the next pioneers. I could not remember a more relaxing holiday. The nearest we had come to disaster was briefly setting fire to the raft in an attempt to smoke out mosquitoes, and losing the letter Q from Mark's Scrabble set. Even my muscles ached pleasantly. Somehow, more than any of my previous adventures to date, the combination of simple, primal tasks in the open air, the company of my brothers, and the enforced slowness of our pace had created a sense of both intimacy and contentment. We never did find out what the mystery graffiti scribbler meant by 'hell'.

'Perhaps he was just too blissed-out to finish his sentence,' suggested Mark, as we drove back towards the airport.

'Yeah,' grinned Dan. 'It's a hell of a way to let go.'

II

Cryptic Clues

London

'The family – that dear octopus from whose tentacles we never quite escape, nor, in our inmost hearts, ever quite wish to.'

DODIE SMITH

It's the first weekend of September, and the day of my parents' ruby-wedding lunch party. In the garden of their suburban home, Ali is helping Dad stake out a cluster of B&Q gazebos in case of rain, and I'm working out a way to force all the guests to talk to one another. An 'ice-breaker', I think Mum calls it. Basically, it's a hand-out list of cryptic clues for people to investigate as they mill around with their glasses of wine. Stuff like 'Who was Chitty Chitty Bang Bang's emergency repairman?' (my theatre technician cousin, Ben), 'Who gets her olive oil straight from the family tree?' (my Spanish sister-in-law, Angeles) and, at Mum's gleeful insistence, 'Who walked round the Eden Project stark naked?'

'Are you absolutely sure you want that on the list?' I ask,

exchanging worried glances with Ali. 'I mean, there are people from church coming ...'

'Oh, stop worrying!' smiles Mum. 'Aren't you supposed to be learning to let go?'

It's a recurring problem with this project – people keep holding me to it. August was a cinch by comparison – a month of anonymous hustling for work in the freelance jungle that is the Edinburgh Festival, where I surprised myself by retaining at least a modicum of the peaceful self-acceptance I had so recently discovered. But letting go in a family gathering is a different matter. It's all very well baring your soul to a sharing group in Sweden, or even baring everything else to strangers on a Cornish campsite, but the average family gathering functions on the basis that everyone agrees to revert back to the safe, familiar and slightly wooden roles ordained since the days of potty training. This isn't just any family gathering, either: four generations of relatives ranging from my two-year-old nephew to my eighty-nine-year-old grandmother, family friends who have known me since I was born and members of the church in which I have been raised, all packed into my parents' garden with nowhere to escape. Could there be any more intimidating forum in which to relax and 'come out' as oneself?

But watching Mum giving her speech to the gathered friends and relations later on, it occurs to me that she is leading the way in that respect. I've always focused on her anxiety, perhaps because it's a trait we share, but today I have the strange sensation of meeting her almost for the first time on her own territory. She makes no reference to her own travails, or the fact that she's even now in the midst of a radiotherapy course. Instead, she uses the opportunity to talk about the development project she visited with Dad in Tanzania shortly before she was diagnosed, and to thank the guests for making donations to that charity instead of bringing gifts. She exudes not just concern, but passion.

For a moment I am overcome with pride in her, and a disconcerting sense of the ineffable mystery of other people – particularly those we think we know best. What if 'dropping the story' applies as much to our ideas about other people as it does to our own narratives? The thought is heightened by the slideshow of photos unearthed for the occasion: Mum doing athletic handstands by the pool on honeymoon, or wearing a sixties miniskirt and a coy smile; my youthful Dad captured in mid-air on a space hopper, eyes twinkling with mischief. For the first time I see them as they must have seen each other: young and alluring and full of potential. Yesterday I enquired for the first time how this architect and pharmacist hooked up together back in 1964. Apparently it was at an inter-varsity trip away in the Cotswolds – a thinly disguised singles weekend, from what I can gather.

'I remember your father on the dance floor,' said Mum, smiling ambiguously (my father has about as much panache as I do on the dance floor).

Dad went all wistful: 'Your mum was the only woman who ever fed me oranges while I was driving.'

While I'm at it, I sweep my eye across the rest of my family with the filter of familiarity removed. There's Mark, traditionally labelled as the sporty but disorganised middle child. It's a label I've reinforced over the years, not least by recounting our teenage InterRail trip and our different attitudes to missing trains: I used to fret about catching them, while he told me to chill out; he used to fret once we'd missed them, while I relaxed and told him there was no point worrying now. True once, perhaps, but thoroughly outdated now that he's a family man running international development projects, and with a talent for the complex logistics of bringing people together.

Next there's Dan, already semi-liberated since the raft trip from my caricature of him as chilled-out rebel, having an intense conversation with our only surviving grandma. And of course there's our wee sister Hannah – not so wee at twenty-five, admittedly. After three boys, she was a successful last-ditch bid for a daughter, born just before my mum hit forty. Only six when I left home for university, Han is the sibling I feel I know least, though in many ways we're the most alike. Both academic, perfectionist, thin-skinned, prone to migraines. Both studied English lit at the same college. Now I watch her giggling with her godmother, and see a friendly, funny and deeply intuitive woman in her prime, well on the way to becoming a child psychologist. In fact, it dawns on me that all of my siblings have chosen broadly caring professions, and I feel both a jolt of my difference, and a swell of pride in them. Another opportunity to drop the story.

The ice-breaker also seems to help in that respect – at least it does in my case. The naturism thing raises eyebrows and smirks among those who remember me as a zealous youth leader in the church. Mum appears to enjoy their surprise as much as I do – though Ali is less comfortable with the exposure. Later, we're a little taken aback when a retired headmaster friend of my parents confides that he got his kit off for the American photographer Spencer Tunick. He had to lie down stark naked with hundreds of other brave volunteers, next to the Cutty Sark. 'A wonderfully liberating experience,' he reminisces genially. 'A vision of unvarnished human equality.' We talk about letting go, and the background stresses of life, and he confesses that the hardest sort of stress to cope with is the incidental, everyday sort – as he puts it, the anger and frustration of dropping a file of papers on the floor and having to pick them all up and re-order them – rather than the big crises, the 'harnessed-in stuff you just have to get on and deal with, like illness and bereavement'. He's not so keen when I bring in Byron Katie, and Buddhist ideas of non-attachment.

'That's fine to a point,' he says as we part. 'But you have to be careful that this letting go doesn't just become passivity ...'

That familiar niggle once again. A reminder that, while wonderfully liberating, my recent experiments still seem a little insulated from these broader concerns. Can you relax *and* save the world?

Mark is particularly interested by the question. 'Actually, one of the most laid-back guys I know works with street kids in Durban,' he tells me later on, as we're clearing up together. 'And if you can relax there, you can relax anywhere. You could drop in on him and find out how he does it.'

Ali and I are going to South Africa next week, strictly speaking for a safari holiday to celebrate our tenth wedding anniversary. But I can't resist Mark's idea. Surely a little extra fieldwork won't take us too far from our itinerary?

'Just don't tell Ali it was my idea,' grins Mark. 'It's probably not quite the kind of safari she had in mind.'

12

Surf the Fear

Durban, South Africa

'We must travel in the direction of our fear.'

JOHN BERRYMAN

The tourist authority of KwaZulu-Natal offered the following advice to motorists:

Always know where you're going.

Don't stop at a body or a seemingly injured person lying on the road. Rather drive on.

Don't get out of your car if bumped from behind under suspicious circumstances.

Try to time traffic lights so that your car always remains on the move.

Be alert when leaving and approaching driveways.

Be on the lookout for people on bridges who may want to throw projectiles at your vehicle as you pass under.

When driving through urban, industrial or suburban areas, lock doors and close windows.

If you still found yourself one of the 3500 or so unlucky drivers to be dragged from their cars each year by armed robbers, it was essential to remain calm, surrender your vehicle and possessions without resistance and avoid direct eye contact, 'which may be interpreted as a threat'.

'I thought you were supposed to *keep* eye contact, so they feel worse about killing you?' I mused, gripping the wheel of the hire car as we sped towards Durban's silhouetted skyscrapers. 'Or maybe that's just in hostage situations ...'

We had both been feeling more excited than nervous when we touched down in Johannesburg on a bright September morning the previous week. We had spent a wonderful first few days in the highlands of Lesotho on horseback, before recrossing the border to reach a safari lodge in the Drakensberg mountains the previous evening. But even in rural areas it was hard to ignore the vast inequalities of the country, with its breezeblock settlements and shoeless kids. And now here we were a few hours later, driving towards Gotham City with a steadily sinking feeling.

'Just keep looking out for the next off-ramp,' snapped Ali, stuffing her daypack under the seat.

She had responded graciously to my temporary hijacking of our anniversary safari, but was trying not to be angry with me for booking us into a hotel in what our travel guide described as one of the city's 'no-go' areas. In turn, I was doing my best to affect the breezy reassurance of the seasoned traveller, while feeling distinctly clammy about the whole thing.

Fear could make you do irrational things. I had heard of one car-load of British lads so determined not to let carjackers catch them stationary that they ignored all red lights and stop signs as they drove through Durban, even devising a system of in-flight refuelling which involved one of them hanging out of the back window with a petrol can. Back in Britain I had sniggered at such ludicrous paranoia, wondering quite what the point had been of coming in the first place. But today I was beginning to sympathise. To quote William Burroughs: 'Sometimes paranoia's just having all the facts.'

Dubbed South Africa's 'robbery capital' by its own newspaper, I later discovered that Durban had notched up an annual total of ninety-two murders in the streets around our hotel. We were thirty times more likely to be murdered here than in central London. The regional total topped almost five thousand victims in a population of ten million. The fear felt different here. We were on the wrong side of a polarised society. I felt that our skin colour defined us as rich pickings as surely as if we had a flashing neon target on the back of our hire car.

'Next left, I think,' shouted Ali. 'No, sorry, right. RIGHT!'

I scythed across two lanes of honking taxis to make the turn. *Always know where you're going.* Suburban security fences had given way to sprawling malls and blocks of chain-link fencing and, despite my attempts to be level-headed and calm, I could feel something clawing at my guts.

'I think that was the wrong turn,' said Ali, crumpling the map in her search for street names. At what looked like the back of a hospital, an old woman sat in a nest of cardboard, swigging at something from a paper bag. Further along, a huddle of young men loitered at the intersection, watching the traffic. As we stopped at the red light, one of them nodded briefly in our direction. Immediately a man in a singlet and baseball cap walked purposefully towards us. 'Watch this guy ...'

Try to time traffic lights so that your car always remains on the move. Before I'd even registered I was doing it, I had stamped on the accelerator and jumped the red light to a cacophony of horns.

'We'll get pulled over by the police!' shouted Ali.

'Great! An armed escort would be nice!' I heard the hysterical tinge to my voice and tried to slow my short, shallow breaths. Then, by some miracle, Ali spotted the name of our hotel and we pulled up in front. I was just taking off my seat belt when a man appeared at my window so suddenly that I yelped.

'Can I take your car for you, sir?' he asked mildly. 'I am Henry the concierge, and we have a secure lock-up.'

Looking down onto the seafront from the safety of our room a few minutes later, I felt relieved but sheepish. Below us was a relaxed lunch-time scene: tourists wandering along the promenade arm in arm, haggling with market vendors over brightly coloured sarongs or T-shirts. The Indian Ocean rumbled and sighed on a sandy beach spotted with the occasional sunbather.

I wondered what Byron Katie would have done in our shoes, remembering her conviction that every terrifying snake is ultimately a piece of old rope. Not in South Africa, I thought. And yet our fear, however well founded, had only hindered us that morning. What was the alternative?

Perhaps Tom could help.

'You guys picked a pretty dicey part of town,' said Tom Hewitt cheerfully, pulling up in his 4×4 about half an hour later. 'Just behind your hotel is where the Nigerian drug dealers hang out. You should have stayed down my end of the beach.'

He was a tanned, freckled surf-dude type with a muscular torso and a pair of wrap-around shades pushed up onto his sun-bleached collar-length hair. Climbing into the passenger seat, I spotted a Thomas the Tank Engine CD on the dashboard and felt grateful for its innocent familiarity. In the back, Ali was making the acquaintance of a couple of street kids. We both did our best with the hip-hop handshakes.

'That guy is a bad guy,' said a sixteen-year-old called Lucky, beginning his own no-gloss street tour as we pulled out into the traffic. He pointed to a thin youth emerging from an alleyway behind the hotel. 'He'll rob you.'

'The big boys are always robbing people,' added Wanda, an eleven-year-old with big eyes and a runny nose. I noticed a tang of something chemical under the general odour of unwashed bodies.

'Yeah,' said Lucky, 'but when one boy steals off tourists, *all* the street kids get the blame. If the police catch us on the streets, sometimes they send us far away.' It happened mostly on public holidays – night raids on an abandoned building, where sleeping kids were sprayed with water or gas and bussed out of town. 'They don't want to see street kids when the tourists are around, eh, Tom?'

Tom nodded grimly in the front seat. Arriving from Surrey in his early twenties with an earnest desire to do something practical, he had quickly lost most of his illusions. The authorities were distinctly tepid about his pioneering outreach project, which was run by the very people it helped – particularly when it unearthed evidence of abuse, theft and fraud within government-run shelters.

'When we first started here, nobody wanted our organisation to survive,' he said. 'The NGOs didn't want us, the municipality didn't want us. A lot of people had a lot they didn't want to be exposed.'

In nearly twenty years of work both in Durban and farther down the coast in East London, he had been beaten, threatened and held at gunpoint – not by the kids, but by those who wished to exploit them or hound them out of existence altogether.

'That stuff takes me to my lowest ebb,' he said, turning from the beachfront down a side street. 'But it also makes me most determined not to back down and desert these guys.'

The kids seemed determined to return the favour. As we slowed to a halt in the side street, the car was suddenly mobbed by children, shouting and waving, banging on the windows. I tightened my grip on my daypack, but Tom just got out into the crowd, gesturing to us all to follow. We were in a kind of street dormitory: the pavements were lined with prone figures lying under bits of newspaper or on an abandoned sofa, while others played soccer in the street, parting grudgingly to let the occasional car past – though traffic seemed generally to avoid this route. Several of the kids were sniffing from cut-down juice cartons, or breathing into crumpled rags that gave off the same sickly chemical smell I had caught in the car. Others gathered round us, eyeing my camera, sizing us up. Tom high-fived a couple of them, and then fished a laptop out of his bag.

'Gather round, people,' he said, crouching down on the pavement as he flipped the lid open. 'Who wants to see their picture?' Immediately, he was engulfed in an excited mass of kids, pointing and laughing at their faces on the screen.

I stood with Ali taking photos, thinking about how many of the tourist safety rules we were openly ignoring just by being there. And yet I felt moved and a little shamed by the spontaneity and affection on show before us – two very different worlds of poverty and privilege somehow overlapping in a place of hard-won trust. A twentysomething man noticed our discomfort and ambled over.

'Tom's like a role model to most of these guys,' he said, nodding at the scrum of bodies. 'He was the one who saw that we were being short-changed.'

Sipho was one of Tom's early success stories. He had left his Johannesburg home at the age of ten because his uncle was abusing him, but found that the treatment was much worse on the streets.

'The first night was terrible – it always is,' he said, looking at his shoes. 'The streets are very violent places. You run away because you want to be free, but you find you're not really free because the people on the streets may be worse than the ones you left at home.'

But, luckily, one street acquaintance was Tom. Decades later, Sipho was a co-worker in his project, offering legal advice to rape victims, kids the authorities treated like trash.

'Glue is a big problem,' he said, watching a small boy with rheumy eyes, ragged shorts and no shoes, who kept putting his nose in a crumpled orange-juice carton. 'These kids are using it for the same reason I did – so they don't have to think about the problems they face.' In the short term it was a cheap high. Longer term, this child might face hearing loss, limb spasms, liver, kidney or brain damage. It could eventually kill him, if AIDS didn't first. 'We teach the kids about these dangers, but some of them think, "I'm going to die anyway." Most of the girls are HIV-positive, and probably most of these guys, too, but they like to keep it to themselves.'

It was horrific – an existence that made my own anxieties seem utterly redundant by comparison. I tried to imagine what the psychological effects must be of living in almost permanent fear for your life – knowing that at any moment you could be attacked or raped, or worse. Faced with all this, why *wouldn't* you sniff glue? Death had claimed many of Tom's friends over the years. As he drove us back across town to the charity's headquarters, I wondered how he maintained such a cheery positivity. He looked surprised at the question.

'I guess I know we're making a difference,' he shrugged. Every year, he and his co-workers persuaded an average of 350 kids to leave the streets, monitoring their return to families or carers in cases of domestic abuse. Of course, it was a drop in the ocean compared to the swelling population of AIDS orphans, runaways and child addicts – which had grown from four hundred when Tom had first set up his charity in 1998 to more than five thousand today, in a city of 3.5 million. Many businesses were moving out of the city centre as the tide of poverty flowed in from the townships. But even that was an opportunity for Tom.

'We've taken advantage of white flight,' he said, as we drove down the basement ramp of a glass skyscraper. 'People expect street kids to be chaotic and informal, so we've taken offices in a smart block to make a point.'

We sauntered in our jeans past liveried doormen and took the lift to an unexpectedly corporate-looking suite overlooking the docks. The charity took its name and logo from the indigenous Umthombo tree, a symbol of hope because of its uncanny ability to sink its roots to invisible wellsprings and grow in even the most arid places. But what springs fed Tom?

One obvious source of his contentment was Mandi Ngantweni-Hewitt, who greeted us on arrival at the office. A friendly black South African with a big personality, she had grown up on the municipal rubbish dump, but ran away from her family's shack to take her chances on the street. Somewhere along the way she had met Tom. And now, two decades later, she was married to him.

'The first time I saw Tom was in a church on Christmas Day, 1996,' said Mandi, now the operations director of their charity, pushing her sunglasses up onto her head. 'I still remember noticing this tall white guy with long hair, shorts up to his knees. I don't think I'd ever seen a surfer before.'

Tom smiled. 'It was the surfing that first brought me here. Then I got involved with street work, and Mandi and I just became friends really, and after a while a whole group of us lived in one place for a while in Durban. It was a bit like a commune.' He blushed a little. 'That's when the, er, romance began.'

Mandi's past was anything but romantic. Her family had scraped a living sorting recyclable trash, but her alcoholic mother and stepfather had done nothing to prevent her repeated rape and abuse by neighbours. Things weren't much better when she escaped, aged ten, to the beach front with a gang of girls. 'We all knew each other and stayed in a group for protection, but we couldn't protect each other from the older guys. They came in from the townships and ...' She paused, and Tom put his arm around her shoulder. Accustomed as she was to telling the story, it never got any easier to stomach. 'To be honest, the memories are too painful. It's why we used glue, or benzine or paint – anything on the dump that we could sniff or smoke. It makes you forget about your fear, your hunger, your cold; you don't feel anything, you're in your own world, nobody can harm you – or at least, what-ever people do, you won't feel it.'

Eventually she managed to find a place in a shelter, but her experiences had a profound effect on her. While her mother and sister still lived on the dump, and her younger brother was in prison for attempted murder, Mandi vowed to bring some good out of her difficult start in life.

'Even when I was at the shelter, I wanted to be a social worker. I never met a good social worker – they were all in it for the salaries. I thought, One day I'll do it better, I'll make a difference.'

She had begun to work as a volunteer in shelters, which was how she got to know Tom, and began to consider the structural causes of poverty. 'Studying black consciousness and listening to Nelson Mandela woke me up that it wasn't my fault. It made me realise that I didn't have to be ashamed of being black – black was beau-tiful.' Nowadays the best thing about her job was seeing the faces of street kids light up when they realised that she understood their life from the inside. 'It is rewarding work.' She looked at her husband with a half-smile. 'Not that people like Tom can't highlight the issue, too – but I've been where these kids are.'

Tom nodded. 'The future for Umthombo is clearly for it to be run by the former street children themselves.' It reminded me of Summerhill School, this conscious empowerment of those who were usually denied it. As the only white non-South African involved, Tom's plan was to fade gradually into the background and, like A.S. Neill, finally relinquish control of the organisation he had helped to nurture. A very real form of letting go.

But there were a few problems to be ironed out before then. Many of the fifteen-strong staff had recurring issues of addiction and had to be coached through sticky patches. Several had AIDS.

'There will be times when people aren't quite ready for the responsibility,' said Tom. 'Some people like to point out how far we are from perfection, but we like to say, "Look how far we've come."'

It was a typically glass-half-full statement from Tom. How did he keep so airy and cheerful in the midst of this urban battleground? I watched as he tied up some staffing problems, waved Mandi off for a weekend social-work conference, and then whisked us to a rendezvous with the childminder. I had forgotten Tom and Mandi had children. Tom threw two-year-old Sabelo delightedly into the air and caught him again, while Ali took Sandino – a contented baby named after the Nicaraguan revolutionary leader, with olive skin and curly black hair like his mother.

There was something almost balletic about the way Tom switched from high-tension situations to relaxed banter, all the time monitoring his surroundings, taking calls on his mobile, keeping things moving. I wanted to pin him down and ask him how he did it. But it was like following the stillness at the eye of a storm. And the storm never seemed to let up for long: we arrived at Tom and Mandi's seafront flat to find Tom's pregnant lodger lying bleeding on the floor.

'I think she might be miscarrying,' stammered another friend, who had been waiting for his return.

'Right, try not to panic, but we'd better get you to hospital,' said Tom, keeping a level head. He passed Sabelo to me. 'Sorry, guys, do you mind looking after the kids while I scoot to the hospital?'

As their voices faded down the corridor, Ali and I sat in shell-shocked silence, watching cartoons with the kids. Without the usual distancing effect of my role as reporter or any impending deadline to distract me, the brutal stories we had heard that day replayed endlessly and somewhat surreally in my mind alongside Noddy's innocent on-screen adventures. *Is the universe friendly?* It seemed ludicrous even to ask the question here. But what were we supposed to do about it?

Sandino started to grizzle in my arms, so I got up and went over to the window to rock him, feeling a familiar lump in my throat as his little fingers tugged at my hair. Such an awesome responsibility, a tiny life in my hands. 'Better get used to this, eh?' whispered Ali from the sofa. And she was right: while I had limited power to help Durban's dispossessed, there was almost certainly at least one child in the world for whom we could provide a loving home. A wave of yearning washed over me, with its familiar undertow of fear. Did anyone ever feel truly ready for this task?

Looking down on the city, I followed the blue lights of an emergency vehicle along the seafront below, listening as its siren faded into the tightly packed circuitry of roads. I wondered what the street kids were doing right now – or what was being done to them. It seemed such an arbitrary division, that we were up here, while they suffered. How on earth did Tom live with it all, day after day? Over the years I had met and interviewed many people driven to change the world. I found such people irresistibly interesting, fed off their energy. Sometimes they were angry, sometimes they were loving. Always they lived in a kind of constant flux in which it was impossible to predict what would happen next. Many were workaholics. Some burned out. Some got bitter. But Tom seemed nourished and energised from within, able to catch new momentum in the midst of a crisis. I wanted to know how. He arrived back an hour or so later, full of apologies for keeping us waiting.

'It's looking okay – not a miscarriage, but they're keeping her in overnight for observation.' He had taken the opportunity to see a friend with AIDS on the way home, too. 'He's not looking too good ...'

We went out together to pick up some supper while Ali babysat the now sleeping kids, and I finally got his full attention.

'Don't you ever get freaked out by the chaos?' I asked as we sat waiting for three burgers at a suburban takeaway.

Tom nodded. He looked tired. 'You try and influence life as much as possible, but there are times when you know that you've done as much as you can.' He sipped ruefully on his beer. 'It might be a child who has committed a crime, fallen out of the programme, been hit by a car, or murdered. I've seen it all, and I've learned the hard way that there's a point where you just have to let go.'

Was it a religious thing? I knew from my brother Mark that Tom shared our roots in the church.

'Faith perhaps, but not religion these days,' he said, wrinkling his nose. 'The biggest challenge to my faith has not been seeing the suffering, but the irrelevance of many church activities to this stuff.

People can have a wonderful time on Sunday, drive past street kids on their way to church, but not connect the two at all. It made me sick, to be honest.' He liked to quote Desmond Tutu: 'I am puzzled which Bible people are reading when they say that religion and politics do not mix.'

He retained a deep-seated faith in God, but if he had a regular place of worship nowadays, it was the Indian Ocean. Every day at 5 a.m., Tom got up, put on his shorts and carried his surfboard one block towards the beach. Dropping onto his front, he paddled out through the breakers towards the rising sun, using the rip current along the pier. After duck-diving through the biggest breakers, he'd be beyond the impact zone and riding only lazy swell, waiting for the right wave.

'It's almost a spiritual experience for me,' he said. 'If you can imagine translucent blue water, rising sun, chatting to other guys out there, or just thinking about things – you're in surf mode but at the same time you're relaxed.'

He'd wait for the best kind of wave – a six- to eight-foot swell, a glassy appearance – and start paddling hard to catch it just as the crest was beginning to crumble, before pushing up into a crouch and feeling the adrenalin surge. 'You don't think about surfing, you just do it, like an artist, drawing lines and curves across the wave, playing with it.' It was where the energy was, one step ahead of the collapsing wall, a dance in the jaws of chaos. 'The more radical you can be, the more the adrenalin pumps. There's a rhythm to it. Surf in, paddle out, wait at the backline, choose your wave . . . It's a huge part of what I do and who I am.'

I was struck by how elegantly this sport encapsulated his life here, with its necessity of living vigilantly in the moment, relaxed but alert. It was yet another illustration – like so many of my own adventures that year – of the way that physical engagement not only distracted from the gnawing anxieties of the mind, but could in some mysterious way transfigure them. Action was key – whether surfing a wave or saving a life. Or even doing both at the same time: Tom had introduced surfing sessions for the street kids, and it was no surprise to learn that they took to it instinctively. 'They're not scared of the water, so our surfing programme aims to minimise the time they're sniffing glue, give them another kind of high.'

In fact, much of Umthombo policy could probably be attributed to his valuable daily session on the waves. 'When I'm surfing, it's a place where I can think strategically. We see some pretty harsh realities, and there's a tendency to overwork, so it's a great tool for keeping my life in balance.'

We were back at Tom's flat with the food at last. Ali looked relieved to see us – it had been a long day, and I suspected she was quietly thankful that I was not drawn to this kind of front-line work. In fact, I could think of very few who could keep their heads above water in this tsunami of human suffering and need. And yet if I had learned anything from Tom, it was that it was that letting go was the very thing that freed him to give more deeply of himself. Perhaps I would find the same, in time. Passing his waxed board in the hallway, I asked if he had any final surfer's wisdom to pass on before we parted.

He thought for a moment. 'I don't necessarily surf the biggest waves,' he said. 'I know my limits after all these years.'

I suspected Tom's limits were rather different from mine – the sort you found through trying and failing, rather than fearing to try in the first place. In the end it always came back to fear and how to learn to let go of it, even when the rope was almost certainly a snake. I realised this was not some cerebral puzzle to which Tom could give me the solution – it was a way of life, an intuitive balance that I could only learn through experience and daily practice. I had, eventually, to live it all – right down to the inevitable moment when the following wave just ate you alive and all was flailing helplessness and boiling surf.

'When you take a pounding, the key is not to panic,' said Tom. He had once broken his leg after misjudging a wave – but now he wore a philosophical expression that suggested he was talking less about surfing than life in general. 'The minute you let fear take you over, you're in trouble. Just go with the flow. It'll spit you out eventually.'

13

Relax or Die

KwaZulu-Natal, South Africa

'The tracker must stay completely attentive to his animal responses ... While attuned to this flow he feels a deep sense of well-being. He is ready to respond, alert yet relaxed.'

PETER LEVINE

A few days later, I zipped up my wetsuit and took my own first steps into the Indian Ocean. After our frenetic blast of Durban street life, I wanted to find a way, like Tom, to unwind, rebalance and learn that trick of paying attention while not panicking. Going with the flow. Rather than riding the waves, however, I was interested in exploring beneath them.

I had been determined to do the whole scuba thing properly, ever since getting briefly and existentially lost during a taster session on the bottom of a murky Scottish loch a few years previously. Since then, I had taken a training course in order to qualify for open-water dives in a slightly more exotic location. I wanted reefs of multicoloured sea life, mysterious wrecks, iridescent bubbles, flattering wetsuits, that sort of thing: a little less

Kafka, a little more Cousteau. Today, I felt sure I had found the right place for my first open-water dive since qualification. We were staying at an eco-lodge built into the dunes on a beautiful and desolate stretch of the Maputaland coast, with direct access to some of the most pristine reefs in South Africa. This was one of the prime migration routes for humpback whales and whale sharks, and it was not uncommon to see manta rays gliding over the rich coral beds.

First, however, I had to remember the training. In many ways, scuba diving required the same cool head as surfing, but the stakes were higher. The water would not just 'spit you out' if things went wrong – at least, not alive. Apart from dangers such as sharks, shipwrecks, rip tides, and so on, there was the simple overwhelming fact that the human body was not designed to survive underwater, and was entirely reliant on complex equipment to do so.

It was not an adrenalin sport in the same way as, say, cliff-jumping. In fact, adrenalin could be fatal ten metres below the surface. Because if anything was more dangerous than snagging your foot on a piece of coral, or running out of air, or encountering a shark, it was panicking about it and doing something stupid. If you made a sudden break for the surface from a certain depth, for example, you could expect the infamous bends, an agonising and potentially fatal condition caused by nitrogen bubbles forming in your body tissue. Or even in relatively shallow water, if you held your breath while ascending, as I tended to do in situations of panic, the decreasing water pressure would cause your lungs to burst like over-inflated balloons.

No, it seemed that in diving, as in surfing or life in general, a kind of peaceful vigilance was required. The motto might be 'relax or die'.

Ask divers why these potentially deadly constraints should elicit peace and enjoyment rather than terror, and they go all Zen on you. 'Once you're down there you'll understand,' said my blond dive buddy Werner, as we dumped our tanks and fins in the RIB and pushed out into the surf.

Ten minutes later, we were bouncing through the glitter of the low-risen sun with B.J. the skipper and his assistant Erasmus.

'So you reckon we might spot a whale?' I shouted to B.J. above the roar of the engine. I felt buoyant and happy, ready for an encounter, if a little nervous, too.

'Maybe,' said B.J. non-committally, throttling down to a halt in the gentle swell. 'The trick is to enjoy whatever's down there ... You ready to dive?'

I clipped on my tank and buoyancy-control device (BCD), did the various safety checks with Werner, and, on his signal, dropped backwards over the side.

We were in deep but sunlit water, looking down through clearing bubbles to a reef some fourteen metres below. As I deflated my BCD and began to sink slowly away from the heaving, mirrored surface, I felt myself stilling with joy. Landing gently on my knees in coarse white sand between two heads of coral, I looked around and did the 'okay' hand signal to Werner, listening to the peaceful sound of my own breathing. The reef location we were diving was called Gogos – meaning 'old angel fish' in Thonga. They drifted past placidly, many of them the size of dinner plates, yellow and white and black. Little shoals of tiny fish parted like bead curtains to let us through.

Filling my lungs to increase my buoyancy, I rose effortlessly up and over the reef head, moved my legs gently and began a low flight through a psychedelic forest: purple fan coral, brain coral, mustard-coloured fingers quivering in the current.

Occasionally there were swirls of turbulence that pushed me towards the coral. My breath tightened and quickened as I kicked my fins to keep clear of its sharp edges. Relax or die, I thought, trying to get my breathing back under control. I checked my air gauge – 1800 p.s.i. – and mimed it, charade-like, to Werner: a fist and then eight fingers. About forty minutes of air.

Werner kicked away gently and drifted slowly over the reefs, examining them, his hands crossed on his chest, his whole body exuding relaxation and control. I watched his bubbles rising and realised I was rising with them. Feeling my breathing quicken again, I let some more air out of the BCD and tried to swim down again. It was a tricky business, but the aim was to find the perfect balance, leaving you floating effortlessly in mid-water, and thereby using less air. They called it neutral buoyancy, the key to relaxed diving – and perhaps to life – finding the still point, the place of total harmony with one's environment, where no wasted energy was required simply to inhabit one's own space.

Nearby a parrotfish chewed on a piece of brain coral with an audible crunching sound. No less audibly, a familiar voice muttered in my mind: *Is this it?* I felt the first stirrings of impatience, and tried to squash the disappointment, and then the disappointment in myself for being disappointed. *Where are the whales, the sharks, the rays?* I tried to convince myself that it didn't matter if we saw them or not, imagined saying to Ali: 'We saw these awesome ... parrotfish.'

And then I saw the turtle. It was a beautiful loggerhead swimming slowly over the reef away to my left, its green shell mottled with sunlight. With a surge of excitement I began to swim after it, craving the sort of close encounter that featured routinely on wildlife documentaries. The turtle saw me and began to swim faster, and I accelerated to keep up. It must have been four feet long. My breathing was deep and fast, but if I could just get a little closer ... I caught a glimpse of its leathery flippers, its sideways glance over its horny shell, before it disappeared into the middle distance. I stopped swimming and hung in the water, breathing hard, then looked around to see if Werner had witnessed my find.

He was nowhere to be seen. A wave of panic rose like nausea. I turned quickly to scan the blue void. Nothing. *You idiot!* I had committed the cardinal scuba sin of going it alone and forgetting to keep in touch with my dive buddy. I glanced at my pressure gauge and couldn't believe what I saw. It was nudging the red, only 500 p.s.i. left. My breathing was getting wheezy, but I wasn't even sure which direction to swim in. How could I have been so stupid? Then, straining my eyes through the empty water, I glimpsed a luminous fin beyond a coral head. Werner was swimming towards me in a leisurely manner, making what looked like a 'slow down' hand signal – though it's possible it was a much ruder one than that. After all, Werner still had a good twenty minutes of air left, while I had used most of mine up chasing a turtle. Now I might never see a whale! When I mimed my pressure reading, he took pity on me. Unclipping his emergency mouthpiece, he shared his remaining air with me for a final ten minutes, as we swam in tandem.

I did my best to adopt a more Zen attitude to the whole thing after that, keeping myself relaxed while keeping my eye on the gauge. Werner pointed out a few interesting fish, including the fat, blunt head of a moray eel guarding a hole in the coral like a bouncer at the door of a club. Then we began the slow surfacing process, hanging around at five metres for a while to make sure we decompressed properly.

It was a curious paradox: all this meticulous planning and control for fifty minutes of awed weightlessness. Every tank like a little life, consumed at leisure in the constant face of death. A mind neither clenched nor flaccid, but peacefully vigilant, ready to respond to whatever came up, dangerous or delightful. In the business of contentment, bursts of euphoria could be as unreliable as waves of depression. I thought of the ancient mantra: This, too, will pass.

We were back in the boat, shrugging off our tanks, when B.J. touched my shoulder and pointed behind me. About 50 yards away, something vast and grey wallowed at the surface, spitting spume into the air with an abrupt hiss.

'A humpback!' whispered Werner.

'With a baby,' said B.J., as the shape sank below the surface again. 'She's been teaching it how to jump for the last half-hour. I can't believe you didn't see her down there!'

We strained to make out the shadows, until suddenly a barnacled muzzle broke the surface and the mother launched herself into the air. At her side, the small form of her calf bellyflopped an imitation before the mother hit the surface again and both disappeared in the explosion of spray.

The two of them faced a long journey, up towards the warmer waters around the Equator – a journey fraught with danger as killer whales and other predators would try to separate them. Watching the mother preparing her, I was struck suddenly by the beauty and fragility of life. Would this vulnerable infant ever make it to the feeding grounds, I wondered? And would I ever get to show such sights to a child of my own? We watched, awed and silent, from the boat as the mother repeated her lesson several times. As we turned finally and headed for the beach, her flipper was visible sticking straight up out of the sea, and pounding the surface over and over again, like a slow, sad farewell.

'Ever wondered what it feels like to be at the bottom of the food chain?' I asked Ali, as we sat on the veranda of our hotel room, gazing out over the dark savannah. She looked at me over her wine glass.

'What do you mean?'

'Well, think of your average antelope – imagine trying to live with the knowledge that at any moment you could be torn apart by a lion. That the bush is full of animals desperate to eat you. How on earth would you relax in the face of that?'

It was a week since our day in Durban, and we'd seen a lot of wildlife on our meandering drive north. Black and white rhino, elephants, buffalo, hippos and a bloated male lion sleeping off the remains of an unfortunate zebra, whose carcass we smelt before we saw it. It was the first time I had seen these magnificent creatures in the wild, but strangely, after the initial thrill of seeing four of the 'big five', I was finding it was the smaller, more vulnerable animals that fascinated me more – those most likely to be dinner for a lion or leopard.

Perhaps I was really still thinking about the street kids, always on the move through the maze of alleyways, trying to keep one step ahead of those who would harm them.

Or perhaps it was the reality of the fear we both felt driving through quite isolated stretches of KwaZulu-Natal, picturing the possibility of a carjacking or fatal crash. This was how I had always coped with fear – by pre-emptively conjuring up all the things that might happen to me in the hope of being ready for them. But I had only to feel the cumulative stress of two days of low-level worry to know it was an inefficient way of doing things.

Even in South Africa, the imagined events rarely took place, leaving us all keyed up with nowhere to go.

'I don't think animals get stuck like we do,' said Ali.

'It's not that they don't experience fear, but that they have the ability to move in and out of it using the adrenalin to escape from danger, then relax again.' We had seen it only that morning, watching an impala grazing, relaxed in the dawn mist as a cheetah approached on the other side of a thicket. Suddenly the impala stiffened and sniffed the air, alert to a possible threat, then exploded into motion like a tightly coiled spring, bounding away until it was far enough from the cheetah to resume grazing. The adrenalin kicked in, did its job, got the creature out of danger, then receded.

'There is total attention at the moment of danger, physical or psychological,' wrote Krishnamurti, the Hindu mystic. 'When there is complete attention there is no fear.' It was what I had experienced for that split second of flight on the wings of the biplane – total attention, total absence of fear, total presentness. It wasn't that people who let go never felt stress – it was that they had found a way to move in and out of stress and relaxation. It was why extreme sports 'worked', taking you through the cycle of stress and recovery, why frenetic dancing had been so good for me at Ängsbacka, why Tom's surfing enabled him to recover from the stresses of his street life.

I had seen something like it in big Joe, our Zulu tracker, who perched silently on the front of the Land Cruiser, completely alert for any sign of animal life. The previous night he had spotted a three-inch chameleon in pitch darkness while travelling at 30 m.p.h., simply by swinging the narrow beam of his torch across the foliage. Little escaped his attention, and yet he was not a tense man – more a gentle giant, always ready to switch into high alert if the situation demanded it. That peaceful vigilance, once again.

'That's what we're going to need as parents,' I said, glancing over at Ali sitting relaxed and pensive in her rattan chair. 'But I guess we'll pick it up as we go along, eh?' She smiled back, and I had a sudden flashback to our first date, and that same freckled face leaning across a table in a little French restaurant. I kissed her now as I had then, and we sat in the darkness, listening to the cicadas.

'Remember Ventry Beach?' said Ali. We had been collecting seashells along the shore near Dingle in Ireland when I asked her to marry me – and she didn't answer the first time, just grinned and asked me to repeat the question. 'Seemed worth hearing twice,' she had explained, as we wandered back, drunk with joy, to find that the tide had come in and cut us off. Wading trouserless through the shallows, I had dropped the car keys. 'And we had to get that dodgy-looking guy from the pub to break into the car with a coathanger!'

I looked at her, and felt a familiar wave of thankfulness – relief that we'd found one another. We'd been lucky, but we'd also worked hard to understand each other. In fact, sitting under the stars that night, scrolling through the many scenes from our decade of marriage, I was surprised to find that it wasn't the holidays, the travel, the mountain-top experiences that stood out. Instead, it was on the ritual of Saturday mornings around our worn kitchen table, grazing on bagels and bacon and coffee. It was here that we had given ourselves the time it took to listen, argue, engage with our unfamiliar preoccupations. To explore the uncharted territory of each other.

It was never easy. There had been laughter, frustration, tears, defeat, silence, hope, recovery – over and over again. While Ali always wanted to talk, share, feel our way forward, my instinct was to stall and retreat into a kind of mental cave until I had worked out the right answer. It was the depressingly familiar male-female ping-pong of logic versus emotion, pithily précised by a (male) songwriter friend as: 'I tell you what's true; you say how you feel; I tell you what's fair; you say what you need.'

The temptation was to keep tightening the unyielding knot, expend useless energy deepening the abyss of communication failure, rather than carefully respecting the need for either intimacy or space. It was the hardest place to let go and trust the process – but why? Was it my own inadequacy I feared – that Ali might need a level of emotional engagement I couldn't give her? I struggled even to remember what the arguments were about, only the clenching of my gut as I invested more and more in being right. Fight or flight, once again.

The way back from such stand-offs was a tricky but familiar dance of vulnerability, as one or other of us – usually Ali – gave some ground, graciously spared a bruised ego, enabled the other to find a 'sorry' and some kind of compromise. Once we had faced our fears, these resolved conflicts seemed ultimately to strengthen us both. It was avoidance that was the problem.

'Remember that old poster from the seventies?' I said. 'Love is ... never having to say you're sorry!'

'Aye,' chuckled Ali. 'What a load of shite that was.'

Early the following morning, shortly before beginning the long drive back to the airport, we chanced upon the Zen masters of the animal kingdom. It was just after dawn and we were sitting motionless in the back of a Land Cruiser, watching a kind of bush ballet. On the far side of a sun-dappled clearing, two male nyalas – members of the antelope family – were circling one another in exaggerated slow motion. Each step was delicate and deliberate, their white manes and tails raised in competition as the animals stared at one another.

'Nyalas are famous for their trance dance,' whispered our guide, J.D., as we all held our breath. 'They're not territorial, but they have an incredibly evolved form of dominance hierarchy.'

It was haunting and utterly beautiful to watch. The winner was the animal who most impressed the other with his poise and stature – as unexpected as if members of rival street gangs abandoned their blades for competitive t'ai chi. 'This way they don't use up energy fighting or putting themselves at risk, which means they're a lot more aware of other predators.' Sure enough, within a few moments, the smaller of the two males obviously decided he'd been comprehensively out-strutted and conceded the dance, skittering off through the undergrowth to munch breakfast somewhere else. Both had saved their fear for more dangerous enemies.

It felt an important lesson to take to heart as we flew home. For the further I went in my quest, the more I was encountering a paradoxical truth – that true letting go, in both human and animal kingdoms, was about engaging with things rather than avoiding them. Instead of a way of escape, it was like the shedding of cumbersome armour in order to respond more flexibly to whatever lay ahead.

What kept the nyala safe and healthy – and Tom, in the midst of his urban jungle – was a focused immersion in the moment, and an instinctive ability to move in and out of fear without being paralysed by it. Adrenalin sports had given me a crude way to release tension, like the reflex shudders of an antelope who had escaped being dinner – but I knew my core fear was not physical but emotional. A fear of being trapped, not physically in a thicket, but emotionally by the demands or expectations of those around me.

And, like all fear, it could not be overcome from outside. I had to face it and pass through it – or perhaps, more accurately, allow it to pass through me.

14

A Good Hypothesis

The L'Arche community, Edinburgh

'There is, in practice, no such thing as autonomy. Practically, there is only a distinction between responsible and irresponsible dependence.'

WENDELL BERRY

A week later, back in Edinburgh, I found myself performing my own 'trance dance' with a man called Pete. Like the nyalas, we circled one another slowly, keeping eye contact, but the similarity ended there. Instead of a jungle clearing, we were in a community hall in the suburbs. And whatever else we were supposed to be establishing, it certainly wasn't a power hierarchy.

Pete was probably the most uninhibited person I knew. A fun-loving thirtysomething with Down's syndrome, he had first grabbed my attention in the church I attended by performing James Brown-style hip gyrations to an African hymn. Solidly built, with a shaved head and a friendly grin, he generally made it his mission to high-five anyone he encountered on his way back from the communion altar. He had a particularly heart-warming intolerance for sermons. If the Bishop of Edinburgh were visiting, for example, Pete could be relied upon to yawn, giggle or belch fulsomely from behind his copy of *Inside Soap*, or mutter a distinctly audible: 'Gah! Bloody hell . . .' If somewhat startling to a newcomer, his contributions had become part of the liturgy for many regulars. We warmed to him quickly, in my case partly because he so often echoed out loud what I was thinking in private. I envied the way Pete was so richly and unapologetically himself. It occurred to me that he had something to teach me about letting go.

But today we were both on unfamiliar territory. The workshop was titled Communication Without Words – part of a weekend event in south Edinburgh. There were fifty of us in the room, including some with learning difficulties and a limited vocabulary, others with physical disabilities who found it hard to make themselves understood. The theory was that these two groups were practised in less verbal ways of communicating, which the rest of us could usefully explore with them. But twenty minutes into the session, the reality was proving quite stressful.

So far, guided by an enthusiastic 'facilitator' from Finland, we had sat in a circle and pulled faces that reflected our frame of mind (I tried unsuccessfully to mime removing my brain, to general bafflement) and watched two women releasing helium balloons from a sack to symbolise letting go of their worries. And now we had all been invited to pick a partner. I made a beeline for Pete, and discovered that he came with his helper, a nun called Mary.

'Now, I want you to look into each other's eyes,' said the facilitator.

Having done this a few times since the clowning workshop, I was expecting it to be a cinch – a proof of how much I had loosened up over the year. But whose eyes should I choose to look into?

I began by focusing on Mary, but Pete tapped me on the shoulder, so I looked at him instead. There was something disconcerting about the way he stared back at me, open-mouthed and unblinking. Was that a question playing in those unwavering eyes, or even an invitation? Unlike Mary, I knew nothing of Pete's inner world. The two of them had a mutual understanding built slowly over their years of shared community. I had only guesses and assumptions.

'Now I want you to keep eye contact and move around the room,' said the facilitator.

The three of us joined hands and improvised a sort of lopsided waltz. Then we did the nyala thing, circling one another slowly. Pete continued to demand my gaze, grinning broadly when I gave it. But what else was he communicating, if anything? I felt like a tourist in a foreign country, struggling to understand the signs.

'Now, I want you to give the person something – a gift,' suggested the facilitator.

Offering my best Marcel Marceau approximation of picking up a box, I pondered the tricky diplomatic question of who to snub with my entirely non-existent gift. Pete looked unimpressed at my empty palm and deftly picked Mary's pocket instead. 'Hey!' she yelled, as he waved her crumpled handkerchief above his head, giggling. The only other sound was the occasional crack of a knee joint and grunt of withheld breath as twenty other couples gave each other handfuls of thin air. I was seized with the sudden urge to go home and do something reassuringly solitary and predictable, like eating Marmite on toast in front of the telly.

'Okay,' said the facilitator, at last. 'Now I want you to break eye contact and do something entirely different. I want you to move as fast as you can around the room without making eye contact or physical contact with anyone. Go!'

Oh, the sweet joy of self-containment! Tucking my arms stiffly along my sides, I headed off like an Irish dancer on speed. Suddenly, something I was good at, like weaving through shoppers on Princes Street – a sort of assault course in which humans were obstacles to be physically avoided rather than connected with. The room boiled like a slide of magnified protozoa, everyone taking responsibility not to bump into anyone else. I think it was supposed to be a vision of hell, individualism at its most rampant, but I felt mainly a wave of relief.

Then I noticed Pete. He was standing on his own, confused amid all the chaos, and beginning to panic. A woman with cerebral palsy shrieked from her wheelchair as her helper pushed her around the room like a runaway train. 'Gah! Bloody hell!' shouted Pete, and walked huffily off to the side, throwing his arms in the air. He was soon slumped in a chair, his lower lip jutting out in anger.

After a bit of coaxing, we got him to rejoin us for the inevitable 'circle of reconciliation' at the end, and he was soon grinning and high-fiving everyone again. But the session left me uneasy. Far from learning to let go *with* Pete, I had felt most free when I let go *of* him. What did that say about me?

'Martin Luther King said people will always despise other people,' began the speaker at the front of the room that afternoon, 'until they begin to accept, to love, what is despicable in themselves.' Before us was a tall man in his late seventies, sitting on the edge of a table, peering out from beneath extraordinary bushy white eyebrows. The room was hushed, hundreds hanging on his every word. 'We keep people with disabilities at arm's length because we haven't yet accepted our own disabilities – our inner brokenness, our inability to forgive, our need to have power over others.'

Jean Vanier could easily have chosen to have power over others. Son of a former governor general of Canada, born in 1928 amid the trappings of privilege, he had the potential to be almost anything he wanted. But his riches-to-rags tale was the antithesis of everything the powerful might recognise as success. After a promising career as an officer in the British and Canadian navies, he had suffered a spiritual crisis, a sense that he was simply pursuing the wrong life. He left military structure behind and for years drifted through various possibilities – an academic flirtation with Aristotle, a spell in a Trappist monastery, a possible vocation to the priesthood. But in 1964 he had finally stumbled, aged thirty-five, on the experience that broke him open.

Visiting an asylum near Paris in 1964, he found eighty men with severe learning difficulties living together in two chaotic dormitories, perpetually unoccupied, endlessly circling and often violent. Shocked and galvanised, he did the only thing he could think of to make a difference: after negotiations with the asylum, he rented a house in a small village just north of Paris and invited three profoundly disabled men to come and live with him there.

The idea was as naive as it was idealistic: on the first night, one of the men – deaf, mute and given to aggressive spitting – began to hallucinate and threaten villagers, and had to be sent back to the asylum. But Vanier continued, chastened, to build a faltering friendship with the two who remained. It was difficult, often demoralising work, but as the months passed, what most surprised the serious-minded young man was how much fun it was.

'When I lived with Raphael and Philippe, I discovered there was a child inside me wanting to fool around,' recalled Vanier, who still lived in the same community. 'It's been a healing experience.'

This was something of an understatement. More than four decades after that first, faltering gesture, his experiment had grown into more than 130 small communities in thirty countries on five continents. Pete was one of several members of an Edinburgh community, while others had come from Glasgow, London, Inverness and Japan to hear their founder. Collectively they were known as L'Arche, 'the ark', and the set-up was always the same: able-bodied helpers joined those with disabilities to enable them to live independently in shared houses, rather than institutions. For parents struggling to make responsible long-term provision for dependants who would outlive them, it was a godsend. For the residents it was often their first real experience of a community of peers – and in some cases the only 'family' they would ever know.

'Many here have lived beyond relationship,' said Vanier gently. 'They've been the source of tears and arguments, put into institutions where nobody really wants them. One of the men in my community, who has Down's syndrome, told me: "If I was conceived today I would be killed." And he's right. We terminate such pregnancies because we do not like difference.'

There was no anger in the statement, only sadness. But it made me feel very uncomfortable. Only the previous week, our social worker had asked us to think about whether we would consider adopting a child with a physical or mental disability. Our complex inner debates on such issues were no use to Avril. She needed us to tick one of three boxes in every category: a) would accept, b) would not accept, or c) would discuss. The list seemed endless: Down's syndrome? Cerebral palsy? Severe emotional difficulties? HIV? Foetal alcohol syndrome? Autistic spectrum disorder? And so it went on. The social worker had sat with her pen poised as patiently as possible, as we agonised over each of them in turn, trying to think ourselves into a life looking after a disabled child, or a youth who might inherit schizophrenia, or a baby born addicted to heroin or with terminal cancer. There seemed no

stress-free way to tick a box. Inevitably we opted for 'would discuss', which simply deferred the difficult decision.

Now, glancing at Pete, I found myself wondering what I would
do if we were offered a child with Down's syndrome. It was true
that not many such children were even allowed to come to full term
nowadays – but to be offered the care of those who did felt like a
terrifying degree of choice. I wondered how Pete felt about what
Vanier was saying – but his face was hidden behind his copy of
Inside Soap.

'The truth is that we're not in control of our lives,' continued
Vanier. 'Anything can happen today or tomorrow. We're living in a
beautiful, dangerous world. And we hide, because we don't want to
show people how vulnerable we are. But we are all broken people.'
He paused and looked out at us. 'And yet if God is living in us, we
can let down the walls.'

I found his words unsettling and demanding. I wasn't sure it was
humanly possible to let go of one's boundaries in the way he was
suggesting. Why all this talk of 'brokenness', this attribute he
constantly praised, and which I so feared? I didn't want to be
broken. I wanted to find a way to let go that would mysteriously
perfect my life. It was absurd when I thought about it. Perhaps,
even after everything I had experienced that year, I didn't want to
let go at all.

It had seemed easier back in my passionate teens, when religious
certainty was there in six-foot-high flaming letters, and I was
glowing with an ardour I believed came direct from heaven.
Nowadays I was fanning a few last embers, increasingly using 'God'
as a kind of 'X' to stand for what I couldn't quite fathom. It didn't
help that the world seemed to be at almost constant war over
people's rival interpretations of 'X'. But I noticed that Vanier rarely
tried to define God, except as a sort of love-generator in human

relationships. In fact, he used 'love' and 'God' almost interchangeably.

'Love requires that we take a risk, without the safety net,' he was saying. 'As soon as we give our lives to anything there is a risk. There are many things we can't control.' He paused and gave that unsettling, sad smile again. 'But true transformation is about welcoming reality as it is and not as I hoped it would be. Be in harmony with reality – don't be angry with reality, whatever it is.'

And what was the reality? It had become convenient for me to point to religious wars or theological conundrums as my reason for holding my once fervent faith at arm's length. But was I really just afraid to look at the core message of all religion?

'The work of God is very simple,' said Vanier. 'To love people just as they are. The way we look at them, the way we share with them – to reveal to them that they are precious to God. People need us to be with them without trying to change them.'

To need help, or to be needed: it was difficult to know which was more terrifying. These were the twin risks I found so difficult to take, much harder than stepping onto the wings of a biplane, or out of my clothes – risks that required me to put aside my cherished self-sufficiency and open myself to the possibility that I could not do it on my own. I knew simultaneously that this was the hardest risk of all – and that it was the risk that lay behind all others.

I managed to buttonhole Vanier himself in a back room at lunchtime, over sandwiches and soup.

'I've been very moved by what I've seen here,' I began, as we sat down together. 'And I really want to learn to let go, to learn to open myself more fully to other people, like you're suggesting. But . . .' But what? I was babbling garrulously like a child desperate for acceptance. '... but I'm afraid that if I open the door to this stuff I'll never be able to close it again. You live with all this need. But don't you have any escape hatches?'

Vanier nodded thoughtfully. 'We are not God,' he said presently. 'God has no protective barriers, but of course we need protective barriers because otherwise we could hurt ourselves.'

It was amazing what a relief it was to hear this from a man whose life of self-sacrifice both awed and appalled me. I had feared he'd be pushing the full-immersion model of Christian martyrdom. I told him about my experience in the workshop and, conversely, my observation that Pete and others with learning difficulties had no problem keeping eye contact.

'They're amazing,' agreed Vanier. '*Our* problem is needing reputation, needing success; but people who live with disabilities have let go. Their big secret is living in the present moment. They don't have to prove anything because they are loved by God.'

I passed him another plate of sandwiches, which he put away with a quite remarkable speed. It occurred to me that his vocation took more out of him than he publicly let on. Feeling reassured by his gentleness, I rambled on self-deprecatingly about the attraction of committing myself to others – and the risks.

'But you've already taken a risk in getting married,' said Vanier, eyeing my wedding ring as I passed him a second cup of soup. 'That's a great risk, because she could change, you could change. When you start getting committed to people you discover covenant relationships, and they lead you places you don't want to go. That's when you really have to let go ... Tell me, do you have children?'

'Um, no. Not yet.' Even here, the risk of vulnerability. 'We're thinking about adopting.'

He looked at me. 'You cannot have your own children?'

'It doesn't look like it, no.' His gaze was laden with compassion and, mortifyingly, I felt my eyes filling. I didn't want to talk about parenting – it was too raw. Instead, I told him about my experimental forays into community – about the sense of belonging that had come from sharing groups and workshops and, previously, from hitching around my adopted country or rafting to Easter Island with seven other men. 'I think I'm the sort of person who needs to be forced into community. It's behind almost every truly adventurous thing I've ever done.'

He nodded, unimpressed. 'You did that in the Pacific – but that was a bit of a dream, a temporary thing. The biggest risk is when it's in your own village, with your own neighbours. What's important is that you grow and let roots down and open up to others. The big thing is to "let go and let God".'

The G-word again. I felt a fraud for nodding. Vanier's world rested on an Almighty I wasn't sure I believed in. Knowing I had only moments before his minder arrived to whisk him away for the final afternoon session, I took a risk.

'I don't want to insult you,' I said carefully. 'But I wondered if you ever doubted God's existence?'

He looked up sharply, as if I had slapped him. 'No, never.' There was a pause and he seemed to soften and grow pensive again. 'Look, don't waste time worrying about God's existence,' he said, with a twinkle and a shrug. 'It's a good hypothesis.'

We ended the day with another strange ritual. We were to wash one another's feet, just as Christ had washed those of his disciples. (The women had been warned in advance to wear socks, presumably to avoid the necessity of removing tights in public.) I could see why St Peter himself was sceptical when Jesus tried it first time round.

'Peter's reaction was understandable,' said Vanier, as little plastic bowls were passed around with painted jugs of warm water. 'We have difficulty imagining the all-powerful knocking on the door of the vulnerable. But this story shows us how counter-cultural is the Gospel. It's about the place of suffering, the place of weakness, the place of littleness.'

A pianist tinkled away, accompanied by flute and violin, as we divided into circles of ten or so, and nervously began to take off our socks. The etiquette seemed to vary between groups. Some whipped both socks off enthusiastically, others were more token-istic and kept one on. We seemed to be a two-sock group. It turned out I was sitting next to the head of security at a well-known Scottish institution. I felt a little self-conscious, revealing my large white hobbit feet in front of her, but she washed them in silence and with care, pouring on warm water, even making an attempt to wash between my toes. It was a surprisingly intimate act – more so than a whole day at a naturist convention. I blushed and thanked her as she rinsed and then dabbed me dry with a towel. The feet next to me were hairless and dainty, belonging to a tired-looking male Japanese care worker. I made sure I washed them carefully, and he nodded his thanks to me with a wry smile. I felt a sudden rush of fellow-feeling towards this strange impromptu community, mutually vulnerable in this odd way. As the bowl continued round the group, along with warm jugs of fresh water, I allowed myself to look at the other groups. I couldn't see Pete, but Shirley, the woman with cerebral palsy, was a vision of ecstasy in her wheelchair, gazing at the person washing her feet, tears running down her face.

Nearby, Jean Vanier was himself towelling dry the feet of an admirer. I was struck simultaneously by the absurdity and profundity of this ritual. In an atmosphere touched by reverence and slight foot odour, our worn and uncared-for extremities were being handled tenderly by strangers. Feet in all their imperfection lay before us: white, corny, some with crooked toes, some with cracked skin or knobbly joints, pointing inwards or outwards. Mutually vulnerable, washed by another, we were temporarily losing the distinction between able-bodied and disabled.

As each group completed the circle and the musicians played on, Shirley began to howl in anguish. She was realising, like others, that this little oasis of acceptance and communality was about to end. Normal service would resume on Monday: the averted eyes, the embarrassed strangers, the indifferent streets. Pete had his head on the shoulder of his helper, but it was impossible to see whether he was sleeping or crying or just sheltering. Suddenly I knew I had to get away from all this heightened emotion, this peeled vulnerability. More than anything else, I now needed space. I hugged my fellow group members and left the room like a man staggering from heavy surf.

15

Choice Cuts

Edinburgh

'Anxiety is the dizziness of freedom.'

SØREN KIERKEGAARD

It's an autumnal morning in October, and I'm walking the dog by the Forth, pondering the future. Charlie runs down to the water's edge and back, sniffing excitedly at seaweed and rocks and other dogs, his breath hanging in the chilled air. The salty tang of the sea mingles with a smell of leaves burning somewhere. Out over the water, an eerie wall of mist hangs motionless, obscuring the far shore.

What lies ahead? Only a few weeks remain of my experiment, and then – assuming the adoption panel approves us in December – we will face the task of choosing the child who will join our family for the rest of our lives. It's a decision that feels almost too huge to contemplate.

Sometimes the unsettling thought strikes me that the child we will eventually adopt is already out there somewhere, waiting. I wonder what he or she is doing just now? Have we already unwittingly seen his or her face in those magazines? Or is 'our' child still to be taken into care — and if so, what is happening, or about to happen? I find it haunting, this sense of parallel lives — and our powerlessness yet to help a life almost certainly already in motion. How will we know when we've found the right one?

Sometimes Ali and I sit around a candle and pray silently that we'll know in our guts when we encounter the child we will adopt. Or that if, for some reason, adoption is not the road we should be on, then this will become clear. Praying is a rusty but familiar ritual for us both. Despite the fact that we don't know for sure if anyone is listening, it still seems to mute the endless jabbering of possibilities, if only for a moment. And besides, what do we have to lose?

It's an almost heretical thought in a society that habitually equates freedom with choice, but sometimes I wish it were out of our hands.

There's a conundrum, a paradox here that I keep feeling for like a missing tooth. Philosophers or theologians might call it something like the weight of free will. Clearly, the ability to exert some control over our lives — or at least over our response to what happens — is crucial to our most fundamental sense of well-being. Americans enshrined it in their constitution: life, liberty and the pursuit of happiness. But once you're free from oppression or poverty, you still have to work out what to do with that freedom. In a society that enjoys a range of choice unthinkable even to our parents' generation — and certainly to most of the rest of the world — we must decide where we live, who we love, what we believe in, how we earn our money, how we present ourselves to others. Surely we should be the happiest society on the planet?

But newspapers and statistics say otherwise. It seems there is a marked conflict between what it is we think we want, and what actually brings us contentment. The majority of us say we want more control over the details of our lives – and yet the majority of us also say we want simpler lives. And despite our professed love of freedom, the things proven to bring us most happiness are social ties. Those who are married, who have good friends, or who participate in religious communities are statistically found to be happier than those who do not, even though those commitments paradoxically decrease our freedom, choice and autonomy. I know instinctively this is true: my marriage to Ali is the single most consistent source of happiness in my life, despite – or perhaps because of – the fact that it requires me to rule out other partners.

I suppose that's also why Charlie has been such an unexpected gift. Initially, I baulked at Ali's suggestion that we get a dog, not wanting to be tied down to a daily walk, or to have to worry about kennels if we went away. But in fact, dog-walking has proved more of a lifeline than a restraint, pulling me away from the pallid light of my computer screen and into the fresh air when I might otherwise have worked myself back to a standstill. Strange but true: commitment is good for you.

I call Charlie, watch him running excitedly back to me along the breakwater, his ears flapping madly. Much as he enjoys chasing after balls and discarded chip wrappers, his species long ago accepted basic subservience in return for food, shelter and protection. His wolf cousins may be freer to roam, but even they have collaborated and evolved their own pack hierarchy in order to ward off unnecessary conflict and, one suspects, loneliness.

A few rungs up the evolutionary ladder, we twenty-first-century humans often forget that limiting our options can actually bring happiness. But everyone trades freedom for security one way or another – the only question is exactly how much of one to give up for the other. Which brings me back to Vanier's 'good hypothesis' – and the way religious people talk so cheerfully about submission or obedience, like dog trainers. For although I now feel unable to commit wholeheartedly to a rigid system, I can't deny that the days when I could were some of the happiest in my memory, with their exhilaration of purpose, of certainty, of knowing where I was going. I envy Vanier his commitment, his calling, the way he has freed himself from the paralysis of too many choices.

Perhaps he is right, that this most fundamental of choices – the choice of how to orientate one's life, which philosophical lens to use, which story to believe, if any – is really the most important of all. I've discovered a lot this year, perhaps most importantly that even when I can't choose what happens, I always have a choice in the way I respond to it. And yet, in some paradoxical way I'm only just beginning to glimpse, I wonder if it is my very independence I need to relinquish if I am to find true freedom.

This isn't what I thought I meant by letting go. But on the threshold of one of the most far-reaching decisions of my life, I need some space to decide exactly what it is I've freed myself to do. That's why I'm taking one last trip, a kind of retreat, a crucible in which to boil it all down to a working philosophy. A high and steady place from which to survey the horizon, and decide which way to jump.

16

When Pigs Fly

Albuquerque, New Mexico

'Faith is a lump in the throat ... less a sure thing than a
hunch.'

FREDERICK BUECHNER

I woke in the darkness with a raging thirst. Inches from my face,
red neon digits: 4.33 a.m. Gulping from a bedside glass of water,
I fell back onto the pillow and watched a hotel room materialise as
my eyes grew accustomed to the darkness. Then I remembered.
Albuquerque. The wide-open spaces. A freight train lowed mournfully in the distance, right on cue.

I had been planning this trip for months, coveting the stretched
skies in the brochures, feeling my heart expand at the merest photo
of a cactus. Where else but the desert to seek a bigger vision? Now
that I was here, there was no question of fooling my disorientated
body into going back to sleep. I got out of bed and went in search
of coffee.

I had more or less sleepwalked through Albuquerque's Sunport
airport the previous night, bagging the only hire car that didn't

have its gearstick on the steering column – a bright red Pontiac Grand Prix with leather seats and a spoiler. Climbing into it now, I was struck by how laughably inappropriate it was for a spiritual quest. It was also evidently made for smaller men than me, because my head touched the ceiling.

On the other hand, it felt perfect for cruising the darkened freeways of Albuquerque in search of a cup of coffee and the best view of the sunrise. I pulled out into a river of tail lights and began scanning the speckled horizon for a familiar neon brand. Since Route 66 first carved a line through the Rio Grande valley in the 1920s, Albuquerque had become a city geared to car travel. Sprawling across the wide plains between the black lava mesa in the west and the Sandia Mountains in the east, its compass points were scored into the landscape at the place where Interstates 40 and 25 formed an unholy cross. The sky was fractionally less dark in my driving mirror, suggesting I was heading west, away from the dawn.

By the time I found a gas station, it was 5.45 a.m. Putting my coffee and muffin into the fast-food holders on my all-American dashboard, I cruised back towards the eastern mountains, now silhouetted by the glow of approaching dawn. A razor-sharp crescent moon hung above them, flanked by what looked like dark planets.

Planets? I stared at them, doubting my own eyes, until one of them glowed orange. I caught my breath and grinned. I was look-ing at hot-air balloons, sporadically illuminated by their own gas jets, rising to meet the dawn. One was brightly striped, the other starred. I kept them in view in my windscreen as long as I could, but eventually lost them behind trees. Never mind. It felt like a good omen, this first sighting. And minutes later I found myself in a queue of SUVs towing wicker balloon baskets, turning down a lane marked: Albuquerque International Balloon Fiesta. Waved on by a traffic cop, I caught a glimpse of a vast field filled with semi-inflated balloons, like an enormous sheet of bubble wrap. I pulled into another gas station, got myself another coffee and stood awed as dozens of them began to rise above the grey urban plain. Far beyond, a dazzling sheet of light was advancing slowly as the sun rose behind the mountain. The balloons ascended and ignited one by one as they left its shadow.

I waited until I could count a hundred airborne, then headed back to the hotel, cold-fingered and flushed. I had a sense of something in me rising slowly towards the light.

Deserts had a certain symbolism for me, even as a child. I had grown up learning about the Israelites wandering for generations in the desert, and later Jesus' forty days of temptation by the Devil. It was partly why I had come here – to find the space to wonder, and possibly confront a few inner demons of my own. I craved a line in the sand, a rite of passage – something to test and consolidate the lessons I had learned in the previous year. I had originally planned simply to hike out into the wilderness with a tent, but discovered that in October the nights were already freezing. So after a little web-browsing I had instead booked a guest cell for three days and nights with a silent order of monks. The Benedictine monastery of Christ in the Desert lay a few hours north of Albuquerque in the middle of nowhere, and welcomed all genuine spiritual searchers. But apart from its various daily offices chanted in Latin, I obviously wouldn't be getting much input from its silent inhabitants. It was down to me. So before I set off, I planned to spend a few days soliciting advice from a few different spiritual traditions on what exactly to do when I got there.

My first stop was a low-roofed building set back from the road in a poorer neighbourhood on the far side of the Rio Grande river.

I was drawn as much by its paradoxical name as anything else – the Center for Action and Contemplation. Its founder, Father Richard Rohr, was a Franciscan priest with a reputation for blending Catholic social activism with Buddhist practice. It was a spirituality I could respect – a bit like Jean Vanier or Tom in Durban.

'So, what can I do for you?' asked Father Richard, pulling up a couple of plastic garden chairs under a tree in his shady backyard. What indeed? I gave him a potted summary of the past year and my ongoing quest, and he nodded patiently – a monkish-looking fellow, with a neatly clipped goatee, a close crop of silvery hair, and circular spectacles.

'I'm just tired of trying to control everything,' I concluded. 'Does that make any sense?'

'Plenty,' said Father Richard. 'It sounds like you know yourself pretty well. And you're right on schedule: late thirties? Yep, that's the onset of the second half of life.'

Apparently the psychologist Carl Jung believed that human experience could be divided chronologically into two halves – and that the task of the second half of life was to dismantle, voluntarily or otherwise, the structure by which you had understood the first. Hence the term 'midlife crisis'. Ideally, according to Father Richard, you had to relinquish control and allow life to be as it was: self-contradictory and full of mystery.

'Actually, you can't even decide when control is going to be taken away from you,' he added, almost apologetically. 'The real test is how you react to the unexpected person at the door, or the child who wakes you up in the middle of the night. That's what really teaches you letting go.'

I thought about my carefully planned cliff-jumps and wing-walking. 'So choosing when you give up control is just another form of control?'

'Exactly right,' said Richard. Now in his sixties, he chuckled compassionately at much of what I was saying, as if listening to a younger version of himself. I liked him immensely. I sounded him out on my plan for a silent desert retreat.

'It's funny, I've spent most of my life searching for some over-arching philosophy that will make sense of it all – and maybe I'm still hoping for that in the desert. But, actually, all my best moments this year have been about doing rather than thinking.'

'Good!' said Richard. 'Really, all meditation is an attempt to get back out of your mind and into your body. So when you're out in the desert, take some long walks, do some physical labour – anything to relativise the mind, so that it becomes your servant instead of your master. And just keep witnessing the stuff it comes up with. Don't try to control it, fix it, explain it, or feel guilty about it. That's how the detachment will happen. You'll start to see your life as a drama you're creating – a mental construct.'

It wasn't quite the promise of a spiritual epiphany I was hoping for, but then I probably wouldn't have trusted him if he had offered a three-step plan to happiness. He nodded and smiled.

'It'll be boring and strange and scary at times, and you'll want to get away from that much spaciousness. But as long as you know that in advance, then you won't be afraid of it.'

But I was.

Spits of rain were falling as I drove into the vast, darkened balloon park at 5 a.m. the following day. Before I knuckled down into my silent retreat, I couldn't resist the prospect of something more immediately uplifting, and had arranged to go up in one of the early-rising balloons I had seen the previous day. But the snapping flags on the closed-up fast-food vans didn't bode well for a flight, which relied on calm conditions. I checked in at the press tent anyway and was met by a woman wearing pink furry pig's ears on her baseball cap.

'You're here for dawn patrol?' she said. 'Lucky you.'

Out on the field, I joined a small crowd of pig-eared people gathered round a black trailer. They were the ground crew, waiting for the pilot to come back from a safety briefing, and their eyes were on a small weather balloon slanting over our heads carrying a luminous green light. 'That balloon is trucking it,' murmured someone, 'I bet you ten dollars we're not going up in this.' Somewhere a distant flash of lightning lengthened the odds.

Ever since its invention in 1783, when the Montgolfier brothers sent a cockerel, a sheep and a duck aloft from Versailles before hazarding their first human passengers, the hot-air balloon had in turn enchanted and frustrated by its dependence on prevailing winds. And perhaps that was the whole point.

'For once you have only limited control,' explained a man in the group. 'In today's health and safety culture, it's just fantastic to be at the mercy of the elements – you have absolutely no idea where you're going to land – you just go with the wind.'

Doug Gantt, the pilot with whom I was supposed to be flying, gave me a slightly more scientific explanation – though no more reassuring. 'Winds flow at different speeds at different altitudes, and in different directions,' he said. 'The only control we have is vertical, going up and down. My job as a pilot is to maintain heat in the balloon. We have to be hotter than the surrounding air to get lift, and we're always going to lose heat through cooling.'

The idea of dawn patrol was for a few balloons to test the wind before hundreds of others launched. Yesterday, people had ended up in hospital after their balloon was blown into a wall on landing, and the day before that a woman had died falling from a basket. It seemed unlikely that we were going to go up at all today – and perhaps that was for the best. But suddenly a radio crackled into life.

'That's a go-ahead,' said Doug.

Pig Ears shoved a clipboard under my nose. 'I need you to sign your life away before things get too crazy around here.' Surrendering to the adrenalin, I signed the indemnity without reading it.

Crowds were gathering round us – a strange breed of festival-goer willing to get up at five in the morning to hang round the balloonists. They stood at a respectful distance while Doug's volunteer ground crew unrolled a long pink tongue of nylon across the dark field and switched on a powerful fan. Soon the billowing nylon was hollow enough to take the first blasts of propane flames, and the vast canopy floated tentatively upright revealing itself to be a 125-foot pig.

'"When Pigs Fly" – it was my father's favourite phrase when I was growing up,' explained Doug, as we clambered into the wicker basket. 'I'd say: "I'd like a new bike," and he'd say "When pigs fly." I guess this was a kind of response to him.'

We watched the tethers tauten in the hands of the ground crew, waiting for Doug's signal. Apart from a local newspaper photographer, I was the only one actually accompanying him on the flight. Finally he gave the command, and my stomach dropped suddenly as the basket lurched upwards into the pre-dawn darkness. Below us the cheering crowds receded quickly in a sparkle of a hundred camera flashes.

'See you in an hour, folks!' shouted Doug, his gloved hand hanging from the propane release as if from a handrail on the subway. 'Okay, Nick, soon as we're clear of obstructions, dangle these aircraft lights over the side.' He handed me a coiled flex studded with blinking red and solid white lights. 'You're also going to look for power lines, hills, towers, any kind of obstruction. Don't be afraid to tell me, even if you think I may already have seen it. Okay?'

There were a dozen balloons rising around us, only sporadically lit. Below us, the rivers of car headlights were moving along the freeway again. We must have been a disconcerting sight for a bleary-eyed commuter. Shivering with a familiar chemical rush of fear and excitement, I took my cues from Doug as he moved seamlessly between altimeter, visual checks and sporadic bursts of propane. Occasionally we exchanged grins.

Once upon a time Doug had been a plastic salesman. Then, twenty-five years ago, he'd stood in a field much like the one we'd just left and marvelled for the first time at the audacity and grace of these floating planets.

'My first balloon flight was awesome. I hadn't been up for more than two minutes when I said: "I've got to have one of these." Six months later, I had a balloon, I had a divorce, and the rest is history.' He didn't elaborate on his personal story, but it left me thinking how costly and irrational a man's yearnings could seem to those around him. Had it been worth it for this American dreamer? For years he had made a good living running flights for corporate clients, then terrorists steered planes into the Twin Towers and suddenly everyone was nervous and risk-averse and disapproving of frivolity. 'People went back to tried and true things. It was a very unstable time for all of us.' But Doug carried on regardless. 'If I haven't flown in a couple of weeks I get real antsy.'

The air was growing luminous with the imminent sun, already framing the mountains with its glow. We were high above the dim glitter of the flat valley floor, which was bisected by the mirrored steel of the Rio Grande. In the silence between the roars of the propane burner, the gentle hiss of traffic rose faintly, along with what sounded like barking. 'The gas coming out sounds like a dog whistle,' said Doug. 'It drives them nuts.'

In one backyard, someone had laid out white sheeting to spell the simple word 'NO'. It occurred to me that the random descent of nearly a thousand balloons in gardens, farms and schoolyards across Albuquerque must at some point cease to be magical and start getting irritating to its residents. It was that important line between freedom and licence, once again — the potential for one person's letting go to become another's burden. 'I don't understand those people,' Doug was saying. 'But I do try to avoid landing in their fields.' It seemed a useful rule of thumb.

We were two thousand feet above the ground and travelling north-west — almost opposite to the direction we set off in — and the peaks of the eastern mountains were pregnant with light. I watched the sun crawling farther round the curvature of the Earth and felt light-headed with possibility, squinting as it suddenly broke over the top. The sudden warmth and light brought smiles to our faces.

'Yes sir, there ain't no better way to greet the day,' breathed Doug, quiet and reverent. 'Almost mystical, ain't it? It's the closest you'll ever get to being a cloud.'

He was right. And yet it wasn't the sort of mysticism I needed. I was loving the ride, just as I had loved the adrenalin rush of wing-walking and scuba diving, but I knew in my gut that this exhilarating weightlessness was, at best, a distraction from my real work here. I needed roots, not wings.

I watched the ground rising slowly to meet us, and braced myself.

17

Follow Your Bliss

Santa Fe and Beyond, New Mexico

'It's time you realised that you have something in you more
powerful and miraculous than the things that affect you and
make you dance like a puppet.'

MARCUS AURELIUS

I drove north, trying not to be distracted by the balloons still drifting silently overhead. We had only just missed a busy road
ourselves, clearing telegraph wires and a filling station by a few
metres before the chase team grabbed us as we touched down on
waste ground to a chorus of cheers.

By lunchtime I had checked into a hotel in Santa Fe. Dubbed
Fanta Se by those sceptical of its New Age credentials, New
Mexico's capital city had long been the crucible of spiritual activity in the region. Unlike the urban sprawl of Albuquerque, it was
arranged immaculately around a central square in which an adobe
cathedral presided over giftshops and a market. I had a cursory look
around before heading for the Georgia O'Keeffe Museum. O'Keeffe
was one of the more famous secular pilgrims to this place, and I

was keen to examine her sparse paintings: bleached white bones, giant plants, the parched, layered beauty of a canyon wall.

'I have used these things to say what is to me the wideness and wonder of the world as I live in it,' she wrote of her elemental bones and the desert on her doorstep. 'Such a beautiful untouched lonely-feeling place – part of what I call the Faraway.'

Faraway. Was that a positive thing? I had to admit to myself that I was already feeling a little lonely – and that was before my three-day retreat. I phoned Ali and told her about the balloon flight and the fact that I was planning to visit a Zen temple the following morning.

'Covering all the options, then?' she said, ambivalently. 'Well, don't get too enlightened and forget to come home.'

Later, enjoying a good massage at a Japanese-style spa in the mountains, I reflected that I hadn't been the most reliable of husbands, always sniffing the wind for some new quest. I thought of Ali, pictured her ensconced in front of the fire with the dog, and felt a long way from home.

Upaya Zen Center was a low-roofed adobe building at the end of a dirt road up in the mountains. I found it almost by accident with the help of a hollow 'plick' sound coming from a doorway, where a shaven-headed man was hitting something with a small wooden mallet.

I wished I had done a little more research on Zen Buddhism. I knew from memory that it held theory and scriptures to be of relatively low importance, preferring to focus on direct experience of what it called 'mindfulness', which sounded promising. But I had no real idea what the practice actually involved.

At the main entrance people were taking their shoes off and bowing to each other with their hands together. 'Are you new here?'

said a man – in a whisper, so as not to disturb whatever was going on inside. 'You need to sit in one of the guest seats – here or here.' He pointed to a seating plan on the wall. People had their assigned seats, it seemed, which was disappointingly like churches with family pews.

'Any other advice for a newcomer?' I whispered.

'Just follow everyone else – they'll have a walking meditation halfway through. And we bow to the altar when we go through the door.' His level voice gave the impression that he was compassionately tolerating my ignorance. I would have given anything for a little human warmth instead.

I went and sat down, throwing in a bow to the altar. In the dimly lit hall I could see the pyramid shapes of people in the lotus position. As the prayer gong signalled the beginning of meditation, I put my feet sole to sole, sat on the edge of the seat, and tried to keep still. I focused for a while on the breath coming in and out of my nostrils ... *in ... out ... in ...* Was my back straight enough? I restiffened my posture, but soon grew tired. My left foot began to cramp. Would it be like this at the monastery, I wondered, rubbing it as vigorously and quietly as possible. And what if they discovered that I was virtually agnostic? Then again, how could they find out if I stayed silent? I remembered that I was supposed to be stilling the mind, and brought my attention back to my breathing. *In ... out ... in ...*

Eventually, after what seemed like about an hour, the twenty-minute gong sounded. This at least meant that I could use the walking meditation to get rid of my cramp. But the two people who rose to their feet were moving in a very strange, stylised way – heels rising, tiny slowed-down steps – around the outside of the hall while the others remained seated. The first man approached from my right at the speed of a glacier, occasionally clacking two pieces of wood together. When he finally passed me, I stood up, and tried to feel each portion of my foot as it made contact with the floor. I must have been doing it wrong, because the man turned and whispered to me, 'Have you done this before?' No. 'Follow me, and bow to the centre of the room when I do.' Fine. 'When I do this again' – he mimed the clacking – 'you need to walk quickly back to your space – but *not* behind the altar.'

It struck me that all religions must seem like this from the outside – odd and essentially impenetrable to the novice. At the end, everyone got up fairly quickly and headed outside. I would have liked to ask someone what was going on, but people talked in hushed voices, if at all, and by the time I had put my shoes back on, I was alone. Feeling annoyed, I was about to head for the car park when a kind-faced older man appeared and shook my hand.

'I'm Ray,' he said, ushering me into an office.

Grateful for his attention, I told him about my quest, and my Buddhist virginity. 'I'm sorry, I think I walked the wrong way back to my seat.'

'You did fine,' said Ray. 'You were supposed to go in front of him but it's not a problem. Part of the idea of walking meditation is to stretch your legs after the sit. The other reason is just to teach you to pay attention. That's what it's all about.' He looked at me for a moment. 'Say, you want breakfast?'

Ray lived with his wife Nancy – also a Buddhist, and both of them in their seventies – in an elegant house up in the hills above Santa Fe. I followed their lime-green Volkswagen Beetle up the dirt track, and parked outside their home. It was simply furnished with a large table on a rug and a fitted kitchen.

They had not always been Buddhist. In fact, they had started out as Episcopalian Christians, but left the church in disillusionment at what seemed to them to be an outdated patriarchy with a narrow view of truth.

'Remember the 1960s?' said Nancy. 'Well, I took a look at our church and said, "This is a hierarchy, and it's run by men!" If women had been there it would have been different, I can tell you!' She gave me a friendly poke in the chest.

'Sure, but how radical is Buddhism?' I replied. 'There's a perception that it's all about passivity and detachment.'

Ray looked thoughtful. 'My vow is to be of unwavering service to all human beings without any hope of reward.' In practice, this meant he spent a lot of time volunteering at the local jail, visiting prisoners and writing letters: 'What I realised is that in many ways prisoners are just like you or I. We're all inmates, doing time on one level or another, dealing with crazy thoughts in the prison of our minds.'

Apparently Buddhists believe that the origin of all suffering is our attachment — to our thoughts, our desires, our friends and families. I had always felt this was a recipe for cold, distant people. But Nancy was adamant that the remedy for suffering was not to detach oneself from life and loved ones entirely, but to recognise that they were all transient and therefore to avoid defining yourself through them.

'It's the difference between having and being,' she said, stirring the scrambled eggs at the stove. 'If you learn to be, you recognise that you're intimately connected with all beings, just as you are intimately connected with yourself.'

She shovelled bacon onto my plate and we all sat down. We munched companionably for a while, until I decided to broach what was really worrying me: the prospect of spending the next three days in silence in the desert. Neither of them missed a beat.

'Watch your mind,' said Ray. 'Just notice what comes in and let it go. Take some reading, and set aside some time for sitting. Take a walk in the country. There's this idea that meditation is all about going into some trance, escaping from reality. But it's about being absolutely present, not absent. In the end, the key is to find the thing that is to be your practice. Follow your bliss.'

For Ray, this applied as much to driving his car, or playing the cello, as to meditating in the temple. 'It's important to me that I can do it while driving. You're looking at the rain, the cars behind, everything around you. Totally present.'

I felt very at home with Ray and Nancy, as if I were visiting wise grandparents. I regretted my earlier judgements that Zen Buddhists were cold, distant people. In fact I had noticed that most of my judgements turned out to be inadequate to some degree – just the critic chewing on whatever was at hand. I wondered if they had any advice specifically for quietening the mind.

'Sometimes I use mantras,' said Ray thoughtfully. 'One is "moo".'

Moo? 'As in cow?'

Ray smiled. 'I think they spell it m-u. It's nonsensical – a koan or puzzle that can't be solved by the rational mind. So a student asks his teacher, "Can a dog have Buddha nature?" And the teacher answers, "Mu." The idea is to derail your linear thinking, your rational mind.'

I tried to imagine Ray intoning the word for long periods of time, like a melancholy Friesian, and couldn't help smiling. Which was a start. 'And all this has had tangible results in your lives?'

'I've definitely changed,' said Nancy. 'I approach people much better than I used to. I've noticed I have expectations of the world and that it doesn't live up to them. And I'm learning to let that go.'

'That's another of my favourite mantras,' said Ray. He looked at me with a half-smile. '"Let it go." And, just as important, "Let go of letting go."'

I drove north from Santa Fe, thinking about what Ray and Nancy had said: 'Let go of letting go.' The road wove between cliffs of dusky pink rock and grew quieter and narrower as the landscape rose around me. The closer I got to my destination, the more anxious I felt. Refuelling at a gas station in Abiquiú I spotted an advert for a local mosque, and another excuse to delay the inevitable. Besides, it seemed too good a research opportunity to turn down – Buddhists, Catholics and Muslims in the same day. The Dar al Islam mosque lay at the top of a winding rubbly path. Looking at its domed, whitewashed exterior and tiny windows, I had to think for a moment where I was. It reminded me of Oman, not New Mexico.

Nobody seemed to be around except a couple of black dogs and a man painting the roof of an inner courtyard, whom I hailed above the sound of country music on his radio. He waved back. 'Try the office up the path!'

Walter de Clerck was a white-haired Belgian with a beard like Grizzly Adams. He welcomed me into his office and pulled up a swivel chair while I explained the nature of my quest.

He was in his sixties, casually dressed in a green shirt with black trousers and waistcoat, and white sport socks that created a polka-dot effect through the ventilation holes of his black Crocs. Like Richard Rohr and Ray and Nancy, he seemed to find nothing strange in my turning up there, out of nowhere, airing my existential questions like ordinary travellers might unfold a road map.

'What exactly do you want to let go of?' he asked presently.

I thought for a moment, battling a sense of déjà vu. 'I think maybe I'm just very tired of trying to be in control.'

He frowned slightly, and stood up. 'I can control that I get out of this chair, but I have no control over whether I'm still alive by the time I reach the door.' He didn't attempt to walk to the door. 'You do what you can and you leave the rest in the hands of God.' He shrugged and sat down again.

Walter's job at the mosque was to educate non-Muslims about the true meaning of Islam, dispel all the stereotypes conjured up by 9/11. 'Islam means "submission", which has the same root in Arabic as "peace". A Muslim is someone who is surrendered to the will of God.'

I was struck by how often the word 'surrender' had come up in my search. The ultimate letting go, handing over agency to another. It seemed a dangerous sort of impulse, but maybe that was because I was used to hearing 'surrender' used in the context of warfare. Perhaps it was possible to surrender to a benevolent force.

That, apparently, was what Walter had done thirty years earlier — after a stint as a hippie in Amsterdam, where he edited something called the *Cosmic Paper*. 'In those days it was like a hub of New Age forces and trends,' he recalled. 'All kinds of fantastic ideas, but no discipline. Like a revolving door. I didn't touch down till I was exposed to Muslim prayer, which required me to put my head on the ground.' He leapt out of his chair and touched his forehead to the floor. 'You do it literally, see? You can't see anything. It's also the only position where the heart is above the head. Can you think of a more surrendered position?'

Time was getting on, so I asked him if he had any specific advice for the three-day silence I was about to begin. He stroked his beard. 'It could be the most difficult thing you do in your life. You'll hear all kinds of noises in your head: I should have been doing this, or I want to earn this or that money, or I'm hurting, I've got to have this. It's going to be tough. There's nothing out here to distract you. Sometimes people break down in tears and say, "My God, this silence is too noisy, it screams at me! My advice is to allow all the stuff that comes. Don't fight it, don't engage with it, just let it pass by."'

Different religion, same advice. I told Walter I was heartened to have received almost identical briefing from Catholics, Buddhists and now Muslims.

'Of course.' He shrugged. 'It's the same basic message in all the world's religions. All the paths come to the same centre. But it's going to be tough. You need to enter a tradition to receive both its blessings and its protection – you can't just take some part of a culture without paying attention to other parts.' As I got up to go, he looked at me solemnly. 'The spiritual path is the most dangerous journey a human being can take.'

His tone bothered me a little. He spoke firmly but kindly, as an uncle might speak to a nephew he feared was about to go completely off the rails.

18

Surrender

The Chama Canyon, New Mexico

'Pass on from the name, and look closer to the source. The source will show you what you seek.'

RUMI

The track off Highway 84 started well, but soon deteriorated. I had been told that in bad weather it was often washed away, but today was sun-dappled and autumnal, the wispy clouds barely visible high in the air. The monastery lay at the very end of a fourteen-mile dirt track that followed the Chama river, sometimes at the water's edge, sometimes along ledges high above it. My sleek red car felt steadily more ludicrous the farther I got from the city, its low-slung underbelly scraping on humps and bumps. I drove on, crawling around tight corners, skidding occasionally on the cinder surface, until finally, deep in the river valley, I passed a carved wooden sign that said:

PEACE
MONASTERY of
CHRIST in the DESERT
Visiting Hours 8.45am–6pm daily
No Hunting – Watercraft – Camping
Private Property – Dead End Road

And, just over the next rise, it came into view, a little adobe dwelling, presumably the guest house, with the monastery farther down the valley at the foot of vast cliffs. Its adobe bell tower stood, in the words of the writer Thomas Merton, 'like a watchman looking for something or someone of whom it does not speak'.

I thought I had timed it perfectly, arriving at 12.45 p.m. in time for lunch at 1.15. But as I wheeled my case to the front doorstep of the guest quarters, I was greeted by a black monk in a black habit looking at his watch. 'You may be late,' he said. Apparently lunch was preceded by a short service, which he evidently thought I should attend. I nodded, wondering if I had caused him to speak unduly, and hurried straight up the path towards the chapel, slipping in at the guest entrance.

I nodded to a couple of the eight visitors in ordinary clothes. We were huddled in a small transept facing a rustic altar and a vast window set high in the wall near the ceiling, in which was framed a breathtaking view of high canyon wall. It dwarfed us all.

The bell tolled and the monks filed in from behind the altar to sit in two facing rows of chairs, both at right angles to the guests. They had shaven heads and black robes, and were striking for their youth and their multicultural spread. I would later learn that of the men here, seven were from Vietnam, seven from the USA, five from the Philippines, three from Mexico, one from India, one from Madagascar and one from Lesotho. I had expected the dying remnants of an ancient order. But the developing world was evidently producing new recruits.

They chanted their way mournfully through a variety of Latin responses, a standard service called Sext, which I followed on a photocopied sheet, mimicking the other guests for cues about kneeling, bowing and staying silent. I felt as alien as I had done in the Zen temple that morning – but a little less uptight about it. Afterwards, we all left quietly and I followed them round to the refectory. A balding monk showed me where to find my allotted napkin for my stay – blue and folded in a pigeonhole marked with my room number. Then the door opened and we all filed inside.

The refectory was a lovely cavernous space with exposed beams made from tree trunks, the sun lighting its upper spaces through modern stained-glass windows. The guests sat on long tables on one side of the room, facing the monks along the other. Some peered at us like zoo animals, others grinned. We sang a short blessing in Latin (words were provided on a small sheet of paper under my fork), then sat as monks came round with pots and trays of food. The idea was to scoop a portion and nod extravagantly with a smile, in lieu of a verbal thank you. I had expected an awkward silence during meals, with self-conscious scrapings and munchings of the sort you might expect at a family dining table after a dispute. But the monastery seemed to have dealt with this communal awkwardness by serving up serialised daily readings, like a sort of monastic *Book of the Week*.

Today's excerpt was from a harrowing account of the Rwandan genocide, which made our hearty fare of organic vegetables and chicken a little hard to stomach. It was too much even for the reader, who stopped at the end of a sentence and announced:

'Sorry, I can't read any more of this.' Instead he skipped to a brief martyrology of St Callistus I, apparently attacked for his forgiveness of murderers before shuffling off his mortal coil in the year AD 222. When we were all finished, everyone left at more or less the same time and silently disappeared. I followed the reader out into the atrium, where a small huddle of guests was waiting for a rare chat. It turned out he was Brother Andre, the 'guestmaster' in charge of hospitality to outsiders.

'I couldn't read any more!' he told the gathering. 'It was all killing and bodies; it was too much!'

'It was difficult to listen to,' someone else agreed.

A cheery Irishwoman introduced herself as Nora, a former Carmelite nun back for a top-up of silent contemplation. 'I'm a bit of a tea addict, Father – is there anywhere we can brew up?'

'Oh yes, any time you want a cup, just go to the guest-house common room.'

'Oh, Father, you saved my life!' she laughed.

I was just about to introduce myself when Brother Andre looked at his watch and excused himself. So instead I trotted after Nora.

'I haven't done one of these before,' I said.

'Really?' she said, looking at me wonderingly. 'I've done hundreds! I love silence – it's really become my passion.' Her eyes were sparkling and full of laughter, exuding the kind of happiness that advertisers try but fail to conjure up in models who have changed to a new brand of shampoo. 'I get up at five every morning and spend two hours meditating, and later on, too. It's just the most precious thing!'

It occurred to me that I was actually holding her back from her silent cup of tea. I reduced my voice to a whisper to show that I knew this. 'Just a quick question: what do you do if someone else is talking to you and you want to let them know you're doing a silent retreat?'

'Oh, you just wear the wooden pendant like this,' she grinned, holding up an image of a cross on a leather thong. 'Yours should be in your room.' She trotted happily off into silent seclusion as if heading for a warm bath.

In the Pope John Paul II Memorial Meditation Garden, a rather thin-looking horse was munching on the grass. Looking around me at the vastness, the whispering of the wind, I felt both anxiety and an unexpected gratefulness, a spreading ache of longing that moved me almost to tears.

My room was a simple, whitewashed cell with a narrow bed, a cupboard, a small gas heater and a writing desk, on which had been set out a pendant of a dove, an information brochure, and St Benedict's *Rules for Monks*. I sat down at the desk and put the pendant round my neck. The scrape of the wooden chair fell away into thickening silence. Now nobody would talk to me for three days and three nights.

I opened the book at random. Writing almost 1500 years ago, at a time when the Roman Empire was disintegrating under attack from the barbarian hordes, the Italian abbot had resorted to a kind of religious control freakery as he sought to maintain order in monasteries often peopled by peasants and social misfits. Monks were to sleep in their clothes in order to be able to rise early, but should remove their knives 'lest they accidentally cut themselves in their sleep'. Food would include fruit and vegetables, but no meat from four-legged animals. The daily ration of a half-bottle of wine would be withheld for habitual latecomers at meals, and troublemakers would be ostracised and possibly whipped. And, of course, everyone should keep quiet: 'So important is silence that permission to speak should seldom be granted even to mature disciples, no matter how good or holy or constructive their talk, because it is written: In a flood of words you will not avoid sin (Prov. 10:19).'

Absolutely condemned was 'talk leading to laughter'. I chuckled bleakly at the joylessness of it all, imagining how such rules would go down at Summerhill School, or even in the L'Arche community. Where was Jean Vanier's loving God?

Thankfully, there was a gentler interpretation in a modern pamphlet entitled *Practical Prayer Etiquette: From a Guest to a Guest*: 'After coming from a world full of noise, the silence here can be startling. One way this was explained to me was that the monastery seeks to have the silence within its bounds be as commonplace as the noise in the outside world. However, that doesn't mean that communication doesn't happen. A simple smile or wave here can speak volumes.'

There were a total of seven 'offices', or services, starting at 4 a.m. with Vigils and progressing through Lauds, Terce, Sext, None and Vespers before we retired to bed after Compline at 7.30 p.m. Singing seemed to be the exception to the silent rule, though even that was to be a muted affair. 'The goal is not to have your voice stand out but to have it blend in with the larger community of voices. If you can hear your own voice more than the voice of anyone else, you are singing too loudly. The goal is to lift up one unified voice to God.'

By the time I had finished reading the rules, the bell was ringing again for the next office. I wandered back up the path to the chapel, where the monks were again bowing and singing alternately across the sanctuary. Some appeared to be on the verge of nodding off. Others looked very proud of themselves, singing in the way that people do on *Songs of Praise* when they know the camera is on them. I wondered if anyone up there was listening – and if so, whether He was finding this ritual as uninspiring as I was. I felt mildly ashamed of the thought and looked instead up beyond the altar to the magnificent wall of the canyon, where piñon pines clung vertiginously to crevices in the sheer rock, and birds flapped silently past.

When the service ended, I escaped with some relief down a path towards the River Chama, which wound slowly along the floor of the canyon. Birds skimmed its surface, catching insects. I was peaceful for almost ten minutes, until I realised I was still feeling antagonistic towards the silent monks. I imagined running back into the chapel, shouting, 'Explain to me how this is a good way to spend your life!'

The more I tried to marshal myself back into a suitably serene frame of mind, the worse it got. The inner critic seemed to have brought reinforcements today.

I was starting to feel queasy with the violent judgements inside me, until I remembered that this was just what everyone had predicted: 'You'll hear all kinds of voices in your head. The key is neither to fight them or identify with them. Treat your thoughts like clouds passing by.' So I took a mental step back and stopped fighting. Instead, I peered into my own mind as a Victorian might have scientifically observed lunatics through the window of an asylum. It wasn't quite compassion, but it felt a little calmer. And then I remembered where I was. Amazing how I could stand on the banks of a beautiful river and yet still be entirely immersed in my thoughts.

By the time the bell rang for yet another service, I was almost relieved. I could see why silent monks needed such a meticulous timetable – probably to keep themselves from going insane. This time the chanting was followed by a simple supper, accompanied by soothing classical music. Nora, the ex-Carmelite, smiled serenely at me. Others looked as if they were having a trickier time of it. A well-fed married couple shuffled a lot, exchanging glances and nudging one another to stand up at the right time. Meanwhile, a muscular man with a long facial scar seemed to look mainly at the floor, his tattooed hands clenched together as if trying to crush something. It felt strange that I would probably never know their names. But I liked to think there was already a kind of solidarity between all of us that would not be strengthened by speech.

We were all, after all, engaged in basically the same battle.

The second day began in freezing darkness before dawn. Cursing the absence of electricity at the guesthouse (even the monastery had solar power), I brushed my teeth in the washroom using the light from my head-torch. I had already missed Vigils at 4 a.m., but thought I should make the effort to be at Lauds at 5.45 a.m. It was frosty and bitterly cold as I crunched up the track, and the mist from my breath made it difficult to see where I was going until I switched off the head-torch and walked under the astonishing star-speckled heavens. It was good to nod to now familiar guests inside the chapel and begin the chanting, watching the cliff wall slowly materialise from the darkness.

The liturgy began to lose its appeal as the day progressed. Not long after our silent breakfast, we were back in the chapel for Sunday Mass, this time accompanied by a host of day visitors and the nuns from a nearby convent. Despite the beauty of the incense rising slowly in the sunlight, I realised there was going to be a limit to how often I could sing about my sin and unworthiness – even in Latin – before I began to half-believe it. It didn't help that non-Catholics were excluded from taking communion. By the time the service finished, I was itching to get out into the cathedral of nature instead.

Wandering down towards the river, I sat happily on a log in the sunshine for a few minutes until the heat became too intense. Which was when I found my tree. It was a battered-looking box elder hunkered on the riverbank, with two ancient trunks splaying from the ground. In the V between them, someone had nailed old planks to form a seat. I settled myself at its dappled heart and looked around me. It was half dead, and one of its trunks was charred black, perhaps from a lightning strike, but it still harboured all sorts of birds, which fluttered overhead, occasionally shitting an undigested fruit seed onto my sun hat.

I sat there peacefully for a good two minutes thinking how much better this was than the chapel. I decided to make it my special place, my regular haunt for the next two days. I would have to get here early each day to claim it, just in case someone else had seen it, to make sure the other guests didn't pip me to the post. I was halfway through calculating the earliest time I could arrive when I noticed I was now anxious, and it dawned on me what I was doing. In less than five minutes I had gone from peacefully inhabiting my new hermitage to plotting how to protect it in the future. It was so ludicrous that I laughed out loud, and at that moment I believed the game was up for my poor, scheming mind. I could feel only a sad affection for its insecurity.

For the next hour I simply observed. A furry black and orange caterpillar crossing the path. Pawprints on the muddy foreshore, oddly feline, perhaps some kind of wild cat. And yet, in the willow thickets near the water, something had chewed neatly through the stalks to create little pathways. A water creature, or one from land?

Occasionally I'd meet another human. One woman tried to engage me in conversation, and the man with the scar paused and nodded as we passed on the path – but I just smiled apologetically and waved my wooden pendant at them like a crucifix warding off vampires. It wasn't a great way to make friends, but useful for watching the wildlife – both inner and outer. In the absence of chatter, I was noticing much subtler noises – the burr of birds' wings flying overhead, the patter of animal feet among the scrub, my own breathing.

And of course the dramatic prattle of the critic, coming in abortive bursts now. Taking my shoes off to squidge through the mud farther down the river, I found him anxiously imagining my own unobserved death by drowning. Later he gave me a hard time after I squashed a wasp on a rock with my copy of *Being Peace* by Thich Nhat Hanh. I skipped the afternoon service to lie on my back under a tree, watching the gathering clouds between the branches, but the critic informed me that such happiness was trite and shallow in a world where millions were dying of hunger, disease and war. By the time I got back to the guest house, I was in awe both at the splendour of the environment, and the sheer gothic intricacy of the mind.

Poor critic. He really is a tortured wee soul.

Now I'm in my cell, listening to a thunderstorm, the hiss of rain pouring off the roof. I love storms. The view down the valley is apocalyptic: dark thunderclouds tinged fiery red by an almost quenched sun. It's possible the road will get washed away, forcing me to stay here another day or two. But I'm surprised to find that I wouldn't mind. Wouldn't it be wonderful to be able to embrace life – embrace myself and others – without trying to change anything? I think of the old box elder, gnarly and scorched and split by storms, but still providing shelter for birds and humans. There is nothing I want to change about it. Just as an experiment, I think of all the things I don't want to change about myself – instead of the usual litany of shortcomings. I am surprised how long the list is, and how much lighter I feel afterwards, despite the thunder.

It's day three, the rain has passed, and the air is sparkling and clear. I have decided it's time I offered myself for some physical labour, so I turn up at Brother Andre's office after Terce with a knot of helpers, some of whom try to talk to me. I rebuff them as painlessly and benevolently as possible by pointing to the insignia round my neck, but when it comes to Father Andre it is a little more difficult. He seems to have some kind of dispensation to talk to guests.

'How are you finding it?' he asks. I grin and make a thumbs-up sign. He looks a bit confused, so I point to my little wooden insignia. 'You're enjoying the silence, huh?' he says. 'But you know we don't insist on total silence — sometimes you have to converse to get things done.' I nod as pleasantly as possible, but actually I'm feeling annoyed. Standing back from my thoughts, it dawns on me I'm getting a bit perfectionistic about it — a sort of competitive muteness. Now he's forcing me to break it.

'I was hoping to observe silence for the full three days,' I say in as few words as possible without being rude. Brother Andre looks amused. 'Fair enough,' he says. 'I'd like you to join Brother Dominic this morning — he's cleaning the guest rooms and bathrooms. Here's some replacement toilet paper.'

Housework, on a beautiful morning like this? Everyone else is out digging paths through the brush like New World pioneers, and I'm supposed to wield the toilet brush? I can't say any of this, of course, so I smile thinly, give a small nod and leave the room. At least Brother Dominic isn't big on conversation — he doesn't speak English. A beaming, chubby Vietnamese monk, he gestures for me to watch him, charades-style, as he makes the first bed — as if it's the first time I've ever done so. I indulge him as he shakes out the immaculately folded sheet, lays it tenderly over the stripped bed, making fussy little adjustments to its positioning. Then he smoothes it and folds its corners cleanly underneath the mattress as if wrapping a parcel. Next comes the top sheet, lovingly folded over at the edge of the final blanket. I feel drugged by his extreme slowness. At each stage he stands back to survey what he's done, gives a quiet little 'Mmm', and beams at me.

When it's my turn, I speed competitively through my bed-making, anxious to get back out into nature. Dominic inspects the result with a slight frown and straightens a minuscule crease in the fold-over. Then, with a smirk on his face, he makes slow-down signals with his hands. I suspect I'm in some sort of spiritual test, so I give in and slow down. It's true that I've never seen anyone take so much apparent pleasure from such a mundane task, and it's strangely infectious.

By the third bed, I've stopped thinking about hurrying outside, and instead I'm gazing at the motes of dust turning in the sunbeams as I give the same sculptural attention to my sheets as Dominic. The morning advances at the speed of fingernail growth. It takes us approximately two hours to strip and remake ten beds, empty the litter bins and sweep the floors. We would not, I suspect, win a hotel cleaning contract – but I defy you to find more contented cleaners.

In the afternoon, I hike along the foot of the cliffs, then turn and follow a dry creek upwards into a vast amphitheatre of sandstone, where a vulture circles heavenwards on the thermals. I stretch out on a flat rock and feel the sun warming my skin as it has warmed the Earth for millennia. Looking at the canyon walls, you can see the tidemarks of a primordial flood in which unrecognisable creatures swam when all this was under water a hundred million years ago. In centuries to come, my bones will form part of the Earth in the same way theirs do now, and my life will be of as little significance as some trilobite chipped out of the wall by a passing geologist. From dust you came, and to dust you will return. This is the great paradox, how to reconcile this infinitesimal speck of life in a vast universe with the idea of unrepeated variety, of utter uniqueness. It makes me no more or less important than the vulture surfing the thermals, or the butterfly that crosses my path – all precious lives, but ultimately a flicker on the cosmic screen.

Today I feel somehow comforted by that insignificance, by the humility of simply belonging to a vast and ever-changing drama, a bit player whose role might be over at any instant. What if 'God' is simply the name we give to the big picture, the fathomless sum of all reality, the great unending mystery of it all?

It feels such a relief to find that my self-projections are really of no consequence, like the flashings of a firefly in its dance between life and death. How wonderful to be able to feel oneself emptying of all this churning material, to be as light as a husk, simply a witnessing organism, even part of the picture. Part of the wind blowing down the river and setting all those last yellow leaves dancing. Why, seemingly alone of all animals, do we humans have this craving for meaning beyond the immediate present? How wonderful to be relieved of the need to be significant and important and bigger than others. I've been basking in this happiness all day, the happiness of my own insignificant uniqueness, no better or worse than other life forms, here to play a part, give myself to the flow of life, wherever it takes me.

I feel held, somehow. Held by something vast and all-embracing.

On my last evening, I'm standing on the riverbank when a beaver surfaces. It's dusk, and on the mirrored surface his blunt snout carves a V-shaped ripple through the reflection of a low crescent moon that hangs above the dark canyon walls. I stand watching him, barely daring to breathe. A woman guest, whose name I will never know, stands a few feet away and we exchange a wide-eyed, wordless wonder in our glances. We watch in mute awe until the curious rodent is disturbed by the tolling of the chapel bell for Vespers. He dives with a warning slap of his tail on the water, leaving ripples of spreading silence.

In the chapel I savour my last view of the day fading on the sheer rock face of the mesa. Fitting, perhaps, after starting my quest by jumping off a cliff, to find myself dwelling at the bottom of one. Coasteering feels a long time ago now. Listening to the monks chanting their melancholy unworthiness once again, I realise I have lost my antagonism to these men and their harnessed-in lives. I will miss their grins and their yawns, the ascetic beauty of their black robes framed by incense. They have submitted to their humble task in the universe – and perhaps it is time I submitted to mine. I think of the possibility of a child who needs me, waiting out there somewhere, and remember something Vaclav Havel once said: 'Hope ... is not the conviction that something will turn out well, but the certainty that something makes sense, regardless of how it turns out.'

I can feel it now, that fragile hope, bearing my weight.

After Vespers, I find I am not alone as I walk back through the darkness to the guest house. Someone is behind me, keeping pace. I nip into the common room on impulse, hungry for a slice of toast, and the person follows me in. It is the man with the scar and tattoos. I have to admit I've been avoiding him, intimidated by his tough appearance. I nod an acknowledgement, offer him the bread, and we stand alone in silence together, waiting for the toast to pop up.

'Pretty quiet out here, huh?' he says, quite suddenly, in a nervous, gravelly voice.

I'm sure I must have jumped visibly. Fumbling for my pendant, I find it's still tucked invisibly inside my coat. Ignoring him doesn't feel like an option.

'Yes, it is,' I stutter.

'You're British?'

And so, stiff with blokeish formality, we begin my first conversation for three days. I give up my resistance almost without thinking about it, struck instead by an unexpected wave of sadness – the realisation that tomorrow I will leave this place knowing nothing real about those who have shared it with me.

This man, at least, has a name now. His name is Davie, and he's an oil-rig worker in the Gulf of Mexico, currently resident in one of the grittier districts of Albuquerque.

'So, what brings you to the guest house?' I venture, genuinely intrigued.

He looks at his hands for a moment, then turns to look straight into my eyes for the first time. 'I'm an alcoholic, Nick,' he says, his voice emotionless, tired. 'I've been sober for a couple of years, but before that I couldn't go more than three weeks without getting wasted. And I came here because I just had an argument with my girlfriend. I figured I might go on the mother of all benders if I didn't get away.'

I find his honesty disarming and humbling. 'Sounds like a wise move,' I offer. 'It's a good place to hole up.'

'How about you?' says Davie.

'I'm here because I'm trying to learn to let go. I've been exploring different methods for the past year ...'

He looks up, not understanding. 'Who did you lose?'

'Ah,' I say gently. 'You're talking about letting go of a loved one – but I haven't done much of that. I'm just an anxious guy learning to loosen up, let my hair down.'

'Okay, gotcha,' says Davie. He looks at me for a moment, weighing me up. 'You're anxious, you say? I'm anxious, too. I've always been a bit of an introvert.' He takes a bite of toast. 'That's why I drank, because suddenly I could talk to people. And cocaine – man, suddenly I could hold court for hours, I was invincible!'

'In some ways I envy people who can drink,' I say, wanting to offer something back. 'I could do with the confidence, too.'

'But you pay for it, Nick. I've basically lost everything. They took away my kids, I lost twenty-three years of my life in total chaos. Red mist.' He gently brings his fists together. I try not to stare at his scar, imagining the kind of life that might have produced it. It runs from the corner of his eye to the corner of his mouth, as if someone has tried to open his face like an envelope.

'You familiar with Alcoholics Anonymous?' he says quietly. 'It wasn't till I joined AA that I realised I was afraid. I found out plenty of things about myself that I had to admit were true, but it was the fear thing that blew me away. I met a guy with a life just like mine who said he fought his fear by trying to make other people afraid. I thought, That's what I do!'

The echoing space seems suddenly as holy as a confessional. Despite our different paths, I feel an unexpected connection with this man, tied by the soul through our common anxiety. The fear has led him into much darker places than me: while I'm trapped in my head making war on perfection, Davie has been to physical hell and back. While he's lost his kids to social services, I'm on the way to adopting. We are two halves of the same cycle. But we share an understanding of our shortcomings. I ask him how he managed to turn his life around.

He shakes his head. 'I didn't turn it round – I surrendered.' He pauses for a moment, choosing his words. 'I was never religious. But in AA they talk about a higher power, don't get into arguing about whose God is whose – it's just about letting go and asking for help. I asked for help in fighting the urge to drink and it worked. I've been on the wagon for a couple of years now, apart from one or two lapses. One time a debt caught up with me from years ago, then last weekend my partner came in wasted and I just lost it. Someone recommended I come out here to have a bit of a think.' He nods at me, and gets up. 'I'm glad I did.'

I'm glad, too. It feels like a gift that I have met Davie. He is a good man trying to do the right thing after making some bad choices. There's a copy of *The Twelve Steps* in the common-room library, and I take it back to my room to pore over. It's not a fashionable self-help programme in this age of instant motivational cures, and it has no gurus, because it relies on broken people being honest with each other. And yet, across the world today, millions of people are meeting quietly and unobtrusively in back rooms, church halls and basements. It needs no proselytising. It takes guts to surrender to the point where you'd walk into a twelve-step meeting and admit to your addiction.

The first three steps are:

1. We admitted we were powerless over our addiction – that our lives had become unmanageable.
2. We came to believe that a Power greater than ourselves could restore us to sanity.
3. We made a decision to turn our will and our lives over to the care of God as we understood Him.

However you define a 'Power greater than ourselves' – and there seems to be a fair bit of leeway in the phrase 'God as we understand Him' – it might be the crucial component in letting go. If I am truly all I can rely on in the world – if each of us is the sum total of our own potential – why wouldn't we try and control every last part of our lives? It's the logical thing to do. If, on the other hand, there is something larger to tap into, why not sink our roots into it?

This, then, is the decision that still faces me, after all these years: whether I am going to behave as if this higher power exists, or whether I am the end of the story when it comes to shaping my own life.

I know which I want to believe. There is a beauty in the restored life of Davie that continues to move me – a bravery in surrender. An unpopular word, 'surrender'. Funny how often it is taken for the coward's option. Yet in some ways it's the only one that confronts fear head-on. The counterintuitive third option, beyond fight or flight, when you stop running or fighting and turn and face your truth.

I think about this as I lie in the darkness, hearing Davie turn over in bed on the other side of the wall between our rooms. Only a thin partition of genetic chance separates our lives – how arbitrary it is that the cards are dealt as they are: that I was born in Kingston and Davie in Albuquerque; both anxious and introverted men who found different survival strategies.

I meet Davie only once more, the following morning, as he hurries out of the monastery cloisters. He's been to confession – or 'making a fearless and searching moral inventory of ourselves' as the AA people put it. He looks as if he has been crying, but he's lighter somehow. He nods at me briefly, heads for the car park, and is gone.

But walking by the river, I have the strangest sensation. Looking down at my trainers as I pick my way along the muddy path, I have a fleeting sense that these are Davie's feet. That I am, in fact, Davie.

I stare at my feet, my hands, then the trees around me, the mist clearing from the river. And I realise: it's all the same thing. It's a moment of pure interconnection that flashes onto my consciousness as briefly as a subliminal image. But it's enough. Because suddenly I know it's true. What separates us from one another is fear. What separates me from life is fear. Fear of losing control. But if something bigger is holding us, and that thing is love, what is there to fear?

I pack my bags slowly, smiling to myself, leave my silent pendant on the desk for the next guest. Then I get into the red Grand Prix and scrunch along the canyon road, heading for the stretched horizon.

Epilogue

'The curious paradox is that when I accept myself just as I am, then I can change.'

CARL ROGERS

'Daddy?'

Every time I hear that word, something in me dissolves into joy. Daddy. That's me!

'Yes, love?' Story time is over, and the lights are out – but lying next to his bed on the darkened floor, I sometimes find that my son uses his last waking moments to tell me what's really troubling him.

'How many sleeps am I staying here?' He looks down anxiously from his Bob the Builder pillow, with the eyes of one who has had three dads in as many years and still can't quite believe that this one isn't going to prove as temporary as the others. He's been with us three months, and it's a ritual question.

'We're your growing-up family, love. No more moves.'

His wee hands scrunch and unscrunch absently on the down of his favourite soft toy dog as he considers this, his eyes still wide open.

'But what will happen if you die?'

I bite my lip in the darkness, trying not to show the emotion I'm feeling. 'We're not planning to die any time soon,' I say carefully. 'People usually die when they're much older than me or Mum.'

'Will you go to heaven like Misty?' Misty is the name of the much-lamented dog of his foster family.

'Yes, love, eventually. But God holds everyone in his hands — and none of us can fall out of God.'

In the end, we didn't have to search for C. He found us. Approved by the adoption panel a few weeks after I flew home from the desert, we spent several months leafing through the magazines, never quite feeling right about the children who were available. By the following summer, we were beginning to wonder if we had made a mistake applying for adoption at all. And then one day the social worker phoned with a referral. 'I've got a feeling you might be interested in this wee chappie ...'

Sure enough, as we read through the papers, we both had a strange sensation in our guts. 'A lively, sociable three-year-old with a sunny personality and a streak of mischief, C loves to talk about his feelings and listen to story books ...'

'Are you thinking what I'm thinking?' said Ali.

I nodded. 'Is this what they mean when they say you'll know?'

It was a huge emotional gamble. As he had not got to the stage of being advertised in the magazines, there was no picture — and it was policy to ask potential adopters to commit before they actually saw the child. Would we like him when we met him? But the sense of something right, something *meant*, was strong enough for us to proceed anyway. We had some fun making a short DVD to introduce ourselves and our house, and sent it off to his foster parents. Driving over on the morning of our introductions, I missed a call on my mobile and pulled over to listen to the answer machine. There was the sound of muffled breathing, and presently a little Scottish voice said: 'Hello? Are you there, Mummy Ali and Daddy Nick? Where are you? I'm waaaaiitiiiing . . . !' Two minutes later, he opened the door in his Scooby Doo T-shirt and grinned at us from behind his foster mum's legs — and somewhere in my guts the last ramparts of anxiety collapsed into love.

Within minutes we had met C's favourite toy (a much-loved dog called Woof), had a sticky-fingered tour through his photo album, and promised to remember all his favourite food, including 'strangled eggs and pasghetti'. Rarely does he run out of words, we discovered — and if he does, he just invents a new one. Bob the Builder's spanner is, rather wonderfully, a 'wigglefence'. And don't rain clouds seem much kinder as 'soggyfers'?

We played most of that first, wonderful day, and we haven't really stopped since. We have played as if our life depended on it — which in the very deepest sense, of course, it does. It's the Holy Grail, the magic glue, as natural as breathing — ceaseless, serious, funny, boisterous, tender play. C has us building camps, nursing teddies, blowing bubbles like the primary-school children we once were — and, apparently, still are on some level. In the process, he bowls the sort of questions that might stump a philosophy graduate. Is the Evil Vilgax all bad, or just listening to his naughty part? Is Charlie the cocker spaniel actually thinking something when he stares? And, of course, what happens when we die?

The story of C's early life before we met is his rather than mine to tell — but he's since thrown himself enthusiastically into the important work of unleashing all his contradictory emotions and pushing every boundary in his new home, as is his job. There are some days when it all feels as blessed and natural as if this lively, funny child has lived with us for ever. There are others when I'm so tired I could crawl into bed and sleep for years. But it's different from the exhaustion of the day when I first lost control – it's my body, not my mind, that's spent. And I'm delighted and surprised to find that the effects of my year of experimentation remain profound and long lasting – and tested with a conscientious rigour by our new family member.

Richard Rohr was right. It's the unexpected letting go that counts. The supermarket tantrum, the abandonment of leisurely plans, the realisation that I simply don't know what to do. I've learned to ask for help a little earlier, and discovered that what I perceived as weakness is actually an opportunity to connect with a friend. I still thank the critic, often through gritted teeth, and find that he is becoming unexpectedly helpful in return. *Can you absolutely know that's true?* he now asks, playfully, when I'm clinging furiously to an unexamined belief: 'C should just do as he's told,' for example, or, 'This book shouldn't be taking so long to write!'

I've stopped travelling altogether for the time being, in order to be a better father, and am surprised to find that I don't miss it. Nowadays, I get my adventure closer to home, courtesy of some of the methods I picked up along the way. Encouraged by Bengt and Mikael in Sweden, I've invited Ali and a few friends to a monthly sharing group in our front room, a candle-lit silence interspersed with six-minute bouts of unfettered honesty. Nobody has yet requested we play 'raccoons' – but I rule nothing out. And one Saturday a month, when C is tucked up in bed, I also sneak off to a wood in central Scotland where a group of men sit round a campfire and talk about our places of hope or despair. In both settings we circumvent the small talk, and dip straight into what's really going on beneath the fast-moving surface of our lives. It's addictively real – and often as exhilarating as wing walking.

I still can't commit wholeheartedly to a single religious system, though I do make it along to our friendly little Anglican church once or twice a month. I don't always feel comfortable with what I'm hearing, but it's not generally a sign-on-the-dotted-line kind of place, and I appreciate the sense of extended family, the shared seeking, the way the tribe of other kids have taken C under their collective wing. Compassion will always trump doctrine for me.

Likewise, the body, rather than the mind, continues to be the best guide to what I need, as it was on the day I first lost control. Thanks to regular yoga and fewer hours in front of the computer, my migraines have receded drastically, to a point where I even allow myself the occasional beer, with no ill effects. After all the spiritual searching, the most effective tools seem to be the simplest. Grinning at myself in a mirror continues somehow to unseat the operatic complexities of my fears, and cheers me up. And if the brain chatter is getting too loud, I head to a Five Rhythms dance class and let rip for two hours with a crowd of folk who couldn't care less what any of us look like. It remains my ideal nightclub – anonymous, alcohol free, and all over by 9.30 p.m.

When it comes to work, I rather like Henry David Thoreau's dictum: 'The truly efficient labourer will not crowd his day with work, but will saunter to his task, surrounded by a wide halo of ease and leisure, and then do what he loves best.' Like world peace, this is something to aspire to rather than a realistic blueprint, and I'm fairly relaxed about the fact that I'll never be quite that laid-back.

Increasingly, it seems to me I will never really change who I am. Instead, my job is to stop the inner war and accept myself as I am – which is, of course, the most radical change of all. On the days when I can't accept who I am, I accept that I can't accept it. Let go of letting go. Sometimes that's as good as it gets.

Ultimately, I've discovered that letting go is less like jumping off a cliff than joining an intricate, intuitive dance. There's no simple way to do it other than to relax and forgive yourself when you fluff your steps, and stay open to the changing rhythm of the music. C has a natural yen for it, this dance of attachment. Sometimes he needs holding close in the certainty that he is loved, whatever happens. And yet there are other times when he needs me to let go, as he reminded me in the park this afternoon, doing his first slide down a fireman's pole. At such moments I must relax and step back, trust the dance.

C is no different to the rest of us, really. For all our supposed love of novelty, most of us like to be in control of what happens to us. It's a survival instinct that has served us well as a species. The simple fact is that it's hard to let go until you've learned to hold on. We're all looking for a safe place to stand, whether physical or spiritual. We are homesick until we find our home.

'Daddy?'

I hadn't realised he was still awake. But, turning over, I see his eyes are on me again, those wide hazel eyes that hollow me out and flood me with compassion.

'What is it, love?'

'Can I hold God's hand?'

Oh blimey. A theological question. 'Um, well, yes, sort of – if you go into your imagination …'

'No! Not like that!' he interrupts. 'I mean God's *real* hand!' C doesn't like being fobbed off. And who can blame him? In his straightforward way, our three-year-old son has just identified one of the more obvious shortcomings of religion.

'Well, God doesn't have that kind of hand,' I admit. 'But you don't need to worry – God's big enough to hold us all.'

Even a year ago, I'd have baulked at such simple assertions, but

three-year-olds have no tolerance for doubt or vague mysticism –
not this three-year-old, anyway. I wait in the pregnant silence.

'Can I hold *your* hand?' he says finally.

I don't trust my voice not to crack, so I just gently reach up and
stroke his wee fist, feel his little fingers curling eagerly around mine.
He yawns and murmurs: 'I love you, Dad.'

'I love you so much, son,' I manage. I prop my arm in position
and keep gentle hold, listening to his breathing. A tear rolls across
my face. It's a responsible job, being God's hand.

C squeezes experimentally a couple of times, checking I'm still
there. Then his breathing deepens, slows. And gradually, inex-
orably, like a flower opening, his fingers loosen into the kindness of
sleep.

Acknowledgements

A huge thank you to all those who featured, knowingly or not, in my adventures. I have tried to be as objective and faithful to the facts as it is possible to be in a highly personal account but, where appropriate, I have used pseudonyms and changed other identifying details to protect privacy.

Behind the scenes, many others helped practically to make the various journeys and encounters happen. Thanks to Christine Walker, Joan McAlpine and Gillian Harris on *The Sunday Times*, and Michael Kerr on the *Daily Telegraph*, for commissioning pieces on my travels in Sweden, South Africa and New Mexico – and to Visit Cornwall, Vertical Descents, Visit Sweden, Nature Travels, Tribes Travel, the North America Travel Service and the New Mexico Tourism Department for helping to get me to my destinations in the first place.

The writing of the book was a journey in itself, lasting longer than any other I've undertaken. This was partly because I took a significant and necessary break from full-time writing to focus on welcoming C to our family. But perhaps it was also inevitable, in a project based on letting go, that the hardest thing to relinquish would be the finished manuscript. Thanks therefore to Tim Whiting, Victoria Pepe and Steve Guise at Little, Brown, and

Camilla Hornby and Felicity Blunt of Curtis Brown who supported me patiently and with great enthusiasm until it was finally time to wrestle it from my grasp.

Huge thanks also to my faithful friends who have provided tea, sympathy and/or textual feedback well beyond the call of duty: Lisa Clark, Fadeke Kokumo Rocks, Marc Marnie, Louisa Waugh, Elspeth Murray, Richard Medrington and Jim Ferguson. Others buoyed me with consistent enthusiasm for the idea: Cole Moreton, Gareth Higgins, Robin Connelly, Mark Rickards, Alan Bell, Judy Hepburn, Maralyn McBride, Daphne Martin, Wendy Ball, Geoffrey Stevenson and others at SJTL, Socrates Café and the Solas Arts Festival. More recently, Mike Jones and others at the Mankind Project, who brought the kind of creative energy boost every writer craves. Thanks also to Steve Butler, Charlie Irvine and Dot Reid for permission to quote from *In a Different Voice* (After Virtue, Sticky Music, 2006). Nirved Wilson has been an unflaggingly wise soul-guide and sounding board at key points in the writing process, while my mum, dad and siblings – Janet, Graham, Mark, Dan and Hannah Thorpe – have shown unstinting support, not to mention benign tolerance for the unsought and subjective exposure they've all received in my story. Thanks to all of you.

Most of all, however, I want to thank my soul-mate Ali, an essentially private being who went well beyond her comfort zone to accompany me on an often exposing journey simply because she passionately believed in what I was trying to do. Thank you for encouraging me to take the most important risks, for your incisive and detailed suggestions for the text, and for living with its enduring imperfections. I couldn't have done it without you.

And to my beloved C? You have captured my heart, son, and changed my life for good. xxx

Select Bibliography

Adams, John: *Risk* (UCL Press, 1995)

Batchelor, Stephen: *Buddhism Without Beliefs* (Riverhead, 1997)

Bradley Hagerty, Barbara: *Fingerprints of God* (Riverhead, 2009)

Damasio, Antonio: *The Feeling of What Happens* (Vintage, 2000)

Gazzaniga, Michael: *The Mind's Past* (University of California Press, 1998)

Hewitt, Tom: *Little Outlaws, Dirty Angels* (Hodder, 1999)

Hillesum, Etty: *An Interrupted Life: the Diaries and Letters of Etty Hillesum 1941-43* (Persephone Books, 1999)

Katie, Byron: *Loving What Is* (Rider, 2002)

Layard, Richard: *Happiness: Lessons from a New Science* (Penguin, 2005)

Levine, Peter: *Waking the Tiger* (North Atlantic Books, 1997)

Mitchell, Stephen (translator) & Lao-Tzu: *Tao te Ching* (Harper, 2006)

Neill, A.S.: *The New Summerhill* (Penguin, 1992)

Rogers, Carl (ed. Kirschenbaum, H. and Henderson, V. L.): *The Carl Rogers Reader* (Constable, 1990)

Rohr, Richard (with John Feister): *Hope Against Darkness* (St Anthony Messenger, 2001)

Rohr, Richard: *The Naked Now* (Crossroads, 2009)

Schwartz, Barry: *The Paradox of Choice* (Harper, 2004)

Spink, Kathryn: *Jean Vanier & L'Arche: A Communion of Love* (DLT, 1990)

Various authors: *Summerhill: For and Against* (Angus and Robertson, 1973)

~~

If you enjoyed *Urban Worrier* why not start a new journey with another of Nick's bestselling titles . . .

~~

EIGHT MEN AND A DUCK

An Improbable Voyage by Reed Boat to Easter Island

Nick Thorpe

Nick Thorpe was innocently travelling around South America with his wife, Ali, when he came across an American adventurer planning to sail from Chile to Easter Island on a Bolivian boat made of reeds. Inspired by the great Thor Heyerdahl, Phil Buck had recruited seven men to join him on this experiment to discover whether it might have been possible that Polynesia was first settled from South America rather than Asia. But when one of them dropped out a place in the crew became available for Nick.

What followed was a somewhat bizarre expedition undertaken by a rather makeshift vessel, a couple of ducks (one of which could have only guessed at its fate) and a group of men, who, when all said and done, weren't quite sure how to sail a boat . . .

Brilliantly told, *Eight Men and a Duck* is a feel-good, hilarious tale of storms, amateur seamen and the occasional shark.

'Thorpe may be a poor sailor but he is an accomplished storyteller . . . he chronicles the voyage of *Viracocha* with an easy, unforced humour. It's hardly surprising that it's an inspiring story'
Telegraph

'An exciting, involving read'
Independent on Sunday

978-0-349-11454-5

ADRIFT IN CALEDONIA

Boat-hitching for the Unenlightened

Nick Thorpe

One clear morning in May, Nick Thorpe left his Edinburgh flat, ducked off the commuter route and hitched a ride aboard a little white canal boat, heading west towards the sea. It was the first mutinous step in a delightful boat-hopping odyssey that would take him 2,500 miles through Scotland's canals, lochs and coastal waters, from the industrial Clyde to the scattered islands of Viking Shetland.

Writing with characteristic humour and candour, the award-winning author of *Eight Men and a Boat* plots a curiously existential voyage, inspired by those who have left the warm hearth for the promise of a stretched horizon. Whether rowing a coracle with a chapter of monks, scanning for the elusive Nessie, hitting the rocks with Captain Calamity or clinging to the rigging of a tall ship, Thorpe weaves a narrative that is by turns funny and poignant – a nautical pilgrimage for any who have ever been tempted to try a new path just to see where it might take them.

Part travelogue, part memoir, *Adrift in Caledonia* is a unique and affectionate portrait of a sea-fringed nation – and of the drifter's quest to belong.

'As travelogues go, *Adrift in Caledonia*, is a beautiful entertainment, better than Bryson, as shrewdly observant as Theroux'
Scotsman

'A lovely, humorous, fluid book that anchors itself in the heart'
The Times

978-0-349-11737-9

Now you can order superb titles directly from Abacus

☐ Eight Men and a Duck   Nick Thorpe   £10.99
☐ Adrift in Caledonia   Nick Thorpe   £9.99

The prices shown above are correct at time of going to press. However, the publishers reserve the right to increase prices on covers from those previously advertised, without further notice.

─────────────── ⬭ABACUS⬭ ───────────────

Please allow for postage and packing: **Free UK delivery.**
Europe: add 25% of retail price; Rest of World: 45% of retail price.

To order any of the above or any other Abacus titles, please call our credit card orderline or fill in this coupon and send/fax it to:

Abacus, PO Box 121, Kettering, Northants NN14 4ZQ
Fax: 01832 733076   Tel: 01832 737526
Email: aspenhouse@FSBDial.co.uk

☐ I enclose a UK bank cheque made payable to Abacus for £ . . . .
☐ Please charge £ . . . . . . to my Visa/Delta/Maestro

Expiry Date ☐☐☐☐   Maestro Issue No. ☐☐

NAME (BLOCK LETTERS please) . . . .

ADDRESS . . . .

. . . .

. . . .

Postcode . . . . Telephone . . . .

Signature . . . .

Please allow 28 days for delivery within the UK. Offer subject to price and availability.